PLUNDERING THE NORTH

PLUNDERING THE NORTH

A History of Settler Colonialism, Corporate
Welfare, and Food Insecurity

KRISTIN BURNETT AND TRAVIS HAY

UNIVERSITY OF MANITOBA PRESS

Plundering the North: A History of Settler Colonialism,
Corporate Welfare, and Food Insecurity
© Kristin Burnett and Travis Hay 2023

27 26 25 24 23   1 2 3 4 5

University of Manitoba Press
Winnipeg, Manitoba, Canada
Treaty 1 Territory
uofmpress.ca

Cataloguing data available from Library and Archives Canada
ISBN 978-1-77284-049-0 (PAPER)
ISBN 978-1-77284-050-6 (PDF)
ISBN 978-1-77284-051-3 (EPUB)
ISBN 978-1-77284-052-0 (BOUND)

Cover design by OTAMI-
Interior design by Karen Armstrong
Map design by Julie Witmer

This book has been published with the help of a grant from the
Federation for the Humanities and Social Sciences, through the Awards
to Scholarly Publications Program, using funds provided by the
Social Sciences and Humanities Research Council of Canada.

The University of Manitoba Press acknowledges the financial support
for its publication program provided by the Government of Canada
through the Canada Book Fund, the Canada Council for the Arts, the
Manitoba Department of Sport, Culture, and Heritage, the Manitoba
Arts Council, and the Manitoba Book Publishing Tax Credit.

Funded by the Government of Canada | Canadä

CONTENTS

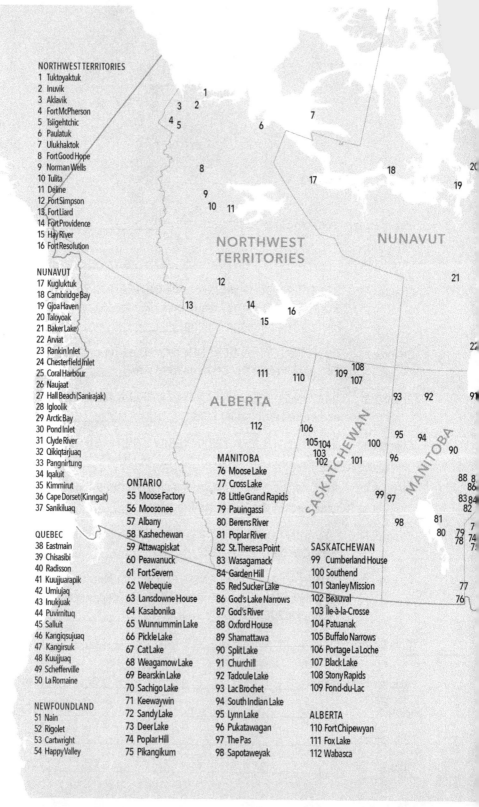

NORTHWEST TERRITORIES
1 Tuktoyaktuk
2 Inuvik
3 Aklavik
4 Fort McPherson
5 Tsiigehtchic
6 Paulatuk
7 Ulukhaktok
8 Fort Good Hope
9 Norman Wells
10 Tulita
11 Déline
12 Fort Simpson
13 Fort Liard
14 Fort Providence
15 Hay River
16 Fort Resolution

NUNAVUT
17 Kugluktuk
18 Cambridge Bay
19 Gjoa Haven
20 Taloyoak
21 Baker Lake
22 Arviat
23 Rankin Inlet
24 Chesterfield Inlet
25 Coral Harbour
26 Naujaat
27 Hall Beach (Sanirajak)
28 Igloolik
29 Arctic Bay
30 Pond Inlet
31 Clyde River
32 Qikiqtarjuaq
33 Pangnirtung
34 Iqaluit
35 Kimmirut
36 Cape Dorset (Kinngait)
37 Sanikiluaq

QUEBEC
38 Eastmain
39 Chisasibi
40 Radisson
41 Kuujjuarapik
42 Umiujaq
43 Inukjuak
44 Puvirnituq
45 Salluit
46 Kangiqsujuaq
47 Kangirsuk
48 Kuujjuaq
49 Schefferville
50 La Romaine

NEWFOUNDLAND
51 Nain
52 Rigolet
53 Cartwright
54 Happy Valley

ONTARIO
55 Moose Factory
56 Moosonee
57 Albany
58 Kashechewan
59 Attawapiskat
60 Peawanuck
61 Fort Severn
62 Webequie
63 Lansdowne House
64 Kasabonika
65 Wunnummin Lake
66 Pickle Lake
67 Cat Lake
68 Weagamow Lake
69 Bearskin Lake
70 Sachigo Lake
71 Keewaywin
72 Sandy Lake
73 Deer Lake
74 Poplar Hill
75 Pikangikum

MANITOBA
76 Moose Lake
77 Cross Lake
78 Little Grand Rapids
79 Pauingassi
80 Berens River
81 Poplar River
82 St. Theresa Point
83 Wasagamack
84 Garden Hill
85 Red Sucker Lake
86 God's Lake Narrows
87 God's River
88 Oxford House
89 Shamattawa
90 Split Lake
91 Churchill
92 Tadoule Lake
93 Lac Brochet
94 South Indian Lake
95 Lynn Lake
96 Pukatawagan
97 The Pas
98 Sapotaweyak

SASKATCHEWAN
99 Cumberland House
100 Southend
101 Stanley Mission
102 Beauval
103 Île-à-la-Crosse
104 Patuanak
105 Buffalo Narrows
106 Portage La Loche
107 Black Lake
108 Stony Rapids
109 Fond-du-Lac

ALBERTA
110 Fort Chipewyan
111 Fox Lake
112 Wabasca

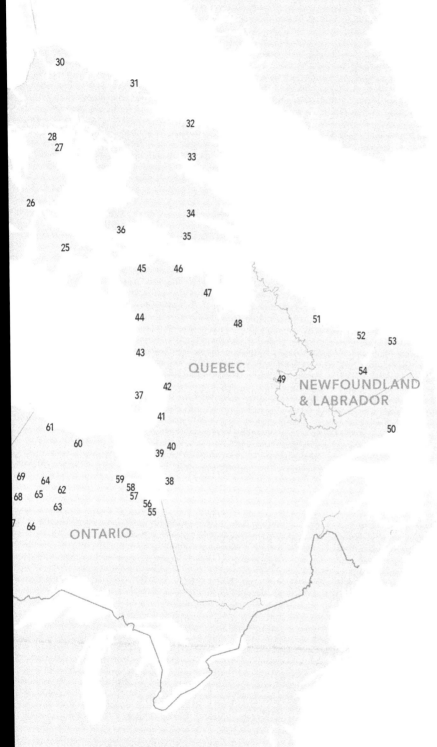

Current Northern Store/NorthMart Locations

PLUNDERING THE NORTH

INTRODUCTION

I think it's just the cost, really. I mean, how can I say this? You know: I am relatively healthy and I try to feed my family in a reasonably healthy way, but I buy ice cream, you know? . . . but like: it's eleven dollars for a tub of ice cream. And so, it's just the overall amount of money that families have to spend on food. . . . It's over fifty percent of your household budget. And that was based on somebody else's nutritious food basket estimate. Most people don't want to eat, necessarily, that food.[1]

—Community Member [Sarah]

Sarah (a pseudonym)[2] is a member of a fly-in First Nation in the geographic area now known as northern Ontario who works to address access to and the affordability of market-based foods in her community. She and her partner are also active harvesters and share the foods they harvest with extended family and friends. Sarah lives out a community reality of securing wider access to food for her family and those around her, but is an autonomous individual who makes her own decisions about what it means to live "well" or "healthy." She is also a person of some privilege in her community: Sarah is well educated, lives in a dual-income household, and helps operate a food market that brings fresh foods at cost into her community on a bi-weekly basis. Nevertheless, food access remains a significant concern for Sarah and her family.

Sarah's community has a Northern Store—a retail chain operated by the North West Company (NWC), the successor of the Hudson's Bay Company (HBC). The Northern Store is frequently the only full-service grocery store in many First Nation and Inuit communities located in northern Canada. The food sold at the Northern Store in Sarah's First Nation is exorbitantly expensive—at least double the cost of the same food sold in southern Canada.[3]

The NWC has consolidated a near monopoly on food sales in the Canadian North and expanded its operations in the early twenty-first century to include financial and banking services, medical and pharmaceutical services, bottled and purified water sales, as well as postal operations. Even though Sarah's First Nation runs initiatives intended to bolster Indigenous food sovereignty and security distinct from the NWC (such as harvester support programs), they are regularly forced to rely on NWC business operations for many state-sponsored programs intended to support the health and well-being of the most vulnerable community members. Sarah explains:

> As far as prenatal programs are concerned . . . we're given these vouchers that can be handed out to pregnant women and women who are . . . breastfeeding their infant for up to one year. And those food vouchers, it's for milk and some food. Those are only redeemable at the Northern Store. . . . Also, one of the programs at the Health Centre would buy emergency supplies like diapers or that kind of thing, and that would come from the Northern Store. So, within [a local health organization], we would just request a purchase order, and that purchase order would be redeemed over there. Technically, I think we could redeem our purchase orders in the other local stores, but we don't do that so much—well, because the Northern Store is the only full service grocery store.[4]

In this context, it is very difficult for people to purchase food and household goods locally or run community programming without using the Northern Store.

We began with Sarah's story because her experience with the Northern Store and, by extension, the NWC reveals the contemporary contexts in which people living in northern First Nations and Inuit communities are forced to make choices about food. First and foremost, the cost of food and other essential goods in northern communities is prohibitive, difficult to access, and available from a very limited number of retailers. Second, what is available at northern retailers is largely predetermined by non-Indigenous people who do not live in the Canadian North. Since the Second World War, the federal government has increasingly sought to govern which foods Indigenous peoples should or should not eat, either directly through forced purchasing lists and food subsidies or indirectly through shame-based nutrition education programs and initiatives that consistently position Indigenous bodies as unhealthy and, increasingly in the latter part of the twentieth century, as obese and in desperate need of intervention.[5] The introduction of market-based foods of poor quality, divorced from socio-cultural meanings, worked alongside provincial and federal governments in the twentieth century to undermine Indigenous food sovereignties through the criminalization of harvesting practices, severing the intergenerational transmission of knowledge, and alienating people and communities from their territories. Third, northern grocery stores occupy a position of considerably more power in the socio-economic life of the communities in which they operate compared to their southern counterparts. State-funded programs and services have long been routed first through the HBC and now through the NWC, enabling corporations to benefit enormously from providing relief, social services, and food programming. Finally, the NWC, like the federal government, dedicates a considerable amount of its resources to sanitizing its operations by employing a discursive chicanery to make it appear as if they are providing a service or "doing a favour" for northern communities that helps rather than hinders Indigenous food sovereignties.[6] We interrogate how relational discourses of service provision, benevolence, and "aid" continue to permeate much of how the state, the HBC, and its successor the NWC position themselves in Indigenous communities and in northern Canada more broadly. The Canadian government has certainly not, as it claims, "made a healthy, modern lifestyle a reality . . . in the magnificent yet stark wilderness" of the Canadian North, nor does it have "preserving quality and freshness down to a science."[7] Instead, the state has done quite the opposite by ensuring First Nations and Inuit communities who have thrived in their territories since time immemorial do so with increasing difficulty. The federal government and its exercise of colonial governance has facilitated the presence and growth of corporate interests in northern First Nations and Inuit communities.

The objective of this book, then, is to unpack the history of federal Indigenous food policies and corporate practices in the provincial and far North in Canada in the post–Second World War period. We seek to elaborate upon how the state in the last century has manufactured food insecurity and retail monopolies in northern First Nations and Inuit communities. A historical examination reveals that the present-day northern retail landscape is not the result of the business acumen of the NWC's executives or the perceived failure of Indigenous peoples to become more like European-Canadians. Instead, settler colonialism and corporate welfare have created the current food landscape. In order to illuminate the history of this problem, we trace the partnership established between the federal government and the HBC in the late nineteenth and early twentieth centuries, focusing in particular on the ways in which food and foodways became a technology of assimilation used by the state in their efforts to destroy the national patterns of Indigenous peoples and ultimately acquire their land. Built on the foundations of the former Northern Department of the HBC and purchased by HBC executives and private investors in 1987, the NWC currently holds a position of market dominance in most northern First Nations and Inuit communities. The NWC inherited many of the relationships and business practices developed and employed by the HBC over centuries of operations on Turtle Island.[8] Building on the foundations laid by the HBC, the NWC leveraged their market share of food sales to include other essential services unavailable elsewhere in many northern communities, like banking and pharmacies. This business model has proven so profitable that the NWC has exported it further south to rural and low-income communities in the south Pacific and Caribbean.

We think it is extremely important to understand the historical conditions of possibility that produced and maintained the current circumstances in northern Indigenous communities wherein high rates of food insecurity persist and the solutions generated by the state to address food insecurity are divorced from the systems in which they were produced. Moreover, what we are witnessing in the late twentieth and early twenty-first centuries in the crafting of federal Indian policy are neoliberal ideologies where "the notion of free market rationalities" have come to inform state food policy, its proposed solutions, and the bodies upon which those policies/solutions are imposed. In other words, notions of "individualism, privatization, and decentralization reign supreme."[9] Such cold rationalities lie in direct opposition to the operation of Indigenous food sovereignties. By placing the discourses of the programs and government officials alongside the histories of state and corporate practices in the North, we can see how the settler state comes to understand itself as a benevolent, scientifically minded, and modern government through its project of assimilating Indigenous food systems to settler strategies of grocery shopping and market-based food consumption.

Indigenous Food Sovereignties and Canadian Settler Colonialism

Our work focuses on those geographic regions in Canada that are currently known as the provincial norths and the Arctic or far North. We did not choose this geographic focus because these arbitrary divisions created by the colonial state accurately reflect the diversity of Indigenous nations and cultures. Rather, we explore settler colonial histories of assimilation and introduced foods in the northern First Nations and Inuit communities that are characterized by the federal and provincial governments as northern, rural, and "remote." Remote is used to refer to those communities that are accessible only by plane for the majority of the year. We examine a northern imaginary wherein the Canadian state casts the North as uninhabitable while simultaneously pilfering lucrative natural resources in the region. Discourses of the North as remote and vast have been (and are currently) used to legitimize the dispossession of Indigenous peoples from their territories, making disproportionate rates of poverty and food insecurity appear normal and neutral.

The provincial norths are the sub-arctic region that runs from the coast of British Columbia (through the provinces of Alberta, Saskatchewan, Manitoba, Ontario, Quebec, and Newfoundland and Labrador) across the Canadian Shield to the coast of Labrador.[10] Directly north of the sub-arctic lies the Arctic, popularly referred to as the far North, and includes the following socio-political divisions: Nunavut, Northwest Territories, Yukon, Nunatsiavut, and Nunavik. First Nations located in the provincial norths briefly have access to more southern markets via seasonal winter roads. This intermittent access is being rapidly reduced due to climate change. Food, goods, gas, and building materials are transported into "remote" northern communities through long and complicated shipping routes, including trains, planes, barges (for communities located along the coast), and winter roads. Heavy materials and foods with long shelf lives are usually shipped during the winter months on seasonal roads.

The Indigenous peoples and nations that have lived in the geographic areas that make up Canada's provincial and far norths occupy diverse cultural, social, ecological, geographical, and climatic realities. Given that "the North" makes up more than half of the land mass now known as Canada, enormous variation exists in physical landscapes, plant and animal life, and Indigenous food sovereignties.[11] However, what remains consistent across these territories and diverse cultures are the significant, and in some cases rapid, changes that have taken place during the twentieth century. For instance, the provincial and far norths have experienced economic and environmental degradation through resource extraction, climate change, and the imposition of federal Indian policies that saw the creation of reserves and forced sedentary living, the internment of children in residential schools, and other violent interventions associated with the Canadian settler colonial project. Provincial hunting laws, deputized game wardens, and criminalized Indigenous food economies all played foundational roles in limiting food choices for Indigenous families in the North. Today, many northern First Nations and Inuit communities' food systems are comprised of a mixture of land- and water-based foods acquired through hunting, trapping, and fishing; locally grown and harvested foods; and introduced market-based foods that are shipped into communities along extended transportation routes. These market foods are sold in what is often the only store in the community at more than twice the price of the same food sold in southern parts of Canada.[12] Discourses around the high price of foods generally focus on long transportation routes and extreme environmental conditions,[13] obscuring the processes of settler colonialism that have been taking place for more than a century.

The assault on Indigenous food sovereignties by the Canadian state has eroded the ability of Indigenous communities to govern and determine all aspects of their food systems, and as a result, food insecurity rates in northern Indigenous communities have skyrocketed. Food insecurity is measured at the household level and refers to "inadequate or insecure access to food due to financial constraints."[14] To illustrate the severity of food insecurity for Indigenous communities in northern Canada, the United Nations Special Rapporteur on the Right to Food, Olivier De Schutter, issued a report on his visit to Canada in 2012. De Schutter notes in the report that 60 percent of on-reserve Indigenous households in northern Manitoba were food insecure, as were 70 percent of adults in Nunavut. These rates of food insecurity, he observed, were six times higher than the national average and "represent[ed] the highest document[ed] food insecurity rate for any Aboriginal population in a developed country."[15] The federal government has described food insecurity in northern Indigenous communities in Canada as a "serious public health issue."[16] More significantly, the long-term impact of food insecurity has grave cumulative physical, social, and mental health consequences on both children and adults.[17]

Indigenous health scholars and those engaged in food studies have been some of the leading academic voices in underscoring the ongoing nature of northern food insecurity as well as its alarming impact on the well-being of First Nations and Inuit communities.[18] Of particular relevance here are scholars who centre Indigenous food sovereignties alongside conversations about food insecurity. Indigenous food sovereignty refers to the capacity of Indigenous peoples to control all aspects of their food systems, including production, distribution, cultural knowledges and practices, and environmental safety.[19] According to Michelle Daigle, Indigenous food sovereignties are both "a resistance against the inter-workings of settler colonialism and neoliberal capitalism, and a resurgence of Indigenous forms of authority and autonomy."[20] Foreclosures of Indigenous food sovereignty have thus been identified as worthy objects of critique as well as examples of settler colonialism.

Settler colonialism operates distinctly from other forms of colonialism, such as classical colonialism or post-colonialism, in that it "considers those political and geographic contexts in which the colonisers never left."[21] The assertion of settler authority and sovereignty is predicated upon the erasure of Indigenous peoples through what Patrick Wolfe describes as a "logic of elimination."[22] Here, Indigenous peoples are targeted by policies that seek to extinguish them as distinct peoples, cultures, and nations through a variety of eliminatory strategies, including those directed at Indigenous food and foodways such as hunting and fishing regulations.[23] Settler colonialism, in Wolfe's formulation, "strives for the dissolution of Indigenous nations and sovereignties in order to erect a new colonial society on the expropriated land base" and introduces alien social, economic, and political orders that are typically, though not exclusively, dominated by settlers.[24] Thus, settler colonialism functions not merely through the attempted elimination or destruction of Indigenous sovereignties or foodways, but through the efforts of settler states and polities to make Indigenous peoples stop being Indigenous. In Wolfe's words, "settler colonialism destroys to replace,"[25] and the construction of a national identity rooted in whiteness, Britishness, heteropatriarchy, and middle-class values remains central to the dispossession of Indigenous nations and communities.[26]

Lorenzo Veracini theorized that settler colonial conditions included targeting Indigenous peoples through assimilatory policies intended to absorb them into the settler body politic through federal legislation like Canada's

Gradual Civilization Act (1857) and the Gradual Enfranchisement Act (1869). Veracini also includes "enforced sedentarisation" and "coerced lifestyle change" as part of the settler colonial toolkit to eliminate Indigenous national patterns and secure settler sovereignties.[27] The destruction and dispossession of Indigenous foodways figure prominently here and are visible within the genocidal policies and actions of the state through the incarceration of Indigenous children in residential schools, the criminalization of Indigenous healing practices and ceremony, the imposition of the pass system, and the non-recognition of treaty rights to hunting and fishing, to name but a few.[28] All of these policies sought to accomplish the ultimate goal of severing Indigenous peoples' relationships with the land. Recent federal supports for Indigenous harvesting and sovereignty must also be viewed cautiously. Glen Coulthard and Audra Simpson unpack these political economies and elaborate on how settler colonialism works to destabilize Indigenous sovereignties by enfolding and prescribing Indigeneity within limited and performative settler articulations.[29] Thus, the state seeks to reduce the operation of Indigenous food sovereignties to a limited and overregulated number of harvesting and land-based practices that do not threaten settler sovereignty or the vast amount of money to be made from selling poor quality market-based foods to Indigenous peoples. Such expressions directly contradict Indigenous articulations of food sovereignties where, as Dawn Morrison eloquently writes: "Food is a gift from the creator. In this respect, the right to food is sacred and cannot be constrained or recalled by colonial laws, policies, or institutions."[30]

Veracini further elaborates on the role played by foodways in what he describes as "settler gastrocolonialism" and the ways in which food became and remains central to the consolidation and reproduction of settler colonial polities. "Settler food is a prerequisite of settler colonialism," writes Veracini, "but also its outcome, because to make settler food, the foodways of the Indigenous populations must be disrupted . . . one social body must starve so that the reproduction of another can be ensured."[31] In this framing, the foodways of Indigenous peoples in the Canadian North and settler colonial locales elsewhere can be read historically as a conceptual battleground on which settler or Indigenous futurities have been secured or foreclosed. Billy-Ray Belcourt explicitly locates the imposition of settler foodways as a bio-political invasion. That is, as a lived experience of settler colonialism and Canadian federal Indian policy, statecraft, and interventionism (rather than as a sociological reflection of free subjects making personal choices about what they eat).[32] Belcourt describes the politics of Indigenous food access by underscoring how on-reserve "junk food invades your diet and ... the convenience store stymies personal agency" under conditions of food scarcity and unaffordability, given that "the protracted craving to eat junk food is stalled by the petty knowledge that those kinds of products are bad for you and that there is little you can do about it."[33] The lack of choice and food freedom in northern communities is a useful example of how settler governmentalities have functioned within the colonial project.

Settler governmentality refers to those spaces and processes when "apparatus[es] of the state come to embroil itself with the business of knowing and administering the lives and activities of the persons and things across a territory."[34] As a concept, governmentality is extremely relevant in the Canadian context, where settlers prefer the façade of political liberalism and benevolence as opposed to more overtly visible draconian modes of rule.[35] For example, Andrew Crosby and Jeffrey Monaghan have gone so far as to argue that, as a concept, "settler governmentality reflects the particular rationalities of governance that animate Canada's relationship with, and governance of, Indigenous peoples."[36] Going further, the pair cite Wolfe's "logic of elimination" to describe how, despite its liberal edifice, Canadian "settler governmentality implements techniques to eliminate Indigenous life-worlds."[37] Here, Canada's Food Guide serves as a fitting example of settler governmentality, given the extent to which it seeks to align the individual and everyday choices of Canadian and Indigenous subjects to the goals, values, practices, and priorities of the settler state. Charlotte Biltekoff notes that "dietary ideals are cultural, subjective, and political,"[38] and efforts to encourage people to eat "right" are inevitably about shaping, creating, and reforming particular subjects, especially those situated as "the other." Thus, what presents itself as rational, normalized, taken-for-granted, and common-sense nutrition advice and praxis, often involves two kinds of violence that operationalize the "logic of elimination." First, as Belcourt observes, foods linked to "dietary ideals" are frequently unavailable or unaffordable on many reserves, ultimately producing death and disease in a necropolitical fashion of physical suffering and violence. Second, eating like settlers represents, for Indigenous peoples, a form of social death or cultural genocide through what Veracini identified as "settler gastrocolonialism" and the destruction of Indigenous foodways.

Situating Canadian food policies and NWC business operations as embedded in settler colonial governmentalities helps us to articulate the embodied as well as the symbolic violence that attends ongoing histories of northern retailing, which have served simultaneously to produce corporate profit for settlers while at the same time assimilating Indigenous peoples so that they eat like white people. If Indigenous peoples become more like white Canadians, then the lands upon which they have lived well since time immemorial will become the possessions of the settler state.[39] Here, whiteness does not refer to skin colour but the adoption of qualities coded as "white" such as civility, rationality, property ownership, and responsible or healthy behaviours like eating those foods associated with European-Canadian culture.[40] As Kathy Squadrito has noted, agrarian labour has been fetishized in European philosophical registers, which caused key thinkers to construct Indigenous peoples as "uncivilized" to the extent that they used their land and fed themselves differently from Europeans.[41] For this reason, whiteness and western foodways are deeply entangled within the political imaginary of settler colonialism, thereby making what Christopher Mayes called an "unsettling of food politics" possible in the Canadian context as well as in other settler-colonial locales.[42]

By naming and critiquing whiteness in the formulation of federal food policies and corporate practices, we seek to make the role of white supremacy more visible within our larger critique of settler governmentality and gastrocolonialism. The supposedly benign labelling of certain foods as "good" and others as "bad" conceals the operation of white supremacy and racism in creating these value-laden categories. The identification of certain foods as "healthier" was and is made possible only through the logics of white supremacy, as white supremacy is the "defining logic as [social perceptions of food] are culturally and materially produced."[43] Our book historicizes how the operations of the HBC, and then the NWC, participated in and indeed benefitted from the exercise of settler colonial governance over northern Indigenous bodies and food systems during the twentieth and early twenty-first centuries.

Canadian Historiographies of Food and Settler Colonialism

Colonial food relations are grounded in much more expansive histories of Turtle Island and the arrival of Europeans on these territories. Upon arrival and for several centuries, Indigenous nations and communities fed

Europeans. The Wendat (Ouendat) Confederacy of the sixteenth century served as the bread basket for the people of New France, and other European communities traded with and learned from Indigenous nations. Fur traders, in particular, relied on the expertise of Indigenous women and communities for sustenance and the acquisition of skills regarding harvesting and food provision on Turtle Island. These skills and knowledges were not singular and, given the environmental diversity of Turtle Island, were shared by many different peoples countless times and in diverse ways. These histories are often overlooked and ignored in the face of ongoing settler-colonial efforts to erase Indigenous knowledges, cultures, and communities and undermine Indigenous sovereignties.

Works by Sarah Carter, Hugh Shewell, and James Daschuk clearly show that the state frequently used food resources and rations to ensure the compliance of Indigenous bodies and nations.[44] Shewell's work, *"Enough to Keep Them Alive,"* looks at the practice of rationing as part of the growth of the social welfare apparatus and a means of chronicling the ways that Indian policy, although appearing outwardly different, retained its assimilatory logic. Significantly, Shewell shows how these social welfare systems had their origins in the practices and policies employed by the HBC. The post–Second World War period witnessed a growing interest in the expansion of the welfare state and the importance of "nutrition related initiatives"; the politicization of food in this period made it a central component in how the state interacted with and managed Indigenous bodies through education, economic, and social programming.[45] Krista Walters's work is particularly foundational here because it reveals how European-Canadian nutrition regimes in the post–Second World War period were central to the formulation of federal Indian policy. Walters elucidates how "Nutrition Canada helped launch a new chapter in the assimilationist project, aimed specifically at nutritionally deviant Indigenous bodies."[46] Indeed, the historiography has thoroughly addressed the assimilatory efforts of the state to bring Indigenous peoples closer to whiteness,[47] especially its gendered nature, through the imposition of European-Canadian domesticities. Similar processes are visible through the regulation of Indigenous foodways. Heidi Bohaker and Franca Iacovetta found that Canadian officials sought to introduce Canadian citizenships by making Indigenous women more like European-Canadians through a range of educational programming, including the introduction of so-called healthy Canadian diets as determined by nutrition experts.[48]

Food is an important category of analysis because it both "illuminate[s] how personal and group identity is constructed,"[49] and can be understood historically as a tool that "reinforce[s] the disciplinary colonial power structures"[50] that persisted in all Indigenous-state relations in Canada. The mass internment of Indigenous children serves as a particularly poignant reminder of how food was used by the state to discipline Indigenous bodies and to try to destroy cultural identities. The hunger felt by Indigenous children was not merely a function of government and church neglect but also conscious action on the part of the state and health researchers using the bodies of Indigenous children to understand malnutrition. Ian Mosby's article on nutrition experiments conducted at residential schools highlights the "false perceptions that [Indigenous peoples] had somehow been left behind by modernity and were therefore in need of the benevolent hand of settler scientists, experts, and professionals."[51] The embodied violence of residential schools is illustrated by researchers like Paul Hackett, Sylvia Abonyi, and Roland Dyck, who explore the body mass index, height, and weight of Indigenous children who entered residential schools in Manitoba and Saskatchewan between 1919 and 1953 and found that children entered these institutions relatively well-fed.[52] The profound and long-term impacts that the residential school system had on both Indigenous bodies and food sovereignties through the disruption of the intergenerational transmission of knowledge and social and cultural community practices remains ongoing and is an important area of inquiry.[53]

Indigenous food sovereignties were also impacted by other settler colonial processes that sought to secure Canada's sovereignty and economic wealth through resource extraction. For instance, Indigenous politicians, activists, and community members, as well as academics, have illuminated the devastating histories of forced relocations in the Arctic during the Cold War;[54] the disruptive effects of natural resource development projects (that can scare or sometimes kill herd animals);[55] the contamination of ecosystems and especially waterways with mercury and other pollutants;[56] and the environmental fallouts associated with climate change.[57] Further work on these forces in shaping Indigenous food sovereignties and securities is ongoing, and we do not explore them in great detail in this book. Instead, we make note of them because they are part of the context in which Indigenous peoples are forced to make choices about food.

Historians elsewhere have found deep connections between the presence and actions of colonial powers and the making of starvation—notably, that there is a history to the creation of hunger and food insecurity,[58] and it is these connections that we plan to tease out in this work. Understanding this history is important to appreciate and unpack the ways in which food and foodways constitute the architecture of the settler colonial project. Indeed, challenging the dominant narratives that continue to situate Indigenous hunger or high rates of diabetes as a function of "transitioning"[59] from a mobile to sedentary lifestyle or as poorly informed choices is essential to addressing deeply embedded racist assumptions about Indigenous peoples.

Position, Method, and Chapter Outline

For us as settler scholars, the path this project took was very much a process of unlearning and learning what constituted good research and the importance of working with Indigenous communities. In doing so, we drew on the knowledges of Indigenous scholars who have long tried to impress upon settler scholars, especially historians, the value of Indigenous methodologies and the importance of embedding ethical and reciprocal relationships in the research process.[60] Carrying out research that engages with Indigenous contexts, histories, and experiences is a process where "knowledge is generated through relationship."[61] In that relationship, we are held accountable for the research questions, methodology, and outcomes.[62] As a discipline, History has been reticent to see the importance of relationship building and ensuring that outcomes hold value for contemporary Indigenous communities.[63] Instead, the discipline of history has long touted that its practitioners are objective witnesses that study the past and refrain from imposing so-called contemporary beliefs or interpretations on historical events and subjects. We scoff at the ridiculous suggestion that objectivity or "distance" is even possible, much less desirable under conditions of settler colonialism and widespread food insecurity across the North.[64] Drawing on the words of Adam Gaudry, we affirm that "research is always a political process," and any mythical claim to objectivity only serves to amplify a colonial system that seeks to obscure its very operations.[65]

This project grew from the authors' broader food security work with Indigenous communities in northern Ontario, which supports resurgent activities engaged in food sovereignty and undertakes policy and anti-colonial/racism work. The former is largely community-based work that centres a politic of refusal[66] within Indigenous food systems. For instance, a biweekly market that sells foods at cost is embedded in community relationships of responsibility and reciprocity rather than corporate profit and settler colonialism. The latter includes work that seeks to illuminate the ways in which settler colonialism and white supremacy inform and shape federal Indian policy. More specifically, this work arose out of our interest in the North West Company and how it came to operate in fly-in First Nations in northwestern Ontario. This interest was generated for Burnett in 2009, after they had worked on an undergraduate thesis with a student from a fly-in First Nation in northern Ontario.[67] The student wanted to understand the relationships between the high cost of food in their community and Type 2 diabetes. The student undertook a food costing comparison between their home community and Thunder Bay—the price differences were shocking for Burnett and demanded further explanation. Even after the student had moved on, Burnett had become invested in understanding how the NWC came to occupy its current position in many northern First Nations. This precipitated an examination of the publicly available corporate records of the NWC: annual reports generated for shareholders, newspaper coverage, and government food costing studies. Initially, we focused on the contemporary policies and practices of the NWC: how the company determined the price of food versus shipping costs, food quality, the role of store managers, and best-before dates, to name a few. From there, the project snowballed to include federal Indian policies that impacted food access in the Canadian north.

We were also asked to explore the historical records of the federal government and the Hudson's Bay Company to understand current federal policies and corporate practices. Our research questions were formulated in conjunction with Indigenous food sovereigntists and community members who wanted to better understand why the NWC operates as a virtual monopoly in many Anishinaabe communities. We were frequently asked during community conversations about non-competition clauses and one-hundred-year leases held by the HBC and, by extension, the NWC. People were especially interested in understanding how such contracts were negotiated without the consent, and frequently without the knowledge, of First Nations. As historians, we were well situated to undertake this investigation within the colonial archive and to draw attention to the histories of government and corporate food policies and practices in northern Canada. To that end, we spent considerable time at Library and Archives Canada in Ottawa as well as the Hudson's Bay Company Archives in Winnipeg. The archival research was informed by interviews with community members, government employees, and employees of the HBC and, later, the NWC. We held a series of community conversations where people shared their concerns and experiences about northern retailers and the cost of food. Here, numerous people we spoke with talked about the long-term relationships and obligations they believed the HBC had formed with their communities. Many people's grandparents had worked for the company as trappers or in the transportation of foods and goods. Others expressed surprise that First Nations had not been part of the discussions involving the sale of the HBC in 1987. We also had countless informal conversations with people that took the form of what Cathy Mattes describes as kitchen table talks.[68] People invited us into their homes and fed us, and they sat with us at restaurants and coffee shops. In these spaces, our long-term friendships, relationships, and obligations were solidified, and our understandings about the intimate impact of federal and corporate food policies crystallized. In other instances, once people found out we were looking into the history of the NWC, they sought us out to share their stories. All of these conversations, formal and informal, shaped how we approached the documentary record we were tasked with examining. In other words, we read the documentary record through and alongside the experiences of Indigenous peoples living in the North.

Most of the sources used in this monograph were texts produced by the state and corporations, and they form part of the imperial archive and a "fantasy of knowledge collected and united in the service of the state."[69] However, we think it is necessary to examine these records as "cross-sections of contested knowledge . . . as both transparencies on which power relations were inscribed and intricate technologies of rule in themselves."[70] We made this decision in the context of looking at the policies and practices of the state and corporations, not because the stories that people shared with us did not matter or were irrelevant. Notably, we wanted to avoid what Eve Tuck has described as "damage-centred research *and* damaging research."[71] The effects of long-term food insecurity and settler violence should be clear, and there is no need to recount those stories here; indeed, a great deal of uncritical food studies literature already takes on much of this work. Debbie Martin offers a useful analysis of studies that focus on the impact of what has been described as the nutrition transition[72] on Indigenous peoples. Notably, these studies attribute rising rates of chronic disease in Indigenous communities to poor personal choices without properly addressing the socio-cultural, economic, and political environments in which choices about foods are made.[73] Our reading of the colonial archive centred community members' conversations and perspectives. Indeed, a history that privileged the perspective of the federal government and the HBC/NWC would look very different from what the reader will find in this book.

Our book is a statist history that reveals the dysfunction and violence of the settler state and the ways it has materially produced food insecurity in the North, normalized by employing specific discursive practices. For the broader settler Canadian public, the current state of affairs in northern Indigenous communities has been naturalized through the settler colonial hegemonies of the state and the NWC. The federal government and its efforts to resolve food insecurity in the North are represented in Canadian media as a noble failure, with the government trying but failing to do all that it can to make life liveable in the North.[74] When criticized for its monopolistic business operations and gouging of Indigenous communities in the Canadian North, the NWC is not above taking to the media to cleanse its image and insist that its immense profits are in no way unduly derived.[75] Further, the NWC positions itself as "serv[ing] communities as good corporate citizens"[76] through charitable donations and localized initiatives. It is important to unpack how these discursive practices distract from the settler colonial histories that have produced and perpetuated food insecurity in Indigenous communities, rationalized the high cost of food, and obscured the enormous profits being made at the expense of Indigenous peoples. Put simply, corporations are representing themselves as "good neighbours" through philanthropic activities that serve the bottom line.[77] This work seeks to destabilize this state of affairs.

Our first chapter briefly charts the criminalization of Indigenous foodways through the imposition of hunting and fishing regulations in direct violation of Indigenous sovereignty and the Treaties. We do this not because an examination of Indigenous foodways is the focus of this work but rather to set the stage upon which the federal government and Hudson's Bay Company introduced market-based foods into Indigenous communities and households. Chapter 2 picks up the history of the HBC prior to the Second World War to establish how the federal government used the company to carry out roles normally performed by the state. We also see the early impact of an emerging interest in nutrition on the retail practices of the HBC and its food sales in northern communities. The third chapter explores the role played by federal policy in shaping food access after the Second World War through newly created social welfare initiatives like the Family Allowance Program. Connections are drawn here between the forced purchasing lists created by Indian Affairs and the shifting retail practices of the HBC in the North.

Expanding on the changes that started in the 1940s, the fourth chapter looks at the establishment of the Northern Stores Department and the development of inland stores in the provincial and far norths. Chapter 5 looks at the history of the Food Mail Program and the ways in which the transportation subsidy schema informed the choices that Indigenous peoples could make about market-based foods. Drawing on hegemonic nutrition discourses, the chapter interrogates the constructions of good food and bad food in the context of food subsidies and settler colonialism. Chapter 6 returns to the Northern Stores Department of the HBC, its sale to company executives and private investors, and its transformation into the North West Company in 1987. In this chapter, we trace the NWC's intense focus on food sales and the accumulation of profit, specializing in retail that focuses on low-income, northern, and rural spaces with high barriers to entry as a business model that produces enormous profit. The last chapter brings us to the present and the replacement of the Food Mail Program with Nutrition North Canada—a subsidy paid directly to retailers with minimal oversight. Our conclusion offers an illustrative example of how these historical patterns, established over a century, remain operative in the current iteration of the HBC—the NWC.

A thread that flows throughout each chapter is how discourses around nutrition deficits in Indigenous communities and bodies are used to justify state intrusion into the intimate and familial spaces of people's lives. In particular, we highlight how market-based solutions to food insecurity and poverty obscure and dismiss the enormous profits being made in northern communities from the sale of food. Although we are dealing with the state, corporate entities, and the operation of capitalism before and after the rise of neoliberalism, we chose to forefront settler colonialism in our analysis, given the extent to which state interventions into northern markets have historically assisted the operation of the HBC and NWC. State support has occurred to such a degree that drawing a neat line between state and market actors becomes misrepresentative of the power dynamics involved in these histories, which have produced and positioned First Nations and Inuit communities as captive consumers of grocery store foods.

CHAPTER 1

SETTLER COLONIALISM AND INDIGENOUS FOOD SOVEREIGNTY:
The Assault on Indigenous Hunting, Fishing, Trapping, and Trading

We draw on the words of Dawn Morrison from her influential 2011 work that characterizes "Indigenous food sovereignty [as] describing, rather than defining, the present-day strategies that enable and support the ability of Indigenous communities to sustain traditional hunting, fishing, gathering, farming, and distribution practices, the way we have done for thousands of years prior to contact with the first European settlers."[1] Morrison further emphasizes that Indigenous food sovereignties can only be exercised through "upholding our longstanding sacred responsibilities to nurture healthy, interdependent relationships with the land, plants, and animals that provide us with our food."[2] This explanation underscores both a responsibility and relationship to the land that, as Adam Barker argues, operates in direct "opposition to colonial forces that would displace Indigenous peoples from their homelands, disrupt Indigenous communities and cultures to attack their sovereignty, and destroy Indigenous territories through extraction and [so-called] development."[3] In this context, Indigenous food and foodways are, and have been, sites of conflict and violence between Indigenous peoples and the settlers who seek to lay claim to Turtle Island. While this chapter does not address Indigenous food sovereignties directly, it offers a brief overview of some of the regulatory regimes that prevented Indigenous peoples from exercising their obligations to and relationships with the land to illustrate how settler colonialism operates in such a way that "one social body must starve to ensure the reproduction of another social body."[4]

The late nineteenth and twentieth centuries witnessed growing efforts by settler-colonial authorities to contain and reduce Indigenous food systems to seasonal and occasional recreational pursuits. Both federal and provincial governments increasingly approached Indigenous hunting, fishing, and trapping as something that might disrupt capitalist economies and land-based resource extraction, and ideologies of white supremacy positioned Indigenous foodways as markers of a lack of so-called "civilization." The result has been a number of legislative interventions upon and encroachments of Indigenous food sovereignties, as well as treaty rights related to hunting, fishing, trapping, and trading. This chapter reviews a few illustrative examples that reveal how Indigenous foodways and sovereignties were targeted for elimination through the abrogation of treaties and the imposition of provincial fishing and hunting regulations. Although these regulatory frameworks are not the focus of this book, we briefly illuminate some of them to make visible the context in which the policies and practices of the state and corporate entities like the HBC took place. As we aim to show, the circumstances in which Indigenous peoples were forced to make choices about foods were never neutral, solely about market dynamics, or divorced from the architecture of Canadian settler colonialism.

The regulatory regimes imposed by provincial governments to reduce Indigenous peoples' access to land- and water-based foods have a long history on Turtle Island and follow earlier patterns established by colonial governments. Thus, it was not surprising that Indigenous leaders and community members made access to hunting, fishing, harvesting, and land management a key priority during the treaty-making processes that took place before and after Confederation. For example, the Wabanaki Confederacy, located on the eastern shores of Turtle Island, worked together to defend their fisheries from settler incursions in several conflicts throughout the eighteenth century.[5] Military resistance, such as the Raid of Dartmouth (1751), forced the British to sign the Peace and Friendship Treaty of 1752, in which King George II promised that "the said Tribe of Indians shall not be hindered from, but have free liberty of Hunting and Fishing as usual."[6] The treaty further stipulated that Indigenous signatories would be able to harvest and sell "skins, feathers, fowl, fish, or any other thing" as well as receive "a quantity of bread, flour, and such other provisions ... half year for the time to come."[7] The 1752 agreement, for instance, protected the right to trade, including in the truckhouses (a type of trading post) that the government had created and subsidized.[8] In

1760, another Peace and Friendship Treaty was signed that later became the focal point of *R. v. Marshall* (1999) in the Canadian supreme court, wherein Mi'qmaw fisherman Donald Marshall Jr. had his treaty rights to a "modest income" affirmed by Canada's Supreme Court.[9]

Although the British Crown guaranteed the Mi'kmaq and Wabanaki peoples access to hunting and fishing through the Treaties, in practice, the colonies immediately moved to annul these rights by enacting fishing regulations that disproportionately impacted the Mi'kmaq and other Wabanaki peoples from accessing salmon fisheries. Foreshadowing provincial hunting and fishing laws passed centuries later, colonial governors established a "closed season for salmon fishing, gear restriction on stationary net fishing in estuaries, and the requirement of providing a fish-way on mill dams."[10] Such measures secured settlers a deeper managerial control of fisheries and set the stage for "modern fisheries administration." These colonial acts of governance did not consider Indigenous sovereignties; rather, settlers sought to establish a locus of natural resource control within the colony that privileged settlers at the expense of Indigenous communities. Unfortunately, this pattern of governmentality centring on the erasure of Indigenous sovereignties was not a coastal but rather a continental characteristic of the settler colonial histories in the geographic area that came to be known as Canada.

The Robinson-Superior Treaty of 1850 serves as another pre-Confederation example of benefits accrued by settlers and corporations at the expense of the First Nations who tried to protect their land and water resources. Covering lands surrounding the Great Lakes, the Robinson-Superior Treaty promised Anishinaabe signatories "the full and free privilege to hunt over the territory now ceded by them, and to fish in the waters thereof as they have heretofore been in the habit of doing, saving and excepting only such portions of the said territory as may from time to time be sold or leased to individuals, or companies of individuals, and occupied by them with the consent of the Provincial Government."[11] As in the previous example, the foodways of the Anishinaabe were immediately impacted by increased mining and timber and natural resource extraction industries. The HBC also benefitted powerfully from both sides of the treaty-signing process: as Indigenous access to the land became enshrined within treaty rights, their potential to extract the surplus value of Indigenous labour in a fledgling fur trade economy was somewhat bolstered if not guaranteed. On the other hand, the disruption to Indigenous foodways wrought by increased mining, timber, and natural resource extraction industries created more Indigenous reliance on goods purchased from HBC outposts. What is more, HBC forts and outposts were key to the westward expansion of settlement into present-day northwestern Ontario and Manitoba. In this setting, fish remained a staple food source for settlers, with sturgeon, whitefish, and lake trout becoming popular food commodities often produced by Indigenous harvesters. As signs of settler encroachment into Indigenous territories, HBC forts were often synonymous with environmental and ecological distress. For example, one Jesuit observer residing in Robinson-Superior territory made the following comments about a regional outpost in December of 1850: "[The HBC] wash and throw their garbage in the water at the shore.... Moreover, even when the fish would be abundant in those regions, the fish flee from the spot because the filth remaining in backwaters prevents the water from being purified quickly enough. In this way, the very finest fishing ground can be lost. This is what brings on famine."[12] Food shortages and even starvation are, sadly, familiar forces in the history of treaty making in Canada, and doubly so in the post-Confederation period.

Post-Confederation treaties witnessed a continuity in the inclusion of provisions related to the protection of Indigenous peoples' rights to hunt, fish, trap, and trade. The Numbered Treaty System, which facilitated settlement westward from northwestern Ontario across the plains, was to some extent shaped directly by fur trade histories in which food and access to food had played a primary role in the complex web of relations between colonists, Indigenous peoples, and companies. Treaty No. 3 (1873), for instance, promised Indigenous signatories "that they, the said Indians, shall have right to pursue their avocations of hunting and fishing throughout the tract surrendered as hereinbefore described, subject to such regulations as may from time to time be made by Her Government of Her Dominion of Canada, and saving and excepting such tracts as may, from time to time, be required or taken up for settlement, mining, lumbering or other purposes by Her said Government of the Dominion of Canada, or by any of the subjects thereof duly authorized therefor by the said Government."[13] The word "avocation" and its associations with labour and occupational hunting and fishing here is key, as the treaties (even in their written variations) clearly protected the right to trade game. Likewise, Treaty No. 5 (1875) included the following passage: "Her Majesty further agrees with Her said Indians, that they, the said Indians, shall have right to pursue their avocations of hunting and fishing

Figure 1. Old Fort William and the Hudson's Bay Company post, near the mouth of the Kaministiquia River, n.d. Credit: Library and Archives Canada, C-020770.

throughout the tract surrendered as hereinbefore described, subject to such regulations as may from time to time be made by Her Government of Her Dominion of Canada, and saving and excepting such tracts as may from time to time be required or taken up for settlement, mining, lumbering or other purposes, by Her said Government of the Dominion of Canada, or by any of the subjects thereof duly authorized therefor by the said Government."[14] Though complicated qualifiers regarding settler economies were included, treaty rights to hunting and fishing were always promised in perpetuity as opposed to provisionally. During the signing of Treaty No. 6 in 1876, for instance, Treaty Commissioner Alexander Morris explicitly guaranteed hunting and fishing rights were to be held by Indigenous signatories "for as long as the sun shines, the grass grows, and the rivers flow."[15] Treaty No. 6 is also notable, given that it contained particular provisions that promised relief from famine should Indigenous signatories find themselves in want of food.

Such inclusions to the treaties were dutifully pursued by Indigenous leadership in what is now present-day western Canada due in part to the decimation of the bison, the skulls of which were used to fertilize the farms of settlers participating in an emerging prairie wheat economy. As a number of historians observe, the 1860s and 1870s were a particularly acute period of Canadian federal authorities using food as a means to control Indigenous peoples, especially in present-day western Canada. As one Piikani Elder recalled of the signing of Treaty No. 7: "They were promised: you will be cared for. I heard they were given beef as rations at the signing of the treaty. They were not very interested in the beef. They would rather have buffalo, which was their main source of food, and it was taken from them. They used the buffalo for their existence in life. That's what I heard the people say. The decision to sign depended on Crowfoot's decision. These were leaders, and they looked to Crowfoot for that one decision. They all cooperated with him once he spoke."[16] Though Crowfoot did not speak for and represent all nations associated with the signing of Treaty 7, the relationship between the disruption of Indigenous foodways and the treaty-signing process was one of coercion. Indeed, the settler state as a representative of the Crown literally and symbolically offered meat to increasingly hungry First Nations, facilitating what was (in the state's eyes) the extinguishing of Aboriginal title to the land. James Daschuk's *Clearing the Plains* details this violent political history, wherein Plains Indigenous peoples were purposefully starved and deprived of food, shelter, and medicine to facilitate emptying of lands targeted for white settlement.[17]

The treaties also included provisions requiring the federal government to provide farming implements and instruction. However, as Sarah Carter illuminates in *Lost Harvests*, while the state wanted Indigenous peoples to become more like European farmers in present-day western Canada, these changes took place under the caveat that the success and productivity of Indigenous peoples remained limited in scope and size and did not compete with white settlers. Indeed, many Indigenous peoples in the Prairie West excelled at farming and ranching only to find themselves "quickly undermined by the federal government through a series of policies and regulations intended to reduce and eliminate agricultural production on-reserve to prevent competition with non-Indigenous farmers."[18] Again, what we see here is not only the relationship between treaty-signing, white settlement, and the foreclosure of Indigenous foodways but a historical tendency for the Canadian settler state to interfere within market economies and to act as a very visible hand that privileges particular forms of land use and food production by white European-Canadians over and above Indigenous nations.

It is difficult to overstate the devastating impact that settler encroachment had on the food sovereignties and well-being of Indigenous peoples on the Plains as well as across the provincial and territorial norths more broadly. As was the case with the Atlantic salmon on the east coast, settler devastation of food sources led inexorably to increased settler control over those same resources. In November of 1877, the North West Territorial Council passed *An Ordinance for the Protection of the Buffalo*, which placed several limits on bison hunting, including the practice of running herds toward cliff edges. Sitting Bull, who was in exile in Canada at the time, asked rhetorically: "when did the Almighty give the Canadian government the right to keep the Indians from killing the buffalo?"[19] In the following decade, starvation on the Plains continued. As Sydney Harring notes:

> The Northwest Rebellion [of 1885] was a watershed moment... that exposed the weakness in the dominion's prairie Indian policy. The Indian Department had determined that its Indian policy was too expensive and only created Indian dependency, and so it decided to cut rations to starvation levels to force Indians to work as small farmers. The plan was cruel and unworkable. . . . As resentment levels rose, altercations between reserve Indians and Indian Department officials increased. Grown Indian men were forced to beg petty Department officials for extra food for starving and sick children. The latter's refusal was not infrequently met with violence as individual Indians took the law into their own hands, striking officials or stealing food.[20]

Though this violence remains understandable, it was nonetheless rarely successful in terms of securing food for starving Indigenous families. Also, such resistance efforts were made manifestly more difficult after the 1885 introduction of the Pass System, which (illegally) restricted the free movement of First Nations people. In this era, the rise of provincial hunting and game legislation began to more acutely impact the capacity of Indigenous peoples to exercise their foodways.

Provincial Hunting Laws and the Criminalization of Indigenous Foodways

In her study of the rise of Canadian conservationism in the twentieth century, historian Tina Loo argues that "until the end of the nineteenth century ... conservation, whether carried out privately or publicly, under state sanction, was a fragmentary set of practices concerned mainly with controlling the kinds and numbers of animals killed."[21] As Loo demonstrates, Canadian notions of conservationism shifted dramatically at the end of the nineteenth century. These notions were reflected in emergent provincial legislative frameworks that viewed game and fisheries as valuable economic resources subject to intensive state control and oversight in order to ensure their long-term profitability. This oversight came at the provincial level and was not uniform in its application across Canada; at the same time, this was a national process, the progression of which can be traced and tracked as it expanded from eastern to western provinces and finally to the territorial north.

Ontario, to some extent, set the stage on which the criminalization of Indigenous procurement practices and foodways was to take place at the end of the nineteenth century. In 1890, the Ontario government founded a Games and Fisheries Commission to help articulate the legal status of wildlife within its borders. Two years later, in 1892, the Ontario Games and Fisheries Commission issued an influential report that attempted to expand the realm of provincial authority to include the hunting and fishing activities of all peoples within the region regardless of whether they were treaty Indians. The Commission's report, without any irony, painted Indigenous peoples as a threat to provincial resources and insisted that limitations must be imposed on their ability to hunt for commercial gain, lest they empty the land of game in a bid to make a profit. In that same year, the government of Ontario passed An Act to Amend the Act for the Protection of Game and Fur-Bearing Animals. The 1892 legislation viewed subsistence hunting as an acceptable activity for anyone to engage in irrespective of treaty rights; nonetheless, it limited the ability of Indigenous hunters, trappers, traders, and anglers to sell a long list of animal-based products. Under the legislation, the number of protected species through closed seasons was expanded; hunting elk, moose, and caribou was banned; and deer season was reduced.[22] Simultaneously, the legislation created an embodied system of enforcement by mandating the creation of game wardens, whose duty it became to level harsh fines for all infringements.[23] This legislation introduced a monetary incentive into provincial conservation efforts where levying fines on Indigenous peoples generated state revenue. As historian Frank Tough notes, the 1892 legislation also imparted a colonial binary between subsistence hunting and hunting for the purposes of market-based activities, especially when Indigenous trappers and traders routinely ate the meat of several fur-bearing animals, such as beaver, whose pelts often ended up on the market.[24] Despite these legislative binaries that ignored on-the-ground realities, Indigenous peoples with Indian status and treaty rights were arrested by colonial authorities for breaking the provincial laws governing hunting and the sale of animal products within Ontario.

The following is a description of an Anishinaabe Chief of the Robinson-Superior Treaty who found himself facing down the fines and threats of the Ontario games commission in 1898:

> Semo Commanda, chief of the Nipissing Reserve just west of the town of North Bay, was angry. His brother Barnaby Commanda and another band member, Wilson Ottawaska, had been arrested for hunting moose out of season in violation of a province-wide ban. Barnaby Commanda had shot a moose for himself and his family, and agreed to sell some of the excess meat to a Canadian Pacific Railway (CPR) survey crew working in the area. He enlisted Ottawaska's aid in transporting the meat to the crew. Joseph Rogers, an inspector working with Ontario's Department of Crown Lands, learned of the incident, arrested both men, and brought them before the local magistrate. At their trial in August, both pled guilty to hunting moose. Commanda paid a fifty-dollar fine, and the court confiscated the moose meat and his rifle. Ottawaska could not afford to pay the fine and was sentenced to thirty days' hard labour in the Sudbury jail. Chief Commanda dictated a letter to George Chitty, the local Indian Affairs timber agent, and sent it to Indian Affairs in Ottawa. The arrest, the chief contended, was an outrage as "Indians had the right to kill moose under the Robinson Treaty."[25]

Throughout this period, other acts of provincial legislation narrowed the possible ways in which treaty rights could be exercised without risk of fines and imprisonment. For example, in 1903, the Province of Ontario prohibited the sale of game fish.[26] In 1907, the Act Respecting the Game, Fur-Bearing Animals, and Fisheries of Ontario further shortened open seasons and reduced Indigenous access to market hunting, trapping, and fishing.[27] The federal government, in 1909, created the Commission of Conservation, and the following year placed a moratorium on the fishing of lake sturgeon in Lake of the Woods in an attempt to allow stocks to replenish.[28] In 1911, the Annual Report of the Department of Games and Fisheries cited industrial expansion and urban sprawl when decrying the "widespread system of pollution of our lakes, rivers and streams."[29] Species of European fish were introduced to Ontario's lakes in 1913 in an effort to stem the tide of over-fishing and the ecological devastation caused by the mismanagement and pollution of lakes and rivers in the province.[30] Although the province had long attempted to bolster populations of sport fish species by mechanically removing species of fish seen as undesirable (such as carp, northern pike, burbot, and sucker fish), the 1930s and '40s witnessed a significant period of such "coarse fish removal" programs.[31] Provincial legislation sought to protect settler sport fishing while also promoting seasonal tourist economies that positioned Ontario's lakes as ideal getaways for American fishermen.

Although this sequence of events represents the rise of Canadian conservationism at the start of the twentieth century, it is worth noting that the election of Theodore Roosevelt to the office of President of the United States was a powerful catalyst for this sudden preoccupation with game, fish, and wildlife in Canada. As Peter Kulchyski and Frank Tester explain, "when Roosevelt assumed office [in 1901], Gifford Pinchot, a German-trained forester and advocate of scientific management and conservation, was chief of the Bureau of Forestry in the Department of Agriculture. Across the border, Pinchot's ideas were to influence Canadian politician Clifford Sifton, who was ... minister of the interior in the Laurier administration" and the first chair of the federal Commission on Conservation.[32] The scientific management of game, fish, and wildlife in Canada thus became a mandate of settler colonial governance on both sides of the border.

Central to this history of so-called resource management is the emergence of fish hatcheries in Ontario and Manitoba in the late nineteenth and early twentieth centuries, meant to keep Canadian lakes and rivers stocked so that commercial activities could persist, including the sale of fish as a staple food product to the United States. For instance, in 1893, the Department of Marine and Fisheries constructed and began operating a whitefish hatchery in the region south of Lake Winnipeg.[33] By 1907, the province had several more hatcheries that sometimes employed Indigenous peoples. While the employment of Indigenous peoples in fish hatcheries shows the relevance of Indigenous labour to emergent Canadian formations of conservationism, what we can also see in these histories is the attempted enfolding of Indigenous relationships with the land into settler institutions premised on particular forms of food production and wildlife management.[34]

Across the prairie provinces, provincial legislation played less of a role in foreclosing Indigenous foodways. This was due to three key factors: first, the influence of the HBC; second, the particular concerns that Indian Affairs had related to relief costs should Indigenous peoples be prevented from hunting and fishing following the destruction of bison populations; and third, the fact that jurisdictional control of natural resources in the prairies was for a very long time housed within federal rather than provincial frameworks (as opposed to Ontario, for example). In 1894, Saskatchewan passed provincial game protection and preservation laws. As Glenn Iceton explains, the HBC was treated as an expert as well as a stakeholder in the preparation of this legislation:

> The Hudson's Bay Company (HBC) actually helped the gov-
> ernment reach some consensus on when and where fish and
> game laws should be enforced on Indian bands. The 1894 game
> preservation bill was submitted to the HBC for suggestions on
> the regulation of certain species and on closed seasons. . . . In an
> attempt to reduce the impact of the legislation on the Indian
> population in the region, the HBC supported the provision that
> allowed Indians to hunt for food in the closed seasons. Like the
> Indian agents further south, the HBC understood the financial
> implications of poor or restricted hunts. The HBC would have to
> supply costly relief in the event of adverse hunting restrictions. By
> the 1890s, the federal government was facing increased costs of
> supplying relief to Indians in regions where the buffalo had been
> destroyed and commercial agriculture was not successful. The
> government was also concerned with the expense of supporting
> Indians who were prevented from hunting for food.[35]

The provision of relief (emergency food supplies) by the HBC was a practice whose origins lay in broader efforts to "encourage" Indigenous peoples to concentrate on commercial hunting to the detriment of food procurement activities. Relief allowed the HBC to step in when the commercialization of food practices reduced the flexibility of communities to continue to draw on a wide and seasonal range of land- and water-based foods or respond to periodic food shortages.[36]

Indigenous peoples in the prairie provinces, as well as Ontario, increasingly found themselves subject to arrest, fines, and imprisonment due to the application of provincial hunting laws. In 1919, a federal commission on conservation expanded this carceral system with the following finding: "that, in view of the destruction of game illegally by Indians of the various western provinces, the Dominion Government be urged to co-operate in the enforcement of game laws in this particular respect, and more especially in the provinces of Alberta, Saskatchewan, and British Columbia, by means of the Royal Northwest Mounted Police or other special officers in districts where damage to game by Indians most frequently occurs."[37] However, the unique ecological and economic conditions of the prairies shaped and inflected this process, and doubly so during the Great Depression when Conservative prime minister R.B. Bennett initiated the Prairie Farm Rehabilitation Administration in an effort to support the agricultural sector of western Canada.[38] Of course, this policy development during the 1930s did not have Indigenous peoples and their access to land- and water-based foods top of mind; rather, this was a response to the ecological as well as economic crisis associated with the Great Depression. In 1930, concurrent Natural Resource Transfer Agreements (NRTAs) made between the Dominion of Canada and the provinces of Manitoba, Saskatchewan, and Alberta enshrined First Nations access to land for the purposes of hunting and fishing within a federal framework that was lacking in Atlantic Canada and Ontario. One oft-cited passage that is rendered identically in paragraphs twelve and thirteen of all three of the NRTAs reads as follows: "In order to secure the Indians of the province the continuance of the supply of game and fish for the support and subsistence, Canada agrees that the laws respecting game in force in the Province shall from time to time apply to the Indigenous within the boundaries thereof, provided, however, that the said Indians shall have the right, which the Province hereby assures to them, of hunting, trapping, and fishing game and fish for food at all seasons of the year on unoccupied Crown lands and on any other lands to which the said Indians might have a right of access."[39] Even so, NRTA agreements have been routinely interpreted by the Canadian Supreme Court as non-inclusive to commercial hunting and fishing, which lessens the protecting impact of their enshrinement within Canadian law. Thus, while there are particular historical dynamics unique to the prairie provinces, there nonetheless remain instructive similarities in that the impact of inter-governmental natural resource regulation wrought the disruption of Indigenous foodways and access to the land and water for both subsistence and market-based purposes.

In 1925, the province of British Columbia instituted a provincial trapline registry, which extended the logic of a burgeoning Canadian conservationism from coast to coast. Echoing the events following the passage of Ontario's 1892 legislation described above, Indigenous peoples found themselves prosecuted by settlers who policed their land use while citing provincial laws. As Glenn Iceton explains, "on-the-ground implementation of trapline registration was mostly carried out by the British Columbia Provincial Police force."[40] Providing evidence, Iceton quotes a provincial game warden who issued the following order to non-commissioned officers and constables who were charged with policing traplines in September of 1926: "in due course you will be furnished with a book containing maps of your district or Division for use in connection with the regulations dealing with the registration of trap lines. These maps have been ruled and divided into small blocks. It is my wish that all NCO's or Constables in charge of detachments do everything possible to keep these maps up to date, in good condition and to see that any work thereon is done neatly."[41] The passage suggests that the trapline registry was one of the primary colonial technologies that allowed provincial authorities to discipline and punish Indigenous peoples for engaging in commercial trapping activities. The logic embedded within this practice mandated the conceptual cutting up of the land into blocks, the policing of which was made easier through the maintenance of continuously updated maps created and maintained by game wardens, their constables, and any other settlers deputized while enforcing and implementing the trapline registry.

In his own investigation of the trapline registry, historian David Vogt offers the following example of a Kitkatla trapper named Matthew Hill to bring some texture to this larger bureaucratic history:

> Between 1934 and 1949, Kitkatla trapper Matthew Hill struggled to gain and then regain British Columbia government recognition of a portion of his house's territory on the Northwest Coast as a registered trapline. Hill won recognition in 1934, at a time when Indigenous trappers, Indian agents, and game wardens had reached a series of informal compromises to protect and expand 'Indian' trapping following the mass displacement of Indigenous trappers during the mid-1920s; he lost it in 1936, when regional game managers decided to test the influence of the federal Indian Department and of the informal agreements by selecting a few test cases (including Hill) for cancellation; and he was ultimately promised it back, but only once the white trappers to whom the land had been ceded in the meantime ceased their operations. ... Hill's struggle was a microcosm of the broader currents of the politics of trapping in B.C. after 1925.[42]

As the example suggests, the provincial trapline registry was not applied in a consistent or comprehensive fashion across the province; even so, however, the administrative grey areas, legislative complexities, and whims of the Department of Indian Affairs placed Indigenous trapping in a very precarious position, and many Indigenous trappers were unable to continue trapping. This precarity was exported to Indigenous peoples across Canada over the following decades as trapline registries were created in Ontario (1935), Alberta (1937), Manitoba (1940), Quebec (1945), the Yukon (1946), and the Northwest Territories (1949).[43]

Conclusion

The ability to hunt, fish, trap, trade, and exercise Indigenous food sovereignties was dramatically diminished by a long list of actors making this history complex. At the same time, the story is also a simple one, wherein white settlement, the growth of industry, capitalism, and the rise of Canadian conservationism intersected with other settler colonial assaults on Indigenous peoples. These assaults destroyed food sources, polluted waters, undermined the intergenerational transmissions of land-based knowledge, and criminalized First Nations, Inuit, and Métis peoples for participating in land- and water-based activities. Although this chapter is not an exhaustive or comprehensive rendering of these processes, we wanted to briefly illustrate the nature of the terrain upon which Indigenous peoples increasingly had their efforts to feed themselves, their families, and communities disrupted by settler colonialism. Though the HBC was directly implicated in this chapter, it is important to underscore that their Northern Store division was a primary benefactor of a larger history in the post–Second World War period, wherein many Indigenous communities had limited retail options from which to purchase market-based foods. In the following chapters, we show how the HBC shifted their business operations to increasingly include food and general merchandise across the North to accommodate these new settler colonial formations of state and economy.

CHAPTER 2

CONSTRUCTING DEPENDENCY:
The Hudson's Bay Company before the Second World War

Here we begin our examination of the Hudson's Bay Company in order to elucidate the blurring of corporate and state colonial interests and activities in northern Canada during the late nineteenth and early twentieth centuries. The previous chapter mapped out the constricting landscape on which Indigenous peoples were forced to exercise Aboriginal and treaty rights in Canada. The abrogation of treaties and the criminalization of Indigenous foodways laid the groundwork for the HBC to become the primary food retailer in most northern First Nations and Inuit settlements after the Second World War. Indeed, in many locales, it was the primary source of food. This chapter explores the shifting roles of the HBC in the pre–Second World War period and elaborates upon how the federal government operationalized the Company's long-standing relationships with Indigenous peoples. At the same time, the role and place of Indigenous people fundamentally shifted within the HBC as the company moved away from the fur trade as its primary mode of business towards one that favoured retail in general and the sale of commercial food shipped from the south more specifically.[1] In this context, Indigenous peoples were shifted within the economic structures of the company from producers and labourers to consumers: the coercive conditions of the fur trade were thus leveraged into the captive conditions of northern food sales.

The state relied on the HBC to provide services that included but were not limited to nutrition programs, basic health services, the distribution of food rations, and the administration and management of annuity payments and family allowance monies.[2] While these services aided the assimilationist agenda of the settler state through the imposition of European-Canadian norms, they also served the interests of the HBC. While we address family allowance benefits in greater detail in the next chapter, the provision of these services guaranteed the Company a dedicated and captive customer base, particularly in a region where the HBC was the only institution selling market-based foods, hunting and fishing equipment, and general merchandise. As Frank Tester and Peter Kulchyski demonstrated in *Tammarniit*, the Family Allowance Program ensured the financial solvency of the HBC following the decline of fur prices on the international market after the Second World War. However, we argue this process started earlier with annuity payments and the delivery of a range of government-funded and -directed programs.

The long and frequently intimate and familial relationships many employees of the HBC had formed with Indigenous peoples and their communities afforded the company (and, by extension, the state) a great deal of power and influence. It enabled the federal government to extend its authority into Indigenous communities in areas where there was little or no formal state presence. In turn, the reliance of the federal government on the HBC for information about Indigenous peoples gave the company unprecedented influence over its primary customer base in northern Canada, especially in communities or locales where the HBC was the only retailer and made available a range of services from emergency food relief to credit. It is in this manner that the federal government bestowed upon the Company an enormous power to influence and transform the foodways of Indigenous people in northern Canada—an influence that was only bolstered by the state's efforts to reduce the access of Indigenous people to land- and water-based food resources through hunting and fishing regulations as outlined in Chapter 1.

The partnership between the federal government and the HBC was mutually beneficial, and while this relationship was more obvious in the late nineteenth and early twentieth centuries than after 1970, the influence of the HBC (as well as its successor the North West Company [NWC]), remained stronger than has originally been understood. Significantly, this partnership embodied the ways in which the federal government's solutions to poverty and ill health in Indigenous communities remained rooted in market-based solutions. In other words, if Indigenous people could be taught how to be appropriate consumers by participating in the capitalist economy, they could be successfully absorbed into the Canadian body politic consistent with the assimilatory goals of Indian Affairs. The HBC was thus hailed as a modern and progressive force in the North through its commercial enterprises and delivery of services. Within the governmental logic of the federal government, the HBC was ideally situated to remake Indigenous peoples into white citizens.

At the same time that the HBC was performing roles usually carried out by the state, the Company continued to function as a business whose primary responsibility was to stakeholders and profit margins. While the HBC continued to purchase furs and operate trading posts throughout northern Canada (just as it does today), it also expanded its retail and financial operations, and, as we see in later chapters, goods and services, after 1987 when another era of corporate retail and service expansion occurred. This earlier shift was a response to broader economic forces as a result of the First World War, the Great Depression, increased competition from independent fur traders, and the decline of global fur prices. The partnership that the Company developed with the government during this period allowed the HBC to remain solvent and to develop an unprecedented retail presence and monopoly in the North over what increasingly became a captive retail population during the twentieth century.

What follows is a short overview of the history of the HBC on Turtle Island and a brief illustration of the Company's market-driven engagement with the burgeoning field of nutritional science in the pre–Second World War period. As we continue through this history of the HBC's centuries-long strategy of trying to situate itself as a trade monopoly in North America and later as the only food source for Indigenous peoples in the twentieth century, the thematics present in the HBC's account of itself (and their cultural functions) will come to the fore.

Positioning the HBC

The Hudson's Bay Company has a long history on Turtle Island, and understanding the complexities of the many relationships and activities that the company has formed and undertaken is an essential part of untangling how the Company's current iteration as the NWC functions in present-day northern Canada. Complicating our understandings and interpretations of the histories of this company are the frequently familial and intimate social relationships that employees of the company formed with Indigenous peoples and First Nations across several centuries. As we know from the important works of feminist scholars like Susan Sleeper-Smith, Brenda Macdougall, Jennifer Brown, Adele Perry, Jarvis Brownlie, and Sylvia Van Kirk, social relations within the fur trade were a central component of its operation and essential to its success and day-to-day functions. Indeed, the familial and personal networks and communities that arose from these economic practices existed across the continent and formed their own cultures, languages, and social modalities. While extremely valuable, these social and family histories have been collapsed into the history of the HBC as a corporation and an entity whose primary purpose was to make money and generate profit for shareholders. It is this piece of the settler colonial history of the state and its relationships with corporations that we seek to tease out.

From its inception as a company chartered by the King of England, Charles II, on 2 May 1670, the HBC used relationships with Indigenous people to establish trading outposts throughout the geographic area now known as northern Ontario and to gain the upper hand over trade and access to furs. According to British law, the 1670 Charter granted the HBC enormous territorial claims to unceded Indigenous territories as well as "established this mercantile firm on a monopoly basis."[3] Specifically, the Charter granted "monopoly trading rights on the 'whole and entire trade and traffic'" to the HBC.[4] From the very beginning, the HBC was intended to operate as a commercial monopoly with state support, first through the British Crown and later through the Canadian state.

In 1673, the Moose Factory outpost was constructed; a year later, the HBC built an outpost at Fort Albany,[5] and posts were established at Fort Severn and York Factory in 1680 and 1684, respectively.[6] Even at this early stage, the HBC worked to exercise monopolistic control and economic power over Indigenous peoples in the region by setting the prices of sought-after items like rifles and gunpowder,[7] and establishing rules and regulations prohibiting fraternization with locals.[8] These prohibitions were later lifted once it was acknowledged by the Company that life and success on Turtle Island depended on the knowledges and expertise of Indigenous peoples in general, and Indigenous women in particular. The operations of the HBC also coincided with the presence and influence of European economic and military powers along Hudson's Bay, sparking upheavals, rivalries, and conflicts between Indigenous peoples in the region. Arthur Ray described these engendered conflicts at length in his *Indians in the Fur Trade*, paying particular attention to how the military, economic, and political landscape choreographed the movements of Indigenous peoples (often in relation to food availability).[9]

Historians have addressed the role the fur trade played in the interior during this period. Sylvia Van Kirk describes the fur trade world as held together by "tender ties"; Richard White chose the conceptual language of the "middle ground" to theorize the co-production of cultural and material histories in the fur trade; and Carolyn Podruchny and Laura Peers write of these historical spaces as "gathering places."[10] In her own contributions to the field, Elizabeth Vibert shows how the histories produced within and around fur trade forts captured only snapshots of the lives of Indigenous peoples and nations and should therefore be viewed with caution.[11] Nonetheless, while we appreciate the complex social realities embedded within the history of the fur trade, a focus on the HBC and its role in the shaping of economic relations helps to underscore the way in which the Company capitalized on these "tender ties" in order to secure profits and absorb competitors who threatened their monopolistic control.

During the latter stages of the eighteenth and early nineteenth centuries, fur trade rivalries between the HBC and the original North West Company disrupted the food economies of those nations embroiled in the fur trade. The North West Company was founded in 1779 and merged with the HBC in 1821. In the interim period, Indigenous peoples involved in the fur trade had a wider range of trade options to choose from, which considerably threatened HBC market dominance. In order to secure the loyalty of Indigenous traders, the fur trade companies began to issue credit advances to trappers and hunters that were calculated on the expected return of their harvest in terms of "made beaver" tokens/coins. This market force encouraged Indigenous hunters and trappers to consume more store-bought foods (such as flour and biscuits), understanding the value of furs in relation to the market price of European goods.[12] After the HBC-NWC merger in 1821, meaningful market competition in most northern locales declined, and HBC was positioned as a powerful entity capable of engaging in more predatory business practices. For example, in 1816, HBC Governor Robert Semple was killed attempting to enforce the Pemmican Proclamation;[13] however, six years later, in May of 1822, Governor George Simpson was speaking of Indigenous peoples in the following terms:

> I am convinced they [Indigenous peoples] must be ruled with a
> rod of Iron to bring and keep them in a proper state of subordi-
> nation, and the most certain way to effect this is by letting them
> feel their dependence upon us ... in the woods and northern
> barren grounds this measure ought to be pursued rigidly next
> year if they do not improve, and no credit, not so much as a load
> of ammunition, given them until they exhibit an inclination to
> renew their habits of industry. In the plains however this system
> will not do, as they can live independent of us.[14]

As this quotation shows, the survival of the bison on the plains prevented the Company from exploiting the credit advance and food relief system to extract the surplus value from the labour of Indigenous peoples in that region (at least in the earlier parts of the nineteenth century). What is more, the merger marks the beginning of the Company's modern formation, characterized by monopolistic control and the absence of meaningful competition.

Credit Advances, Food Relief, and Standing-In for the Settler State

Though it had done so in the pre-merger period, the HBC, after 1821, increasingly sought to leverage credit advances as a kind of food relief, particularly in areas where food sources such as the bison or caribou were significantly disrupted and decimated. Indigenous hunters and trappers therefore began taking credit advances for outpost food products so that they could focus on hunting and trapping game that might fetch a favourable market value with the HBC. As Hugh Shewell explains: "the [Company's] principal reason for providing relief was economic: if the Indians were not given food, they would spend valuable time hunting scarce game instead of trapping, and the company would lose some fur revenue."[15] This shift in the relationship between Indigenous traders and the HBC thus involved the material construction of food shipment routes across the Canadian North in the areas currently served by the Northern Store. It also bolstered HBC outpost operations in a foundational way to the extent that it animated new frontiers of food sales which functioned as an economic lifeline during periods of fur trade market decline. In sketching out this development, Arthur Ray astutely named both food and clothing consumption as a keynote characteristic of trade and labour relations between Indigenous peoples and the Company between 1821 and 1870. In Ray's view, such developments "made the Indian dependent on the company not only for clothing, as had been the case for nearly fifty years by 1870, but also for food—and not just pemmican, but 'store food' as well, such as flour and biscuits. In effect, to a large extent the woodland Indians had virtually become company employees. They trapped for the company and were provided with nearly all their requirements at the company store on credit."[16] Of course, these trade and labour relations did not merely change market forces; rather, as Joseph LeBlanc and Kristin Burnett underscore, "trade and the accumulation of wealth changed the ways in which families and communities related to each other and introduced the idea that resources could go elsewhere and serve very little benefit to the community."[17] The profitability of the Company thus relied to a considerable degree on the ability of traders to persuade Indigenous peoples and the groups they worked with to stop pursuing the land- and water-based foods that had sustained their communities for generations.

This period thus marks the modern emergence of the HBC outpost manager as a powerful and sometimes tyrannical figure in the northern history of the fur trade. In *The Other Side of the Ledger: An Indian View of the Hudson's Bay Company*, the "inhuman actions on part of the company servants" were described as follows: "the company had established trading posts throughout the territory. Each was run by a manager or factor as he was then called. The position was not well paid but many factorers had a way of making extra money at our expense—a practice tolerated and even encouraged by the [HBC]. Short weighting was not uncommon: if the company exchange rate for our rifle was seven beaver pelts, factors often extracted fourteen, keeping the extra profit for themselves."[18] The frequently unscrupulous practice of profit maximization by HBC outpost managers often overdetermined Indigenous land- and market-based activities and impacted the food procurement strategies of many communities. While much of this conduct might have been individual to particular outpost operators, larger economic forces drove this sort of behaviour. For example, in 1860, the International Financial Society acquired HBC "shares from its existing shareholders and sold those shares at a premium to new shareholders who expected more from the company."[19] The new owners expected the Company to operate in a manner that would ensure them a high return on their investments and, thus, the HBC increasingly moved to disentangle itself from its fur trade past to invest in retail and land sales.[20] This also allowed more than mere managers to extract wealth from northern Company operations; rather, through the emergence of a more modern corporate structure, investors from across Canada could now vicariously participate in the colonial exploitation of Indigenous peoples across the provincial and territorial norths.

The Deed of Surrender signed in 1870 between the HBC and Canada resulted in more than 2.9 million square miles of Turtle Island being seized by Canada.[21] While Confederation altered the Company's relationship with Indigenous peoples in the North West through the creation of a federal government that was now regarded as having authority over all matters related to Indigenous peoples, the Canadian government still wanted to use the Company as its agent among Indigenous peoples, especially in geographically rural and northern regions. For example, in a letter written by Prime Minister John A. Macdonald to HBC's Governor, Sir Stafford Northcote, following the acquisition of Rupert's Land, Macdonald described his desire to use existing Company relationships with Indigenous peoples to avoid the experience of the U.S. which relied on expensive military operations to steal Indigenous lands and commit genocide in the western United States in the latter half of the nineteenth century. Thus, Macdonald was anxious to maintain the appearance of good relations with Indigenous peoples and a more orderly process of white settlement and genocide in western Canada. Macdonald thought the HBC had:

> dealt with their Indians in a thoroughly satisfactory way. The policy of Canada is also to deal with the Indians in a satisfactory manner. It would be of advantage to us, and no doubt it would be of advantage to you, that we should be allowed to make use of your officers and your posts for the purpose of making those payments to the Indians which will have to be made annually by the Government of Canada in order to satisfy their claims and keep them in good humour. The Indians had a title to some of these lands which is now extinguished—upon which certain terms which involve annual payments; and it would be of great advantage that we should be able to employ officers who are known to these Indians in order to make these payments and keep the Indians in good humour.[22]

Lacking the infrastructure to deliver many of the services and promises outlined in the treaties, and regarding the development of such structures as prohibitively expensive, Ottawa turned to HBC. As early as the 1870s, the federal government relied on the HBC and its strategically located posts to deliver annuities. Although the payment of annuities was moved onto reserves in the 1880s at the insistence of Macdonald, this policy did not become general practice for those Indigenous communities situated in more northerly locales until after the Second World War.[23] The annuity system helped shift retail practices at trading posts from a trade and barter system to one that relied on the exchange of cash and credit, solidifying the role of the HBC as a creditor in northern regions.

Beginning with annuities and continuing with emergency food relief and later social welfare benefits like the Family Allowance Program, these measures further cemented the Company's financial partnership with the federal government, wherein monies would either be distributed directly by the HBC or held in trust by the Company. HBC's fiscal supervision of Indigenous customers also extended to the wages they earned at government job sites. As late as 1947, the department of Indian Affairs and the post manager at Fort Chimo (Kuujjuaq), located in present-day Nunavik, QC, corresponded about the wages to be paid to six Indigenous employees working at the local Royal Canadian Air Force (RCAF) base as carpenters, bakers, and mess orderlies. Instead of getting a paycheque issued in their names, Indian Affairs—in consultation with the HBC—determined the men's wages would be divided in two ways: a compulsory 25 percent portion would be sent directly to the department to set up a savings account, and the rest would be placed as a credit at the local HBC post, where the men could purchase supplies under the supervision of the post manager.[24] To access their savings, the men had to make a personal request through the local RCMP officer, who was empowered to oversee all decisions regarding their savings.[25] Indian Affairs wanted to ensure that Indigenous people participated in European-Canadian consumer culture, but only in a manner they considered to be responsible and that served to bring Indigenous people closer to whiteness.

Continuing and expanding on earlier practices of providing relief to Indigenous peoples who were connected to the company and its businesses, in 1897 the HBC negotiated an agreement with Ottawa to officially distribute aid and supplies funded by Indian Affairs to elderly and impoverished Indigenous people in northern regions. Arthur Ray describes this practice as serving as a "conduit for the government."[26] In order to move away from the case-by-case remuneration system that the HBC had previously employed,

Clarence Chipman Campbell made an arrangement with Hayter Reed, Deputy Superintendent General of Indian Affairs, to pay for the support of "destitute Indians." Reed cautioned Chipman, stating that the government did not want to get into the general practice of supporting Indigenous peoples, but as long as the company stayed within pre-set limits, it would be reimbursed for the aid it distributed. This practice was also extended to other fur trade companies and missionaries in the region.[27] While these relief practices were built on and informed by pre-existing relationships that the HBC had developed with Indigenous peoples, the formal agreement with the state initiated a new economic order "in which buying and selling furs w[as] increasingly separated and cash transactions became more commonplace."[28] Given this dynamic between the federal government, the HBC, wage labour, and Indigenous peoples, it is necessary to distinguish the historical process we are discussing from the larger rise of a market culture in rural Ontario. Non-Indigenous historical subjects who became enmeshed within this emergent capitalist system in the same period exercised far more market freedom than did Indigenous peoples, whose consumption of goods was vertically integrated into HBC operations through the application of state power.[29]

We also want to caution against emphasizing the totality or evenness of Indigenous peoples' dependence on food resources from the HBC or the role the fur trade played more broadly. This narrative, wherein the fur trade or Indian policy is the only or even the main story playing out in Indigenous histories, serves to normalize the current Northern Store monopoly as natural and inevitable as opposed to the consequence of state policies and corporate colonial practices operating simultaneously over 150 years. It is difficult to gauge the degree of this disruption among different groups and nations as some were more affected than others depending on their particular relationships to the trade and interactions with fur traders. However, many of these efforts to undermine local Indigenous food economies were witnessing a degree of success because of other settler-colonial processes taking place (such as so-called development, expanding settler encroachment, the pass system and confinement to reserves, residential schools, and provincial hunting and fishing restrictions). Always, the HBC benefitted from these shifting colonial relations.

The relationship between relief, HBC, and the settler state was not without tension. Indian Affairs clearly wanted it to be understood by recipients of the state's supposed largesse where the origins of this munificence lay.

Indeed, the settler state became agitated when Indigenous peoples receiving relief from the HBC understood this to be company generosity rather than state-sponsored benevolence. One record from the colonial archive is particularly representative of this tension. Dated 1913, this report discussed the issuing of "sick and destitute funds to Indians" and articulated the state's displeasure at the lack of recognition received from Indigenous peoples for the issuing of such funds:

> The relief should come directly from the hands of representatives of the government so as to impress upon the Indians the exact source from which assistance emanates. At present time, probably 70% of the total Indian population labor under the delusion that the H.B. Co. are the donors of this charity and the sooner such ideas are dispelled the better. It is obvious that the H.B. Co.'s officers will not go out of their way to disillusion them as such a belief materially enhances their position with the Indians. . . . Moreover the trader would naturally be very liberal with relief, when it represents the unloading of some of his inferior foods on the unsuspecting Indian, at a stiff price to the government.[30]

It is perhaps worth noting here that 1913 was the same year Duncan Campbell Scott became the Deputy Superintendent of Indian Affairs. Scott's philosophy regarding the issuance of relief payments was to be so stingy with funding that it would discourage Indigenous peoples from relying on it. Hugh Shewell explains that "Scott's administration continuously attempted to press Indians (mainly adult males) into employment and other forms of self-sufficiency by discouraging dependence on relief (welfare)—at that time issued only as food rations or clothing; hence, if relief was given it was so minimal as to act as a deterrent to remaining dependent on it."[31] The settler state had already worked to undermine Indigenous economic and political sovereignties, and any understanding of self-sufficiency and "real work" existed solely within a context where Indigenous peoples had become just like settlers.

The North West also experienced increased European immigration and settlement; as Steven High recalls, "besides a few mining and logging camps . . . few whites settled the North Shore of Lake Superior before 1890."[32] The arrival of non-Indigenous people in the region marked the shift away from HBC's reliance on Indigenous labour for its survival. After the First World

War, white trappers increasingly encroached on Indigenous trapping during the Great Depression.[33] As we shall see as we review relevant regulatory projects and corporate practices in the post–Second World War period, the goal of the HBC was to make Indigenous peoples dependent upon their retail stores for access to all goods and services. In 1907, the HBC entered into the wholesale business, adding "canned salmon, coffee, tea, and other commodities" to its retail operations.[34] This was not only an expansion of HBC retail market share in Canada, but an entrenchment of the HBC in an emergent global economy deeply entangled with the power relations of racialized labour in the global south.[35] In 1910, the HBC divided its operations into three separate departments, one of which was retailing.[36] After the First World War, the Company became increasingly involved in an emerging network of scientific research and education related to the efficacy of rations, fortified flour, powdered milk, and other novel food products.

The MILK-IT Machine and Other Nutritional Endeavours

The delivery of nutritional education and programming continued the Company's long tradition of involvement in science and the employment of this knowledge within its business and retail operations.[37] It is in this way that the HBC acted as more than a mere extension of empire or a profit-driven corporation (although it was very much both of those things); rather, the HBC was also embedded within a series of scientific networks that enabled the company to employ the appearance of objectivity and scientific empiricism while marketing certain products to Indigenous peoples. We see this increasingly taking place during the 1920s and '30s through the science of nutrition and especially in the Company's informal role as an advisor to the federal government on Indigenous peoples, as well as operationalizing the state's nutritional programs in northern spaces.

By the 1920s, the HBC was employing the language of nutritional science to describe the Company's initiatives in northern Indigenous communities. It is worth noting that descriptions of these retail schemes were contained within the Company's files under "Native Welfare," suggesting that the Company conflated retail activities designed to make money with "doing charitable acts" for or improving the welfare of Indigenous peoples. Company instructions issued to outpost managers in 1928 that outlined a marketing campaign for milk to be employed in northern First Nations and Inuit settlements were couched in the language of "progressive welfare policy."[38] Post managers were instructed to see their relationships with Indigenous peoples as "a living force which cared and looked after them and was not merely an impersonal trading factor."[39] Further, the company urged its employees to "apply modern science" to improve the well-being of Indigenous peoples through the application of hygiene, cleanliness, and proper nutrition (all of which would be sold with an appropriate markup). We see this around efforts by the company to market certain foods, often at the behest of the federal government, which were deemed to be of important nutritional value, like milk, or items specifically produced to address perceived dietary deficiencies among Indigenous communities, like fortified flour.

Echoing doctors and nutritionists during the early twentieth century, the HBC strongly promoted the sale of milk among northern Indigenous populations because "milk contained the constructive materials required to build up bone, muscle, and nerve, if supplied these in the proper amount and in a form which enable them to be easily digested and used. Although other foods contain the substances required to build up the body, no foods other than milk, contain them in the best proportion and in the best form."[40] Identified as a protective food by popular nutritionists of the 1920s, milk was regarded as the "best food for combatting the most common nutritional deficiencies."[41] For example, in 1921, Helen MacMurchy, Chief of the Maternal and Child Welfare Division housed within the federal Department of Health from 1920 to 1934,[42] released a pamphlet that outlined why Canadians needed to drink more milk, declaring that many "children are delicate and sickly from the want of milk than any other cause."[43] The symbolic connections between the whiteness of milk, purity, cleanliness, and moral and physical fortitude served as the perfect therapeutic for Indigenous mothers whose children were regarded as inherently "sickly."[44] Such moralizing nutritional narratives allowed not only for the HBC and the state to obscure their roles in manufacturing food insecurity in northern communities, it also allowed them to offer a market-based solution for Indigenous hunger. If Indigenous parents chose not to partake in this solution, responsibility for the failure of milk to resolve starvation and poor nutrition in Indigenous communities could be laid at the feet of Indigenous parents and not the inadequacy of a beverage to fix settler colonialism and poverty. Indeed, milk was perceived as the perfect food for addressing the ill health of what was believed to be a sickly population. We explore in further detail the role that milk and other fortified foods played in pathologizing Indigenous parenthood, especially mothers, in Chapter 3.

Figure 2. Advertisement for KLIM powdered milk. Credit: *Saturday Evening Post,* 10 April 1920.

The development of nutritional science in the early twentieth century and the identification of minerals and vitamins as central to what was believed to be a nutritious diet led to the identification of milk as the "quintessential protective" food. The Dairy Industry and the Department of Agriculture worked alongside the federal Division of Child Welfare and other organizations in the 1920s to increase milk consumption, especially among children.[45] Fears of the poor health of the Canadian population generally were rooted in the revelation that so many men were unfit for active duty in the First World War and in the return of soldiers from Europe who had suffered the long-term health effects of malnutrition. Campaigns to ensure a healthier next generation were paramount.[46]

To cash in on this nutritional trend, HBC managers instructed their employees to emphasize the importance of including milk in one's diet and that the company's goal was to ensure that milk was made available to all Indigenous children to improve health outcomes. To achieve this goal, the Company invented a machine designed to reconstitute milk by mixing water, milk solids, and butter. To produce one gallon of milk, post employees were instructed to combine the following: "5 3/5 ounces of butter (unsalted butter), 14 3/5 ounces of milk solids, and 7 pints of pure water."[47] The milk solids were KLIM, a dehydrated whole-milk powder designed to be used in locales where it was difficult to ship liquid milk without adequate transportation facilities and storage. Called the MILK-IT machine, employees were cautioned to keep it clean at all times and encourage local Indigenous populations to purchase as much MILK-IT-made milk as they could. The Company capitalized on the advice of health advocates who argued that the "foundations of health [were] laid in childhood"[48] and that proper nutrition standards must be observed from the very beginning. Although milk is a major and recurring example in this regard, it is not the only one that helps to tease out the ways in which the settler state assisted the business operations of the HBC (and vice versa).

The line between nutritional services for Indigenous people and the business practices of the Company were consistently blurred. A report sent by the Department of Indian Affairs to the HBC in October of 1926 advised the company to sell canned tomatoes to First Nations people. Canned tomatoes were described as an:

> invaluable addition to children's diet [because] they were cheap and always available at the Posts. The use of canned tomatoes in out-door clinics of large hospitals is universal, where oranges and fresh vegetables cannot be supplied owing to season and price. The Indians should be urged to use sufficient quantity of canned tomatoes (one can per week per child). I wish to emphasis [*sic*] this point, in view of the absence of vegetables in the Indian diet, especially during the winter months. I would suggest that canned tomatoes be added to the list of "necessities," as understood in Hudson's Bay Company parlance.[49]

In other words, nutritional recommendations positively benefitted the Company's bottom line and were sometimes premised not on the ideal diet but market availability, as determined by extant HBC operations.

Such marketing practices and health edicts were also used to introduce "new foods" into the diets of Indigenous people living in northern Canada. In 1943, Indian Affairs decided to introduce fortified flour to Indigenous peoples living in the North through the HBC. Indeed, Percy Moore, Acting Superintendent of Medical Services, sought out the advice of R.H.G. Bonnycastle, Head of the Fur Trade Department, on how to best market fortified flour to Indigenous people. Bonnycastle suggested that it would be best to introduce the flour slowly and to ensure the packaging was plain, otherwise people would suspect that it was intended to "cover up an inferior product."[50] Indian Affairs wanted to introduce the fortified flour (thiamin, riboflavin, niacin, iron, and calcium) in northern Ontario, the territories, Manitoba, and Saskatchewan, with the HBC as its primary distributor.[51] Indian Affairs even offered to subsidize the additional costs related to the sale of the fortified flour until it became popular among community members. Although such legislation was never passed, Bonnycastle suggested that to ensure uptake of the fortified flour, Indian Affairs could propose legislation which "forb[ade] the sale of other flour."[52]

Solutions to poverty and ill health were imagined and operationalized within a consumer and capitalist framework. In order to achieve good health, Indigenous peoples would need to participate in this increasing consumer society, which included but was not limited to purchasing the "right" foods as recommended by nutritionists and public health professionals, who supported the establishment of a dietary standard in Canada by the mid-1930s.[53] Fortified flour and other foods like biscuits and vitamin tablets would become the cornerstones of the federal government's food/nutrition policies towards Indigenous peoples to resolve the ill health that was a symptom of settler colonialism. The HBC would distribute these so-called solutions to Indigenous peoples at considerable profit. Unsurprisingly, the Company was not averse to taking on these responsibilities because they increased the HBC's capacity for profitable production. In the 1939 annual report for the post at Cape Dorset, the post manager urged the Company to continue to "mak[e] the Natives as dependent, as much as possible, upon the decisions of the Post."[54] Thus, while much had changed in terms of the Company's relationship to Indigenous peoples, the Crown, and the federal government, there is continuity with how the HBC has operated as a benefactor of food insecurity in the Canadian North.

Conclusion

The early twentieth century witnessed increasing cooperation between Indian Affairs and the HBC, especially where interests aligned around the imposition of European-Canadian foodways. The food and goods sold by the HBC served as persuasive vectors of assimilation in the settler state's efforts to make Indigenous peoples more like white people. For the HBC, assisting the settler state in the assimilatory project through the sale and promotion of certain types of foods and a European-Canadian lifestyle made the Company and its stockholders substantial amounts of money. Discourses of benevolence and charity disguised the violence of the settler colonial system that was criminalizing Indigenous land- and water-based practices under the guise of making unaffordable and nutritionally mediocre market-based foods available.

The following chapters pick up and explore the Family Allowance Program and the Food Mail Program and how they helped ensure the financial well-being of the HBC while at the same time furthering the state's objectives in the North. Indeed, we revisit the Canadian imaginary that locates the liberal welfare state in the post–Second World War period as a vehicle for progress and positive action, and instead show that those benefits were only intended for a select few.

CHAPTER 3

"MAKING PROPER USE":
The Family Allowance Program and Forced Purchasing Lists

The previous two chapters sketched out important pieces of the broader settler colonial system designed to erode Indigenous peoples' food sovereignties and access to land. This chapter continues that conversation by exploring the role that the Family Allowance Program played, and in particular, how Indian Affairs drew on the dominant society's understandings of what constituted "nutritious and healthy foods" to alter patterns of food consumption in the provincial and territorial norths and replace them with prohibitively expensive market-based alternatives. Though ostensibly an assistive social welfare program, family allowances also functioned as part of a larger regulatory regime of Canadian governance that emerged in the postwar period that witnessed the implementation of particularly gendered forms of social policy. Like healthcare and education, the Family Allowance Program benefitted many Canadians but had a differential and often violent impact on Indigenous communities. Though we unpack several trajectories of colonial thought and practice in our review of family allowances and their role in the HBC's business operations, it was the program's forced purchasing lists that most acutely manifested settler ideologies of western domesticity and encouraged the elimination of Indigenous foodways. Indeed, the Family Allowance Program in post–Second World War Canada empowered the HBC to transition the role of Indigenous peoples within the company from producers and workers to consumers and customers, which allowed the HBC to increasingly shift towards lucrative retail operations in northern

communities, largely supplanting fur trade operations by the 1950s as the
most substantial profit generator.

In what follows, we explore how Canadian politicians used family allowance benefits to impose their views of how Indigenous peoples ought to
spend their money and feed their families. While our primary focus is on
how gendered norms embedded within social policies played out in terms of
the settler colonial project, we would also be remiss if we did not underscore
how family allowances disciplined Indigenous communities to the logics of
capitalist consumption, opening markets in the Canadian North to expand
the business operations of the HBC. As we illustrate, administrating the
Family Allowance Program in the North required the creation of a regulatory regime that imposed bureaucratic hierarchies and categories into which
Indigenous peoples were placed based on an assumed level of readiness to
shoulder the mantle of Canadian citizenship. Indian Affairs viewed the
ability of individuals to make appropriate market choices as a measure of
assimilation. In contrast, those deemed unable to manage their own money
and spending were categorized as requiring additional and enduring forms
of colonial surveillance and discipline.

The Family Allowance Program: The State, 1940 to 1960

Passed in the House of Commons in 1944, the Family Allowance Act provided Canadian mothers with tax-free monthly payments that varied according
to the age and number of their children.[1] The first payments were issued on
1 July 1945 and required children to attend school.[2] The Family Allowance
Act is considered Canada's first piece of universal social welfare legislation.
It figured prominently in the Canadian state's post–Second World War
planning and reconstruction.[3] More broadly, the Act's passage has come to
be regarded as a pivotal moment in the emergence of the Canadian welfare
state. For many Canadian mothers, monthly family allowance cheques from
the federal government were quite well-received. On the other hand, some
Canadian historians have viewed the Family Allowance Program more
critically as a regulatory project that signified an increasingly complicated
relationship between the Canadian state and its subjects. For example,
Dominique Marshall argues that this new social minimum encouraged
"precise models of childhood and family life that were attached to [an] institution[al] structure" capable of enforcing European-Canadian middle-class
ideals and penalizing those who did not conform.[4] Feminist historians have

Figure 3. Family Allowances poster, c. 1944. Credit: Canadian War Museum, 20070104-009.

also identified the Family Allowance Act as central to the state's efforts to construct a particular vision of postwar Canadian society—a vision rooted in white, middle-class, heteronormative, and patriarchal domesticity and household consumerism that left women largely dependent on male bread-winners.[5] These state initiatives were regulatory in nature and sought to use the nuclear family as a base unit of Canadian governance and social policy formation. In *The Trouble with Normal*, Mary Louise Adams describes this constituent "as represented by married, middle-class, heterosexual couples and their legitimate offspring, the ideal family was at once seen as a source of affectual relationships, the basis of a consumer economy, a defense against Communism, and a salient metaphor for various forms of social organization, from the nation to high school class."[6] Family allowances and other federal policies that used the nuclear family as a basis of governance have been criticized by these historians for their implicit attempts to flatten social differences and visit dominant ideologies of gender and sexuality upon Canadian subjects. As we argue below, family allowances were also constellated within the Canadian colonial project in that they sought to assimilate Indigenous peoples into settler domesticities.

For Indigenous peoples in the geographic area that came to be known as Canada, the Family Allowance Act served as another tool in the state's arsenal to undermine their social and economic lives. Scholar Miriam McNab's exploration of Indigenous women's changing social and economic roles in the latter half of the twentieth century reveals the ways that family allowances and other postwar programs served to "erode the traditional lifestyle and social relations of production"—a state of affairs designed to make Indigenous women more like their European-Canadian counterparts.[7] The Family Allowance Program also joined other legislation and state policies and practices that undermined the roles and status of Indigenous women in their communities. For instance, Indigenous women were not included in treaty negotiations as signatories,[8] and under the Indian Act, Indigenous women were accorded fewer rights than their male counterparts (for example, Indigenous women could not serve as Chief or be a member of band council until major revisions to the Indian Act in 1951). Settler colonialism was a project that worked to alter Indigenous women's relationships to and roles within their territories, families, and communities. As Adele Perry eloquently observes, "gender is where the abiding bonds between dispossession and colonization become most clear."[9]

The implementation of social welfare measures required the formation of state apparatuses on a large scale that mapped and tracked families and created a set of criteria against which to measure and adjudicate people's eligibility and readiness for such benefits.[10] While many of these tools of governmentality were already well established within Indian Affairs for Indigenous peoples and their communities, family allowance benefits appeared during a period of declining access to land- and water-based resources and represented a reliable source of monthly income. Even more insidious was that family allowance benefits operated under the umbrella of a progressive liberal postwar state which masked its more violent and coercive nature. According to Dominique Marshall, those clauses inserted into the Family Allowance Act that empowered authorities to suspend family allowance benefits for so-called negligent mothers or "delinquent" children served as a disciplinary tool against those bodies that failed to conform to the European-Canadian middle-class nuclear family ideal.[11] Marshall found that working-class, widowed, and low-income mothers were disproportionately targeted for surveillance and disciplinary action.

Intersecting with the profoundly gendered nature of family allowances were the ideologies associated with the colonization of Indigenous lands and the racialization of Indigenous bodies. Indigenous women and their families were singled out for additional attention through this growing welfare state apparatus, which operated alongside and in partnership with Indian Affairs. Family allowance benefits and the disciplinary mechanisms included within the Act were added to the growing list of tools employed by Indian Affairs to intrude into the personal lives of Indigenous peoples in ways not experienced by non-Indigenous peoples. As Hugh Shewell argues, for Indigenous communities—and Indigenous women especially—the welfare state in the post–Second World War period signified a broadening of the state's abilities to meddle into the familial aspects of Indigenous communities' culture under the guise of social welfare and munificence, while the settler state was actively reducing Indigenous peoples' access to their lands and taking their children.[12]

In addition to those clauses within the Act that reinforced particular visions of mothering and childhood, further restrictions on access to and use of the family allowance benefits were established exclusively for Indigenous women. These constraints were instituted under the false belief that Indigenous mothers did not properly care for their children and would not use family allowance benefits wisely without further monitoring and guidance. Indian Affairs established strict rules around the types and kinds of food and goods that could be purchased using family allowance monies, and in many cases, Indian Affairs determined that individuals were incapable of spending money appropriately and established trust fund accounts to be overseen by Indian agents, HBC post managers, or RCMP officers. Northern communities were disproportionately singled out for the use of trust accounts and in-kind purchases.

In their design and implementation, family allowance benefits promoted particular behaviours while punishing the persistence of others, thus constituting a project of rule guided by settler colonialism and white supremacy. What is revealed by examining the Family Allowance Program and the ways in which it was employed against Indigenous women, their families,

Figure 4. Nalvana prints her name at the foot of the Family Allowance voucher at the Coppermine RCMP barracks, while Constable Martin Donnan waits, 1949. Credit: Library and Archives Canada, e010934209.

and communities, is that the provision of these benefits had more to do with money and capital interests than health and well-being, as will become increasingly clear as we proceed. According to the Minister of National Health and Welfare, Brooke Claxton, family allowance benefits for Indigenous peoples served as an "initiation into the consumer products of white society."[13] Indeed, as we aim to demonstrate in this chapter, an exploration of the Family Allowance Program and the role it played in northern Indigenous communities is a case study in the co-constitution of settler colonialism, capitalism, and heteropatriarchy.

Administering Family Allowance Benefits in Northern Canada

In early 1945, after a series of ongoing conversations between the Departments of Indian Affairs and National Health and Welfare, an agreement was reached whereby Indigenous mothers could receive family allowance benefits like other Canadian women, provided it was delivered in one of the following ways:

(a) monthly cheques to Indian families qualified for the receipt of Family Allowances in cash;

(b) issuance of cheques to Indian Agency trust accounts where administration is necessary;

(c) issuance of credits monthly to Indian Affairs Branch in favour of Indian families qualified to receive Family Allowances in kind.[14]

During his testimony before the Special Joint Committee of the Senate and the House of Commons in 1947, Dr. Percy Moore, now infamously associated with nutrition experiments upon Indigenous children at residential schools in the same period, further elaborated on the purpose of these categories:

> Indians were placed loosely in various categories whereby an Indian who was sufficiently advanced to handle their own affairs got this family allowance cheque the same as anyone else. The intermediate category took in people who needed some guidance and the Indian agent administered the funds for them. In the third group were the more primitive people and in that case lists were prepared in which we specified only the things that would be supplied under family allowances. The money is not sent to the Indian at all; credit is established at his trading post, where he goes to purchase his supplies, and that trading post manager may issue only certain specific items. These items were selected with great care. The Indian can buy powdered milk products, he can buy cereals, he can buy baby foods and tomato and fruit juices—items which are nutritionally good—but he is not allowed staples such as flour, lard, and tea. Those things should be a matter of relief, not children's allowances. They can buy underwear, rubbers, children's clothing, layettes. This policy has worked very well, and I think it has to a large extent ensured that his money is being spent for the purposes for which it was intended.[15]

Questions about how Indigenous women received family allowances were front and centre during the 1947 hearings held by the Special Joint Committee of the Senate and House of Commons investigating revisions to the Indian Act. Canadian politicians believed that family allowances presented an opportunity to offer further tutelage to Indigenous mothers about properly caring for their families by purchasing appropriate foods and goods. While most First Nations received their family allowances by cheque, there remained a sizeable number of women and families who continued to receive their family allowance benefits in kind. In 1949, for example, 12.5 percent of family allowance benefits were paid to Indigenous peoples in kind, which accounted for 56,924 children.[16]

All applications for family allowance benefits made by status Indians were to be adjudicated by Indian Affairs, and the department's employees in the field supervised the administration and use of family allowance monies. In cases where the agent was serving as "trustee" there was very little avenue for complaint or review open to Indigenous women. For example, it was impossible for Indigenous peoples to write to Indian Affairs directly without the knowledge of the local Indian agent since all correspondence was expected to go through the local Indian agent. In terms of deciding who was capable of properly spending their family allowance cheques, Indian Affairs relied heavily on the advice of Indian agents. As noted by Mr. Case from the Special Committee—"some agencies seemed to have more trustee situations than others. For example, there were several agencies where the agent [was] responsible for administering all the allowances on the reserve."[17]

Indian Affairs also established and maintained a list of specially selected food and clothing on which family allowance monies could be spent or purchased in-kind.[18] Deviations from this list required explicit permission from Indian Affairs, and families were often expected to purchase foods like Pablum long after they were age-appropriate for their children. The prominence of Pablum on the family benefits food purchasing list served both the work and interests of Dr. Frederick Tisdall—the Director of Nutritional Research at Toronto's Hospital for Sick Children and a nutrition consultant for Indian Affairs. Tisdall was one of several individuals who created Pablum in 1931 and sold it to the Mead Johnson company in 1934. Toronto's Hospital for Sick Children received royalties to support pediatric research from the sale of Pablum until the 1960s.[19] The presence, longevity, and importance of Pablum on the family allowance list was due largely to Tisdall's influence. The sale of the Pablum fuelled Tisdall's research agenda at the hospital, and he benefitted directly from the sale of Pablum to Indigenous peoples. As Ian Mosby parsed out in "Administering Colonial Science," Tisdall spent much of the 1940s conducting human experiments on starving Indigenous children in an attempt to develop scientific and proprietary knowledge on the "relative effectiveness of vitamin and mineral supplements on malnourished populations" as well as "the precise vitamin and mineral requirements of human beings."[20] Indigenous peoples, especially children interned in residential schools, presented Tisdall with a captive population. Clearly, a network of colonial actors were collaborating in postwar Canada to try and increase Indigenous peoples' consumption of particular foods.

A directive issued to all field agents by Indian Affairs on 1 January 1950 expanded upon the previous criteria for the receipt of family allowances. These guidelines established a more elaborate series of subjective conditions enabling employees of Indian Affairs to make biased decisions based on personal perceptions about the ability of Indigenous peoples to spend their own money properly. The general rules and regulations of the program operated on a gradual system of responsibility and supervision over how family allowances were to be spent by recipients:

> **Category A:** In cases where the Indian Superintendent feels that the Indian will make proper use of the allowances as set forth in the Act, payment is by monthly cheque mailed directly to the Indian; or

> **Category B:** If the Supt. feels the Indian to be sufficiently responsible, with a degree of supervision, the monthly cheque is made payable to the Indian but addressed in care of the Indian Superintendent. This enables the Supt. to stress the necessity of properly applying the funds received; or

> **Category C:** When the Indian Superintendent considers that although the majority of Indians on a reserve should be paid by cheque, a number should be paid in kind, the payment in kind is effected by means of a monthly cheque deposited to the Indian Agency Trust Account. The Indian Superintendent then sets up a ledger account for each family to whom payment is made in kind, crediting the monthly allowance, and debiting the amount of the vouchers which he periodically issues to the parent for payment in goods; or

> **Category D:** If it is the opinion of the Superintendent that all of the Indians on a reserve are incapable of spending the cash allowances as required in the Act, the allowance is paid wholly

in kind. Monthly credits for each family are issued to the Indian Affairs Branch Department of Mines and Resources for distribution to the Indian agencies. Against such funds the Indian Superintendent issues vouchers authorizing the supply of goods to the Indians. These may be issued monthly or at irregular intervals, depending on the conditions of travel. Lists of supplies which are in lieu of cash benefits have been made under four classifications. Briefly they are:

(a) Nutritious foods that will augment the Indian diet;

(b) Clothing for Indian children;

(c) Foods for special circumstances to supplement items in A;

(d) Emergency List—to be supplied on authorization of the Indian Superintendent.[21]

On full display here is the way in which the implementation of family allowances involved the bureaucratic categorization of Indigenous peoples into a kind of civilizational hierarchy that was drawn upon to organize and facilitate their assimilation into Canadian domesticities. Further, the maintenance of purchasing lists and the issuance of vouchers and in-kind payments allowed Indian Affairs to control and shape the purchasing habits of Indigenous mothers and their families. Of course, the impact of these family allowance policies worked in concert with provincial hunting laws that, in the decades previous, had excluded Indigenous peoples from partaking in the sale of foods. In gendered terms, settlers criminalized Indigenous men for hunting, fishing, and trapping as they targeted Indigenous women with the kind of surveillance and regulation described above.

The Department of Indian Affairs made the decision to begin slowly transitioning from vouchers and in-kind payments to cheques for select First Nations through an order-in-council on 30 March 1955. By 1955, twenty-three First Nations (out of more than 600 First Nations in Canada) were considered by Indian Affairs to be capable of receiving their family allowance benefits by cheque under Category B. In 1958, this number rose to 168 First Nations, but Indian Superintendents continued to monitor spending habits and did not hesitate to step in and impose additional restrictions or conditions for specific individuals if it was deemed necessary.[22] Further, changes to the payment of Family Allowance cheques were made on 1 August 1958, allowing select members of First Nations identified as having "done so well" (otherwise referred to as Category A) to register for Family Allowance benefits under "the same status as other non-Indian payees" through amendments made to sub-section 1 of regulation 11 (1) of the Family Allowance Regulations.[23] In other words, those women determined to be "advanced" or "white" enough were allowed to apply for family allowance benefits directly through the Department of Health and Welfare like other non-Indigenous women in Canada. In this frame of thinking, the highest form of citizenship attainable to status Indians was mapped according to an individual's gradual progression on the family allowance scale. In this way, enfranchisement as a logic of settler colonial assimilation was also manifest in the Family Allowance Program.

Category A was reserved for those Indigenous women determined by the Indian Superintendent to "make proper use of the allowances as set forth in the Act." By making such determinations, Indian Affairs regarded those individuals and First Nations determined to be Category A as "non-Indian." When Fred C. Jackson, Regional Director of Family Allowances, wrote in June of 1958 to J.T. O'Neill, Superintendent of the Sault Ste. Marie agency, he noted that when the "changeover has been completed for those Indian bands designated as non-Indian under the Family Allowance Regulations, the various categories of pay will no longer exist for the accounts."[24] It should be noted that Indigenous communities regularly protested the control and interference of Indian Affairs in the spending of family allowance benefits. Indeed, concerns expressed by First Nations prompted inquiries by Members of Parliament as to what the regulations and standards were and how and why they differed from the rest of Canada. In a letter to J.W. Willard, the Deputy Minister of Welfare, dated 17 August 1964, C.M. Isbister stated that they were regularly getting requests from bands to be able to apply for family allowance benefits on their own instead and not through Indian Affairs.[25] Clearly, if people were precluded from appealing directly to Indian Affairs, they found other avenues of protest.

Finally, in September of 1965, Family Allowance Program regulations were changed, and status Indians were granted the right to apply directly to the Family Allowance Division within the Department of Health and Welfare rather than applying first through Indian Affairs,[26] although a separate form for "Indians" remained. While the 1965 amendment to Family Allowance Regulations made this possible, Indian Agency staff were sent a letter instructing them to enable parents to assume "full responsibility for all

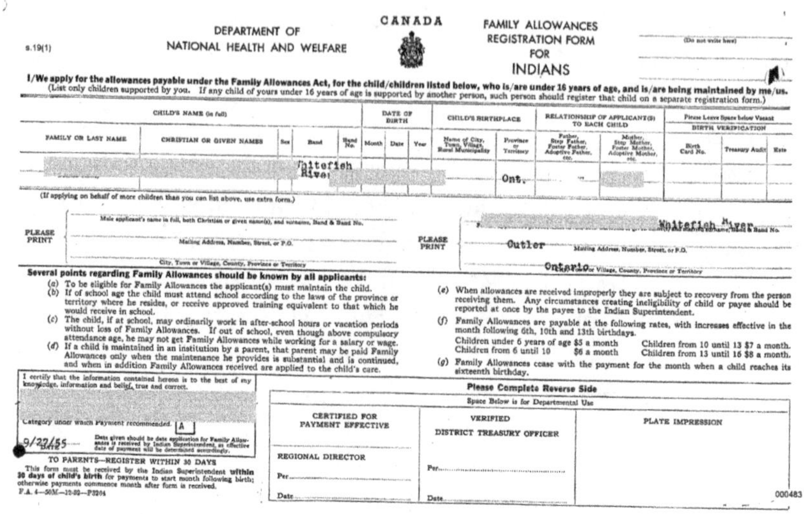

Figure 5. "Family Allowances Registration Form for Indians," LAC, RG 10, file 13/29-8, volume 3, Family Allowances Generally, November 1954 to March 1957.

matters relating to family allowances,"[27] while at the same time telling Indian agents to identify those situations where continued support and surveillance would be required for the foreseeable future. The following scenarios were identified as requiring further monitoring:

1. Parents are illiterate and have no access to other person who could help them complete forms;

2. families living in isolated areas where there are limited postal facilities;

3. nomadic families have problems in notifying Family Allowance Division of their frequent changes of address and family circumstances;

4. parents, for various reasons, request Indian Agency Superintendents to administer their family allowances.[28]

Discussions that began in 1961 about possible revisions to the Family Allowance Act that would enable First Nations and status Indians to receive family allowances directly also need to be viewed with caution. These conversations were undertaken within a context where many Canadians were questioning the misuse of family allowances by Indigenous peoples. As one commentator observed, "one more instance where the general impression of the public is that Indians are wasting their Family Allowances cheques in buying in liquor."[29] The director of the Northern Department, H.M. Jones, agreed to "place strong emphasis upon prompt administration in individual cases of abuse" but noted that the company needs to continue their "policy of resisting pressure brought to bear by Indian and Northern Health Services to retain and extend rigid controls upon the Indian as a class."[30]

The Family Allowance Program and the different categories whereby Indigenous peoples could receive benefits became a measure of "whiteness" to be adjudicated by Indian Affairs. Those individuals who were considered capable of spending their family allowance benefits "appropriately," or more accurately, in ways that conformed to European-Canadian norms, received cheques. The purchase of the "right" kinds of items (food and material goods) was regarded as evidence that Indigenous parents were using the family allowance benefits as intended and were thus deemed good parents, according to European-Canadian standards. Such measures required participation in and the inculcation of Indigenous people within a western market-based economy that used the atomization of the nuclear family as the basis of consumption. However, family allowance benefits were regarded as both a boon and a potential problem, especially when concern was expressed that the benefits had the potential to act as a deterrent to hard work.[31] Thus, constant surveillance was necessary (at least in the eyes of the federal government).

Indian Affairs believed that Indigenous peoples living in northern Canada needed additional assimilatory technologies and guidance to bring Indigenous women and their families closer to whiteness. Testifying before the special joint committee of the Senate and House of Commons, Director of Indian Affairs Mr. Hoey drew on well-worn tropes grounded in scientific racism to describe Indigenous children living in northern Canada as "com[ing] from the bush; they do not know what a chair is; it would be physically impossible for them to sit down on a chair for more than two or three hours a day. Their eyes are not focused for distances from 15 to 30 feet."[32] Hoey noted that family allowance benefits might also serve as an effective means of ensuring Indigenous children living in northern Canada attended school: "The biggest cure we have for truancy is the teeth of the family allowance act which provides that if you do not send your children to school you do not get an allowance."[33] The form used to register children for family allowance benefits stipulated that receipt of these benefits was predicated on school attendance and that the child did not participate in waged labour or receive a salary during school hours. Waged labour included the involvement of children on traplines. Concurrently, parents were expected to register their children for school and remain in one location so that they could attend school.[34] Such expectations drew clear connections between family allowances and the assimilatory objectives of the state. The receipt of family allowance benefits was dependent upon the forced settlement of Indigenous peoples in stationary communities where their children attended state-run schools, women managed the household, and men were the breadwinners.

The churches further reinforced the link between compulsory school attendance and family allowance benefits. In the community of Pukatawagan (part of the Mathias Colomb Cree Nation), located over 200 kilometres north of The Pas, Manitoba and accessible either by plane, train, or briefly by winter roads, community members were informed by Roman Catholic missionaries that if their children did not attend school, then their family allowance benefits would be withheld.[35] Clearly, family allowances operated as yet another tool in the arsenal of Catholic missionaries and the state to coerce people into sending their children to residential schools. A memo from the RCMP located near the community attachment to the HBC noted that this threat was so successful that "families from near and far [were] moving into the settlement."[36] The memo also shared the observations of the local Game Conservation Officer, who had told RCMP officers that the reason families were not "trapping as intensively as heretofore [was] because of the winter schooling with the reluctance of the natives to go in the bush without their families."[37] We see here direct evidence that provincial hunting and fishing legislation worked hand-in-glove with family allowances to disrupt Indigenous foodways. Indeed, the inability of families to go together into the bush during the school year made it so that men went on their own to harvest and brought back the furs for women to treat. The conservation officer further observed that "there was a higher percentage of tainted skins" without the expertise and skill of Indigenous women on the trapline.[38] The disruption of the family and extended family units through the imposition of European-Canadian modes of living and educating children altered the passage of time and affected the seasonal ways in which Indigenous peoples pursued land- and water-based harvesting activities. The enforced sedentary demands to remain in school inhibited people's pursuance of seasonal harvesting and gathering activities.

Drawing on ideologies of scientific racism, Indian Affairs characterized Indigenous peoples living in present-day northern Canada as physiologically different, thus requiring a longer and more applied period of instruction. They were explicitly shown how to spend their family allowance benefits properly to mimic whiteness. To bring Indigenous communities closer to whiteness through activities coded as white, family allowances required Indigenous people to participate in waged labour, live sedentary lifestyles, attend European-Canadian educational institutions, perform European-Canadian parenting and domesticity practices, and participate in European-Canadian consumer culture. This multi-pronged attack came from the province, the federal government, the HBC, the RCMP, the church, and other Canadian actors and agencies deeply invested in the assumed benefits of disciplining Indigenous communities to the foodways and domesticities of settlers.

Although many Indigenous people who were registered as status Indians under the Indian Act were allowed to receive their family allowance benefits directly in the form of cheques, Indian Affairs viewed the "Northern Indian" as an exception.[39] H.M. Jones, the person responsible within Indian Affairs for overseeing the administration of the Family Allowance Program, noted that "there will be a place for allowances in-kind in the more remote and isolated parts of the country for some time to come" in order to ensure the introduction of "new and nutritious foods" alongside the "development of self-reliance and personal responsibility in the Indian parent."[40] Such comments reflected contemporary European-Canadian understandings about the role to be played by nutrition in maintaining good health and the establishment of a shared understanding among European Canadians about the "nutritional status and needs of Canadians."[41] Indeed, the inception of the Official Food Rules in 1942, according to historian Ian Mosby, operated as a means through which the state could impose a particular physical and cultural vision of Canadian citizenship.[42] While Indigenous women had long experienced the state's efforts to impose white European-Canadian domestic norms and parenting, including through the transformation of Indigenous foodways, the Family Allowance Program and emergent forms of nutritional science reinforced the popular belief that ill health and poverty in Indigenous communities could be resolved through education and market-based solutions.

Family Allowances and Purchasing Lists

As Patrick Wolfe theorized, "settler colonialism destroys to replace."[43] If food brings community together, organizes relationships, and encourages the intergenerational transmission of social, economic, and political knowledges,[44] then the success of the settler colonial project demands the destruction of Indigenous foodways and their reconstruction as market-based and settler state–sponsored systems. However, on a symbolic level, settler societies also seek to establish identities that are distinct from their countries of origin; in order to accomplish this, Indigeneity was and is used as an expression of that difference as long as it remains contained to symbolic manifestations like returning Indigenous names to topographical features on Turtle Island.[45] Patrick Wolfe calls this process "recuperating indigeneity,"[46] wherein Indigenous peoples are not eliminated entirely but rather enveloped into the body politic by the application of social welfare measures that impose a particular vision of white society. Participating in this process also enabled the Canadian settler state to claim progressive liberal social welfare as a key component of its identity. Indeed, Canada, and non-Indigenous Canadians more broadly, are deeply committed to a vision of themselves as peaceful democratic denizens. The Family Allowance Program and the generation of purchasing lists was one such technology employed by the settler state to "recuperate" Indigenous peoples or, in other words, bring them closer to whiteness through the imposition of European-Canadian foodways and consumer culture. Dr. Percy Moore, Director of the Medical Services Branch for Indian Affairs, in consultation with Dr. Frederick Tisdall, the Director of Nutritional Research at Toronto's Hospital for Sick Children, created the family allowance purchasing lists.[47] The list included food and clothing that "prioritized middle-class food customs and efficiency regimes derived from capitalist time-management principles, and emphasized cleanliness."[48] Significantly, the lists were generated by men far removed from and without any knowledge of the cultures, experiences, and needs of Indigenous peoples and children who lived in the geographic regions now known as northern Canada. That these politicians were non-Indigenous thus played a large role in the formation of their interventions; however, the fact that these politicians were overwhelmingly men is relevant to an intersectional analysis of the Family Allowance Program. As Indigenous feminists such as Lee Maracle and Paula Gunn Allen have aptly stated, the goal of colonization is itself gendered in that it seeks to have Indigenous men relate to Indigenous women and children in the same way that white men relate to white women and children.[49]

Under the Family Allowance Program, Indigenous women's bodies became sites of conflict and violence for the colonial state. With the intent of withholding their family allowance benefits as a tool of coercion, letters from

Figure 6. Four Inuit women inspect a poster on family allowances, August 1948. The image is part of a series of staged photographs intended to advertise the Family Allowance program. Credit: Library and Archives Canada, e004665201.

Indian Superintendents regularly requested that investigations be carried out into the conduct of Indigenous women believed to be transgressors of European-Canadian notions of domesticity and motherhood. For instance, an Indigenous woman living with three men who did not pay rent or board had her family allowance benefits suspended because she was unmarried.[50] Bianca Isaki describes this constellation of practices as "settler home-making" which includes those "emblems of normative domesticity" like single-family homes, waged employment, property regimes, and in this instance, domestic consumerism and food practices.[51] Isaki argues these practices were central to the "jus sanguinis doctrines of citizenship that create family ties to the settler state, and personal things, such as bodies, feelings, and family."[52] We might also refer to these domestic activities as guided by a settler governmentality that individuals adopt to align their own quotidian life practices with larger notions of utilitarianism and public health that are sanctioned by the state.

Family allowances manifested the ideological conviction that particular activities associated with the domestic sphere serve to create and constitute citizenries more easily governed by a centralized state apparatus.

Indian Affairs established a list of foods and goods that Indigenous women and their families were permitted to purchase using family allowance benefits. Indian Affairs restricted eligible foods to those items considered to be of "high nutritive value" such as "canned tomatoes (or grapefruit juice), rolled oats, pablum, pork luncheon meat (such as Spork, Klick [*sic*], or Prem), dried prunes or apricots, and cheese or canned butter."[53] The list of family allowance foods and goods was divided into four categories: A, B, C, and D. Class A covered those foods that were "especially selected to augment and supplement the Indian diet with foods that will give Indian children proper nutrition." These foods were:

1. Milk—fresh where available. Powered [*sic*] whole milk, evaporated milk, condensed sweetened milk must <u>not</u> be supplied
2. Canned tomatoes, or
3. Grapefruit Juice
4. Rolled Oats
5. Pablum—for younger children, up to 8 years of age
6. Pork Luncheon Meat—such as Spork, Klick [*sic*], Prem, etc Do not supply corned beef. Canned Salmon may be supplied occasionally.
7. Dried prunes or apricots
8. Cheese—canned butter may also be supplied when available.[54]

Classes B and C were a combination of food items and material goods. For instance, a layette was one of the items deemed essential for Indigenous mothers-to-be. A layette refers to the clothing and accessories European Canadians purchased and/or prepared for their newborn child. Layettes typically included several outfits (onesies, socks/booties, vests, hats, sleeping gowns), receiving blankets, bedding, and diapers. All items were very culturally specific to white middle-class Canadian infant care expectations and practices, and the adoption of these articles was symbolic within the assimilatory efforts of the settler state. Class D items were far more familiar and appropriate for Indigenous communities and food procurement practices. Unsurprisingly, such items could only be purchased using family allowance monies with special permission. According to a 1945 circular, Class D items were described as "an emergency list which [was] to be issued on the authorization of the Indian agent to cover special circumstances."[55] This list included the following: "rifles or shotguns, canoes, ammunition, nets, canvas, camp stoves, axes, files, saws, traps and snare wire, and cooking utensils."[56] Obviously, these items were almost exclusively related to land-based food procurement practices, underscoring the extent to which any land-based food production was seen as a supplemental activity only to be approved in emergencies rather than as a staple part of northern diets.

Items from Class D would have done far more to address hunger and food insecurity in northern communities than, for example, those articles considered necessary for a proper layette. The exclusion of those items indispensable to pursue land- and water-based foods on the family allowance purchasing lists parallels the lack of subsidies applied to similar items under the current Nutrition North Canada Program that we discuss later in this book. Indigenous peoples were not allowed to purchase items freely from any of the categories, even from Class A. Indian Affairs instructed superintendents and HBC post employees that additional "steps should be taken to ensure that an Indian does not spend all his allowance on one or two items, but rather that he is supplied with an average of all items in Class A," with milk being the most important.[57] The contradictions embedded in these policies were stark: though they were formulated to turn Indigenous peoples from hunters and gatherers to grocery store shoppers, they did not seek to make Indigenous peoples consumers in the fullest sense. Instead, the use of the in-kind issuance of family allowance goods, as opposed to cheques, speaks to how these policies were riddled with conflict because they sought to simultaneously encourage as well as prevent Indigenous peoples from partaking fully in a market-based food economy.

In northern communities where an HBC post or store was the only place in town to purchase market-based foods or "spend" family allowance benefits, the power of post managers and Indian Superintendents to police and govern the purchases of Indigenous peoples was broad and pernicious. This surveillance was further buttressed by notices and strict feeding guidelines distributed by Indian Affairs medical officers and the Indian agents at HBC posts, nursing stations, and at treaty payment time. For example, notices directing women to buy Pablum and milk were posted at HBC forts and started with strongly worded instructions: "Our King has made a law that all mothers of children will get help in seeing that his children grow up to

Figure 7. In what is clearly a staged photo, Department of Indian Affairs representative S.J. Bailey explains the benefits of Pablum to two Inuit women with babies, 1948. Credit: Library and Archives Canada, a167631.

be strong and healthy."[58] The language used in these notices was little better than a thinly veiled threat; having authority figures distribute the notices gave the guidelines an unstated authority. In some instances, Indian Affairs officials "went so far as to experiment with preventing some families from using family allowance monies to purchase flour, despite the fact that it had long been a key dietary staple."[59] Again, the contradictory way in which these policies played out on the ground is not an uncommon characteristic of Canadian federal Indian policies generally, which often oscillate between the competing logics of exclusion and assimilation.

The broader transformation of Indigenous foodways and the singling-out of Indigenous mothers for additional screening and surveillance aligned with racist constructions of Indigenous communities as places of dysfunction wherein individuals failed to conform to white European-Canadian standards of domesticity. Such efforts fed on and into racist stereotypes about Indigenous women as bad mothers and informed programs established in colonial spaces. Settler logic located the problems of high infant mortality rates within poor mothering instead of the real causes that were deeply rooted in settler colonialism, land theft, and poverty, absolving the settler state and erasing the ongoing dislocation of Indigenous peoples from practising foodways that had fed and supported their communities for generations. This parallels existing literature that feminist historians have produced on family allowances and other postwar social welfare policies, illustrating that these state-based initiatives were regulatory in the heteropatriarchal sense for most women. However, we also see here the ways in which the Family Allowance Program sought to structure the lived relationships between Indigenous mothers and their babies within a particular context of residential and day schooling, outpost shopping, and oversight from colonial institutions. Where gender begins and colonialism ends within our analysis of this program is not exactly clear; nonetheless, the fact that one has difficulty parsing out the intersection of these vectors of state power is, to some degree, our point.

During the decades of the Family Allowance Program and the growing educational initiatives in the North, Indigenous foodways were either represented as the cause of ill health in Indigenous communities or, in later decades, as prohibitively expensive and beyond the abilities and interests of the increasingly assimilated Indigenous consumer whose purchasing activities were cited as evidence of civilizational capacity (or, alternatively, a lack thereof). This extended to those auxiliary foods (in addition to breastfeeding) that augmented infants' diets in the months following their birth. Thus, foods that Indigenous women and caregivers had provided to their children for generations became identified as dangerous. In this context, the state promoted Pablum and European-Canadian auxiliary foods for Indigenous families and children and justified the coercive measures to ensure that these foods replaced Indigenous foods. This practice also ignored the geographical realities of transporting and preparing Pablum in a northern context where fresh milk and safe drinking water was not readily available and often prohibitively expensive.

For families with infants and young children, powdered milk (later infant formula) and Pablum were staples on the family allowance food list.

Figure 8. Store owner Mrs. Sigvaldasson talks to an Inuit woman and her child at the counter, Cape Smith, Nunavut, 1948. This image is part of a series of staged photographs intended to advertise the Family Allowance Program. Credit: Library and Archives Canada, e008446971.

Nutritionists working with Indian Health Services (IHS) in the 1940s recommended Pablum as early as the age of three months, and it became a primary part of many northern Indigenous diets through the family allowance system. As outlined earlier in this chapter, milk products were regarded as the most important food items under Class A, but there remained little flexibility regarding what food items could be purchased with family allowance benefits. In 1955, the general manager for the HBC wrote to Dr. Percy Moore: "the compulsory issuing of pablum is being overdone . . . where families with children ten years of age and over are forced to take it with every payment . . . irrespective of children's age" and questioned the appropriateness of these items for the diet of children.[60] There were times when the perspectives of local HBC employees differed from broader company policy.

As a survey of allowable foods on the family allowance list from 1948 to 1955 showed, the purchase of Pablum and powdered milk by Inuit in the Northwest Territories had gone from sixty to over 1400 units in less than eight years.[61] By 1955, letters between company post managers and the head office revealed that the Family Allowance Program had a real impact on the manner in which people fed their children. Such programs were informed by the belief that Indigenous women and their bodies, including their breast milk, were polluted. Indian Affairs' medical professionals consistently described Indigenous women's breast milk as inadequate and unhealthy, emphasizing the necessity of Pablum for the well-being of Indigenous children.[62] European-Canadian medical professionals identified Indigenous peoples' reliance on country foods as a key reason behind the unhealthiness of women's breast milk and a cause for high infant mortality rates. According to Indian Affairs, Indigenous women needed to purchase, prepare, and eat those foods endorsed as healthy by the so-called experts. Doing so would ensure their children grow up healthy and "whiter."

Intimately connected to the notion that Indigenous women's breast milk was unhealthy was the belief that Indigenous women were bad parents. Anishinaabe and Inuit childrearing practices included breastfeeding children for three years or longer with the addition of auxiliary foods from eight to twelve months. The state identified this practice as part of the spectrum of so-called "indulgent" childrearing practices amongst Indigenous people. To borrow the words of Ann Stoler, it is through the creation of knowledge about Indigenous women and childrearing/motherhood that we see "what makes up the political epistemology of race—the ways of knowing on which racisms have relied ... racisms are not ... only 'visual ideologies.' They are based on how the allegedly visual signs of race are tied to their non-tangible markers ... cultural competencies, moral dispositions, mothering or sexual 'instincts,' inclinations to delinquency or to voracious sexual desires. ... It is in these fungible assessments of cultural distinctions that the power of racisms thrive."[63] The production of knowledge or colonial grammars that marked Indigenous women as "different" and difference between Indigenous and settlers as "bad" have been and continue to be used to underpin settler society and white supremacy, thereby obscuring the real violence of these kinds of programs.

Settler health authorities described Indigenous childrearing practices as lax and neglectful, particularly in comparison to European-Canadian practices. Breastfeeding for three years or longer was seen as the embodiment of that carelessness. It is important to note that these forced purchasing programs were not only part of the larger assimilatory settler colonial project, but also extremely impractical and dangerous. Moreover, "in remote, rural communities 'breast milk is the most secure and economically advantageous' way to feed infants."[64] For communities living in the provincial and far North, many of the items on the list were heavy and prone to freezing; bottle-feeding infants without reliable access to potable water posed a significant and potentially dangerous challenge. Significantly, then as now, the prohibitive cost of food was a serious problem. As early as 1947, the Regional Superintendent of Indian Affairs for the Eastern Arctic wrote about his concerns regarding the high cost of food, particularly in relation to the efforts of Indian Affairs to alter the diets of infants and young children among the Inuit. H.W. Lewis noted firmly in a letter to the Deputy Commissioner of the Northwest Territories (NWT) that the "retail cost of pablum in Ottawa is 45 cents for the standard carton. As a comparison, pablum retailed at Fort Norman, NWT for 65 cents. Milk powder at Fort Norman retails at 50 cents a lb."[65] Declining incomes from furs in the 1940s and 1950s meant that family allowance benefits increasingly constituted a significant portion of families' incomes. John J. Honigmann, an anthropologist working in the James Bay region, "estimated that Family Allowances saw the per capita income in Attawapiskat Cree First Nation—increase by 52 percent in 1946–1947 and by 28 per cent in 1947–1948 . . . [and] . . . in 1949–1950, [it] accounted for an astonishing 54 percent per capita income among the Great Whale River Inuit Community in Northern Quebec."[66]

However, relying on family allowance benefits meant that one had to purchase those foods deemed nutritious and "appropriate" by Indian Affairs (in addition to sending children to so-called "schools"). It also meant that during a period of declining revenues from furs, the family allowance was very timely in ensuring the continued financial solvency of the HBC. According to their study on government policy in the Arctic, Frank Tester and Peter Kulchyski found that "the HBC was more than willing to take advantage of the added income that government relief and family allowances provided the Inuit."[67] Indeed, as we illustrate again and again in the upcoming chapters, the creation of the Family Allowance Program was followed closely in the late 1940s by the HBC's increasing reliance on the sale of foods and goods in fly-in and northern communities to ensure profitability and a return on stockholder investment. While the store continued to purchase furs in northern communities, it increasingly expanded into general merchandising. This shifting focus led the HBC to rename the Fur Trade Department to the

Northern Stores Department to better reflect its changing priorities to the sale of food rather than the purchase of furs in the North.[68] Significantly, this shift was supported by corporate welfare initiatives like the Northern Air Stage Program (popularly known as the Food Mail Program), which subsidized the costs of transporting southern market-based foods and certain non-perishable items to northern communities.

The impact that forced purchasing programs and nutrition education initiatives had on Indigenous foodways, and breastfeeding in particular, is difficult to measure, but considering the currently high rates of food insecurity and low rates of breastfeeding in many northern Indigenous communities, it is not difficult to begin to make some connections. A recent article by Jaime Cidro and co-authors shows that even when European-Canadian cultural perceptions regarding the importance of breastfeeding shifted in the 1970s, this change was not witnessed in Indigenous communities. Cidro makes the important observation that the decision to breastfeed is "not one that always rests solely with the breastfeeding mother and in fact is influenced by the social context of the women and her family."[69] Thus, in a setting where the intergenerational transmission of childcaring activities is interrupted and compounded by food insecurity, it is not surprising that breastfeeding rates in northern Indigenous communities remain relatively low.[70]

In 1977, without any sense of irony or acknowledgement of their decades-long efforts to undermine breastfeeding, impose bottle feeding, and encourage the early use of Pablum, Indian Affairs officials established infant and maternal welfare programs, wherein Indigenous mothers living in northern communities received ten dollars per month from Indian Medical Services if they initiated breastfeeding and sustained it for at least six months.[71] While such programs were designed to encourage breastfeeding rates among Indigenous women living in northern Canada, they obscured the damage already wrought by things like the Family Allowance Program and forced purchasing lists and continued to locate low breastfeeding rates in discourses of bad parenting and negligent mothers. In the same way that state intervention sought to turn Indigenous peoples into modern consumers of HBC goods while simultaneously limiting their capacity to consume in the full and free sense, these interventions into Indigenous motherhood were riddled with contradictory programs and policies.

Over the next couple of decades, requirements were imposed that made it increasingly difficult for Indigenous peoples living in rural and northern communities to either apply for or retain their family allowance benefits. First Nations and Inuit communities located in the provincial and territorial norths that were only accessible by air or winter roads faced even more difficulties when seeking to access social services and supports. For example, in 1975, amendments to Family Allowance Regulations stated that anyone without a Social Insurance Number would cease to receive family allowance payments after 1 January 1975.[72] This regulation came into practice during the summer of 1974. Although Indian Affairs officials raised concerns about the potential barriers this would pose for Indigenous peoples living in the North, the regulation remains in place today.[73] In this way, family allowances further served to make Indigenous peoples countable to the settler state in a way that facilitated control and governance.

Conclusion

In the broadest sense, family allowances were one of the many tools in the federal government's hands that worked to erode Indigenous food sovereignties and solidify a market-based food economy operated by an HBC monopoly. Working in concert with provincial hunting laws that targeted Indigenous fathers (usually constructed as the "head of a household or breadwinners"), family allowances targeted Indigenous mothers, who were often constructed as requiring considerable state-centred help to attain the same domestic state as their white settler counterparts. Thus, whereas family allowances visited dominant ideologies of gender and social relations on all Canadians, they were particularly acute in the Canadian North because family allowance benefits included additional rules and regulations that worked to shift Indigenous foodways towards grocery store shopping and market-based foods. As was often the case, the HBC was enriched by these policies, which increased their market share as well as influence over Indigenous peoples who experienced fewer and fewer alternatives to food production. We explore the growth of the HBC's retail operations in the next chapters alongside state programming regarding nutrition education.

CHAPTER 4

"LEFT AT THE TRADER'S MERCY":
The Hudson's Bay Company and the Northern Stores Department

During the late nineteenth and early twentieth centuries, the HBC joined retailers like Eaton's and Simpsons and established large department stores in urban centres across southern Canada. After the Second World War, the HBC also built small general merchandise stores in northern communities. As we illustrated in Chapter 2, the HBC's location, federal connections, and pre-existing relationships with Indigenous communities gave the Company significant market advantages in Canada's northern regions during the first half of the twentieth century. Such advantages were only bolstered by the Canadian state's relationship with and increasing reliance upon the Company, which was manifest most immediately in growing cooperation between Indian Affairs and the HBC. As the federal government relied upon the HBC to act as the point of colonial contact between themselves and First Nations and Inuit communities, so too did the HBC enforce a set of assimilatory practices for the settler state to replace the foodways of Indigenous peoples. This chapter moves forward in time to explore the Company in the post–Second World War period, the shifting nature of retail in the North in the decades before the HBC sold its Northern Stores Department to private investors and company executives in 1987, and the ongoing role the HBC played in altering the foodways of Indigenous peoples in concert with the state.

Until the late nineteenth century, retail in Canada consisted largely of general stores, trading posts, specialized shops, small grocers, and company stores that relied on a combination of credit, cash, and trade.[1] Following trends in Europe and the United States that emerged between 1890 and 1940, large department stores gradually came to dominate retail sales in Canada by offering a diverse range of stock from clothing, housewares, and groceries, to furniture. Technological developments in the transportation industry made the mass production and consumption of goods both possible and profitable. In turn, department stores could offer a broad range of food and goods at affordable prices for the average consumer. However, retail in the provincial and far norths looked very different. While efforts were made by the HBC and the state to mimic European-Canadian institutions and consumption patterns in the south, geography and long transportation routes in the North made this unlikely. Over time, HBC posts in First Nations and Inuit communities were replaced with small stores that sold both food and general merchandise. The rise of retail capitalism and consumer culture nonetheless complemented the broader goals of the settler state and the interests of the HBC, who began to specialize and differentiate their business practices between department store retailing in large Canadian cities and the provision of food and general merchandise across the provincial and territorial norths. In this chapter, we map out some of the processes whereby Indigenous peoples across the Canadian North had little choice but to participate in the consumption patterns and mores of Canada's postwar market cultures that were deeply gendered, racialized, and classed.

Postwar Market Culture in Canada

As historian Donica Belisle has shown, large department stores like the Hudson's Bay Company or Eaton's came to hold a special place within the imaginary of the dominant European-Canadian society during the twentieth century. Linked to modernity and characterized as an agent of Canadian progress and national identity, these stores were and are regarded as an important part of the nation's heritage. From Eaton's to the HBC, the postwar success of chain-based department stores both shaped and reflected dominant settler ideals of hegemonic gender roles that were seen to embody the white middle-class domestic household.[2] Since retail stores "through their massive advertising efforts, tapped into this yearning [for a national identity/belonging],"[3] shopping and working in these stores came to be seen as uniquely Canadian. If it was uniquely Canadian to shop in these stores, then the HBC

Figure 9. The Hudson's Bay Company store in Winnipeg, c. 1900–1925. Credit: Library and Archives Canada, PA-032842.

(given its geographic location and formative role in the nation's history) was well placed to assist with the assimilatory project.

Simultaneously, the HBC positioned itself as ideally situated to "care" for Indigenous peoples in the North and to bring a modern lifestyle to the region through its stores. In its own company magazine, *The Beaver*, the HBC described itself as paving the way for Canadian society in those regions of Canada where the population remained largely Indigenous.[4] As an institution with a long history on Turtle Island, the HBC heralded itself as an "agent of progress" in northern Indigenous communities through its sale of food and goods.[5] If "white Canadians associated consumption with racial and national belonging," then Indigenous peoples could become closer to whiteness by making the correct purchases.[6] As the largest and often only retailer in the North, the HBC was perfectly positioned to help sell Canadian values, identities, and gender roles to Indigenous peoples in northern communities.

Gender was operative within the assimilatory project and what better way to pursue it than the replication of those contexts and goods that produced a European-Canadian version of domesticity in northern communities. The act of shopping and consumption represented the domestic efforts of women

Figure 10. Cover of *The Beaver*, August 1922.

to become good housekeepers and managers of the household. Within this hegemonic arrangement of gender relations, male "breadwinners" were meant to fund these consumptive commercial activities through wage labour jobs subsidized by the domestic labour of their wives and children. As Tracey Deutsch writes in *Building a Housewife's Paradise*, grocery stores "had long been distinctively identified with women's domesticity and the commercial and public spaces that had become central to domestic life."[7] The question of how this culture of postwar consumption was received in the provincial and territorial norths has not been widely explored. It is also central to our analysis of the HBC in this chapter.

If the settler state wanted Indigenous women to be more like white women, then Indigenous women needed to partake in these activities. Within this model women were positioned as household managers and consumers. Shopping and retail experiences went beyond the mere act of purchasing food and increasingly came to represent a particular national, racial, and gendered identity in the postwar period.[8] In this context, those programs like the Family Allowance Program operated alongside the state and in concert with the HBC to buttress the assimilatory project in northern Canada. Settler colonial objectives, in this manner, were pursued through gendered forms of capitalist consumption strengthened by statist interventions, wherein race, gender, and labour were fused together in the larger forces that encouraged Indigenous peoples to shop at grocery stores. As Deutsch notes, grocery stores where food was sold served as sites "not only for the purchase of food but also for the operations of the mid-twentieth century state and its increased dependence on top-down, standardized, and predictable consumption."[9] Though we track the emergence of a top-down structure of consumption here, we also underscore how the rise of postwar market culture in northern Canada was different from its southern manifestations in certain key respects. Primary among these is the fact that the sale of food and other goods in the south were based largely on consumption patterns and profit.[10] In the North, the kinds of foods that were pushed on Indigenous peoples were based upon a more complex and colonial network of influences that included what was feasible to ship, sell, and promote in existing HBC retail operations. For that reason, the HBC and Indian Affairs used certain tactics, deployed particular modifications, and made some compromises to hasten the assimilation of northern people to postwar market culture. These strategies of assimilation reflected not only hegemonic gender relations of the period, but also racist assumptions about Indigenous peoples as consumers in need of considerable instruction in making the proper market choices. Thus, while the history of HBC retail operations in the postwar period fits alongside the larger history of department store consumption, we explore some meaningful differences in this chapter.

The Northern Stores Department

A slump in global fur trade prices, alongside the growth of the liberal welfare state in the post–Second World War period, led the HBC to shift the focus of its activities in northern Canada from the trading of furs to the sale of groceries and general merchandise, largely to Indigenous peoples and communities.[11] The addition of a "stores" division within the HBC in the second decade of the twentieth century marked a change that gradually came to dominate the company's operations in southern Canada and in the North after the Second World War. Significantly, these retailing operations surpassed the importance of fur sales to the company's long-term profitability. While the Northern Stores Department (NSD) was established as a distinct entity within the Hudson's Bay Company in 1959, its creation was part of a larger re-organization process within the company that had begun several decades earlier. Between 1940 and 1959, the HBC Posts in northern communities moved away from bartering and trade to a cash-only economy.[12] Although the move to a cash economy had started earlier with the distribution of annuities from the federal government, the introduction of the Family Allowance Program and the growth of the welfare liberal state marked the end of bartering and trade at HBC posts. Even still, the issuance of credit by the Company has remained a staple of its business practices to this date.

The transition to a cash/credit economy was just one component of a larger effort within the company to modernize business practices at northern posts and stores between 1950 and 1964 under the leadership of R.H. Chesshire. Chesshire, who rose from assistant manager to general manager during this period, oversaw a program of modernization that included upgrading northern stores and warehouses, updating staff training programs, improving staff housing, and developing centralized ordering and distribution systems.[13] After 1945, the HBC used air transportation to ship perishable foods and goods into communities. Their networks relied overwhelmingly on a system of northern air travel, the early stages of which were premised on the 1933 construction of an airport in Sioux Lookout, Ontario, that served as a major transfer hub between northern and southern communities.[14] Over time, those inland posts in proximity to fly-in First Nations and Inuit settlements with a population of over 3,000 people were converted into merchandise stores—hereafter referred to as inland stores.[15] Although fur purchasing and sales[16] continued within the HBC more broadly, the scale of operations and percentage of total sales declined. Concurrently, food sales increased precipitously in the post–Second World War period, and by the late 1960s, the NSD reported that 59 percent of sales at inland stores came from food.[17] For the NSD, and after 1987 the North West Company, the sale of food not only constituted a highly profitable enterprise, but it also formed a central part of the architecture of the settler colonial project in the North.[18]

The rise of large grocery stores and supermarkets in North America also offered the HBC another retail model on which to draw in northern communities. While inland stores could not match a supermarket's scope, selection, or affordability, the NSD drew on other innovations such as fixed prices for standardized lists of foods, plastic packaging, and refrigeration.[19]

The availability of canned and frozen fruits and vegetables in the fifties and sixties was touted as offering "convenience, and the promise of healthier meals, because they had been 'packed at the peak of freshness.'"[20] By the 1980s and 1990s, nutrition recommendations that encouraged the consumption of canned and frozen foods were reversed by Indian Affairs' nutritionists, who criticized the lack of fresh fruits and vegetables in Indigenous peoples' diets. The Cold War also produced a renewed interest in the gendered ideal of the female homemaker and stressed contemporary European-Canadian ideals that emphasized the importance of time management and efficiency. These qualities, embodied in the convenience of pre-packaged and processed foods purchased at supermarkets, were important in the operation of the settler state in cooperation with a corporate monopoly.[21]

Though postwar market culture shifted, retail and consumption patterns across the North and the role of the store manager remained fairly constant. In fact, it was strikingly similar to the fur trade era: store managers continued to monitor how and when Indigenous customers spent their monies, determined when and how to issue credit, and continued to serve as a conduit between the state and Indigenous peoples and communities. This was especially true regarding how family allowance monies were spent on the pre-approved list of foods, as the store manager was frequently called to pass judgement on customers and determine their eligibility and reliability as recipients of credit. Store managers exercised significant influence in a community where the Hudson's Bay Company was the only active retailer. The NSD also continued to provide educational programming in First Nations and Inuit communities under the perception that Indigenous peoples needed particular forms of assistance in their assimilation to postwar market culture.

The NSD faced little retail competition in the provincial and far norths in the post–Second World War period, even after the establishment of Arctic Co-operatives in some Inuit settlements by the late 1950s and early sixties that were later incorporated under the umbrella of the Canadian Arctic Co-operative Federation Limited in 1972.[22] The NSD's "new" stores were built on the foundations of pre-existing posts and relied on an established shipping and transportation system. This infrastructure, combined with barriers to entry in the north, allowed the HBC to remain largely unchallenged as the primary retailer in the many northern communities.[23] The lack of competition enabled the NSD to establish a uniquely northern model of retailing, unlike southern stores which tailored the foods and goods sold to customers according to consumption patterns.[24] In the North, the assimilatory efforts of the state drove much of what was sold through the forced purchasing lists we addressed in the previous chapter. Over time, these purchasing lists began to reflect purchasing patterns; for instance, Klik and evaporated/canned milk became very popular items. Items useful for harvesting and land-based activities remained part of those items stocked by the store but not approved for purchase under the Family Allowance Program.

In contrast, the NSD's southern counterpart faced increasing retail competition from chain stores, and in the 1960s, the HBC established large suburban department stores. These new stores were housed within the newly created Bay Division and rebranded as "The Bay" in 1965 to appear as a "hip" modern store. The Bay rebranding was part of a larger effort by the Company to disassociate itself from its colonial past, as it faced growing criticism from Indigenous political organizations and communities for its historical (and ongoing) exploitation of Indigenous peoples.[25] The attempts to "modernize" and rebrand the store were part of a broader effort to obscure the assimilatory work of the HBC and signalled a shift within the Company that recognized the distinctions between northern and southern urban retail landscapes.[26] Geraldine Alton Harris notes that, despite its rebranding and efforts to modernize its operations, many of the basic functions of the Northern Stores Department remained largely the same after 1959 as they were still based on transporting materials and goods to and from the North.[27] In some instances, the Transport Division of the Company remained the only means of regularly travelling to and from many First Nations, particularly in the provincial norths. HBC transport networks regularly assisted government and scientific expeditions in travelling to and from communities to carry out their work and activities well into the 1980s. The HBC was empowered to exercise an inordinate degree of control over the lives of Indigenous peoples since it controlled access to market-based foods, government services, and gatekeeping researchers.

Corporate Welfare

As we illustrated in Chapter 2, the HBC performed roles normally carried out by the state, like delivering nutrition education and distributing annuities. In the Cold War period, these roles persisted alongside and often in concert with the federal government's programs and policies, especially regarding the imposition of European-Canadian foodways and domesticity. The retail dominance of the HBC in northern Canada was not an accident and serves as an important exemplar of the ways in which state and corporate interests coincide within settler logic, violence, and the politics of erasure.

The market-based solutions employed by the federal government to address food insecurity and poverty obscured systemic problems and masked the violent architecture of settler colonialism that alienated Indigenous peoples from their lands and foodways. Most importantly, however, market-based solutions placed the onus on the individual and made poverty a function of poor choices and a lack of personal responsibility—all principles that informed the objectives of nutrition experts and Canada's Food Guide. It was in this context that the HBC positioned itself as providing a service to Indigenous peoples in northern communities by making a "modern" lifestyle available through retail selections. As part of its efforts to rebrand itself as a modern and democratic force within Canadian society, the HBC characterized itself as ideally situated to help bring Indigenous peoples in the North closer to whiteness. A sentiment, it seemed, that was echoed by the federal government. In correspondence between the Company and the Minister of Northern Affairs in 1967, Arthur Laing described the HBC as providing an invaluable service to Indigenous peoples through its operation of stores in First Nations and Inuit settlements: "[the] Hudson's Bay Company is prepared to continue providing the people of the prominently native communities of Northern Canada with a modern efficient retail distribution service in return for a fee—a reasonable but not excessive return on invested capital and we are confident that the continuation of this service is in the best interests of the native people and the taxpayers of Canada."[28] In this logic, the Company was entitled to a return on invested capital to the extent that it made possible the assimilation of northern Indigenous communities to food consumption patterns based on an (albeit slightly modified) version of settler strategies of postwar nutrition. Laing characterized the HBC "as a modern and progressive force in the North."[29] Frank Tester and Peter Kulchyski explore the ways in which the federal government used the forcible relocation of the Inuit in the North to assert Canadian sovereignty and the role that relief policies played in this context. Significantly, the authors clearly show that the Family Allowance Program saved the profitability of the HBC in the North in the face of falling global fur prices. What is not addressed in their work is the ways in which the creation of forced purchasing lists by Indian Affairs required the HBC to stock a standardized list of European-Canadian foods with the assurance that those foods would be purchased with family allowance monies. In this manner, the federal government created a captive customer base for the HBC while also assisting the company in shifting its retail model from furs to food.

A circular from Indian Affairs in May of 1945 clarified the Family Allowance Act and its intended objectives as they pertained to Indigenous peoples. The instructions focused on the types of foods and goods intended for purchase with family allowance monies. As we illustrated in the previous chapter, the foods and goods were divided into categories A, B, C, and D that identified "preferred" items on which family allowance monies could be spent. When family allowances were first introduced, it was clear that these items were not regularly stocked merchandise and thus not something that Indigenous customers at the posts regularly purchased. Indeed, Indian agents were cautioned to exercise patience and carefully supervise purchases to ensure that when the preferred items were unavailable, those items purchased were done so within the spirit and intent of the list: "for a period of time after the allowances are first paid there may be times when the merchants, traders, etc may not have the requisite supplies in stock and that during that period the Indian Agent will have to assume considerable responsibility in the matter of substitutions. Stocking preferences for traders should be given to those items in categories A for food and B for clothing."[30] Store managers were also asked to ensure that customers did not spend all of their money in one category.[31] It is in these ways that the NSD and Indian Affairs worked together to ensure that certain foods and goods were available and that they were purchased in a manner that reflected current nutritional recommendations.

To complete this assimilatory goal, agents and store operators practised surveillance and revoked rights from individuals deemed insufficiently prepared to make their own market decisions. For example, Acting Deputy of Indian Affairs H.M. Jones responded to concerns raised that Indigenous peoples were not spending their family allowance monies properly (a charge that the HBC could be seen as complicit in allowing to happen given the control they exercised over how that money gets spent). "With my letter to you of October 29, 1959, concerning the alleged widespread misuse of Family Allowance Payments by Indians," wrote Jones, "I attached reports concerning this matter that were received from Indian Agency Superintendents. These reports indicated that, except for a very small percentage of cases, the allowances are being used as wisely by Indians as by non-Indians."[32]

The testimony of Mr. Gifford Swartman, Indian agent at Sioux Lookout, before the Special Joint Committee of the Senate and House of Commons on the Indian Act in 1947, described the role played by the Family Allowance Program in shaping the retail landscape of the North and the food choices available to Indigenous peoples:

> Had it not been for family allowances, I know the merchants and traders in the remote areas would not have stocked the essential items such as tomatoes, milk in large quantities, pablum, cheese, fruit, vegetables, etc . . . ask any trader or post manager in the inland posts how much milk he sold prior to family allowances and his answer . . . would amaze you. At some posts over a ten year period, records show from one to two drums of powdered milk and no canned milk sold each year. This year these same traders will sell from one and a half to two tons.[33]

Through the forced purchasing lists under the Family Allowances Program, the federal government helped to establish a captive market for the NSD. Over time, this produced and fostered a demand for those foods included on the list. Prior to the introduction of the Family Allowance Program and the institution of forced purchasing lists, people purchased sweetened condensed milk and rolled oats instead of powdered milk or Pablum.[34] As early as 1947, testimony before the Parliamentary committee investigating potential amendments to the Indian Act recorded how food preferences had changed and that "demand" for new types of food had increased: "The band has consumed large quantities of milk cereals and canned tomatoes—phenomenal amounts when compared to their previous purchases. A very interesting feature is their liking for canned tomatoes—an acquired taste. When payment in-kind was first introduced it was difficult to get them to use tomatoes. Now the traders are unable to obtain sufficient supplies to meet the demand."[35]

There was a relationship between how relief rations were issued and how the Company stocked its shelves. Despite testimony that declared canned tomatoes a popular item, following the changes in the issuance of relief in 1959, the Company was left with huge overstocks of cheese and canned tomatoes. Fortunately for the Company, the family allowance purchasing list and Indian agents would assist them with selling this stock. The shift from issuing rations as goods in-kind to cash meant:

> that the food items purchased by the relief recipient will be of his or her own choice. In the past, relief orders have stipulated the items and quantities and in this connection we have carried stocks of canned tomatoes and cheese in order to meet the wishes of the Indian Affairs Department. You are no doubt aware that canned tomatoes is not an item ordinarily purchased by the majority of the Indians. I have been advised on many occasions that canned tomatoes on the relief order were only taken by the recipient because it was compulsory and in many cases were thrown away. While cheese is not in the same category, nevertheless it is not a ready seller.[36]

In March of 1959, H.W. Sutherland, general manager of the Northern Stores Department, advised the manager of the Western Division to work with Indian agents in the field to encourage the purchase of such items so that "our heavy stocks are brought into reasonable line."[37] As we see in these exchanges, the kinds of foods promoted, shipped, and sold in Indigenous communities were not based on market dynamics of supply and demand, but were regularly subordinated to the assimilatory logics of the federal government and the bottom line of the HBC.

It should be noted that Indigenous communities did not meekly submit to the federal government's efforts to alter their foodways or change the ways in which they cared for their children. The 1947 parliamentary committee recorded the frustration of Indigenous peoples who received in-kind family allowance benefits and a critique regarding the behaviour of local store managers and traders, noting the need to change the in-kind method of receiving family allowance benefits. For instance, First Nations from present-day northern Alberta described receiving family allowances in-kind as "being left at the trader's mercy" and that it allowed the "trader to do what he wants when he is sure of getting our credit."[38] One band from northern Ontario made a submission stating that "they regard[ed] [family allowances] as an effort for the federal government to tell them what is best for their children."[39] While the Family Allowance Program may have preserved the profitability of the HBC and created a protected market for the Company, these changes did not occur on the backs of an obedient population. Instead,

Indigenous peoples and their communities used every opportunity to voice their dissatisfaction.

The Family Allowance Program also helped the NSD establish a system of credit that places the NSD in a role where it operates as financial institution, grocery store, and creditor to Indigenous peoples in a region where banks are largely unavailable. Indigenous peoples levelled complaints against the Company that store managers issued advances to customers against the receipt of future family allowances and then, when family allowance cheques arrived, immediately had them signed over. This practice echoes credit practices exercised later under the NWC and discussed in Chapter 6. The issuance of credit by the HBC only became a matter of concern for H.M. Jones, National Director of Family Allowances, when other traders in the region complained about the Company and its practices.[40] The NSD created a cycle of indebtedness for Indigenous peoples living in fly-in communities that persists to this day. Indeed, the NSD was and is often the only place in town where people can "cash" cheques, something we address in more detail in Chapter 6. The shift from goods in-kind to family allowance cheques in the late sixties also created further challenges for recipients. Often Indigenous women did not read or write English and were not present in the settlement.[41] The requirement of needing the woman to endorse the cheque posed a logistic problem for those families actively harvesting. Frequently, women remained in the camp while men travelled to posts and stores to trade. While there, the man would retrieve the mail and try to purchase supplies at the local post.[42] The enactment of such policies illustrates very clearly the disconnect between those who created the policies and the people who are forced to live with them. Indeed, if read within the context of how settler colonial governance is enacted, then both the intent and design of all state policy is to undermine Indigenous food sovereignties through a lack of understanding about land-based realities when formulating state-based interventions.

A series of letters in the 1950s between R.H. Chesshire, General Manager of the Fur Trade Department, Indian Affairs, and the RCMP revealed the extent of cooperation between the state and the HBC. J.P.B. Ostrander, Superintendent of the Welfare Department of Citizenship and Immigration, reached out to the HBC to clarify the Company's provisioning policy for trappers. The HBC wanted to limit the amount of provisions they advanced to trappers, and post managers were instructed to adjudicate between deserving and undeserving trappers.[43] In a letter to Indian Affairs in June of

1954, Chesshire outlined the Company's guidelines for issuing provisions: "What we are primarily concerned about is the character of the man and his ability as a trapper. Next, we consider the distance he travels and the time he remains away from the post, the size of the family, and other pertinent data."[44] Such paternalistic measures and practices allowed the company to insert itself into the intimate and personal lives of Indigenous peoples. Such knowledge was also shared with the RCMP, who, along with Indian Affairs, were assured that any changes to company policy would only be done in consultation with them.[45] The RCMP had the power to order the HBC not to issue advances to Indigenous trappers.[46] Such cooperation provided the state and its watch-dogs, the RCMP, extraordinary influence over the lives of Indigenous peoples and is also illustrative of the intimate relationship that existed between Indian Affairs and the HBC. We also see here the ways in which carceral forms of settler colonial governance were enmeshed and entwined within the emergent welfare-state structure of postwar Canada.

Perhaps the most infamous way that the federal government provided the HBC with access to infrastructure in the North was through the negotiation of leases for on-reserve land where stores and/or posts were erected. Such leases were signed between the Company and the Crown and did not include input from the Chief and Council of the First Nation where the store operated. Although rent has increased in other parts of Canada over the past century, the HBC was fortunate to receive extremely good rental conditions on-reserve. For instance, in Pikangikum First Nation, in 1948, the HBC signed a twenty-year lease with the Crown for twelve acres at a rent of sixty dollars per year; the rent increased to $100 per year in 1966.[47] Similarly, Attawapiskat First Nation had six acres of their land, including a general store and dwelling, leased by the Crown to the HBC for five years at ten dollars a month.[48] In 1994 when the lease originally signed between Sandy Lake First Nation and the HBC and Crown neared expiration, it was renegotiated. The community's leadership negotiated a significantly different lease following the construction of a new store building. Instead of the Crown providing the best deal for the Company, the First Nation ensured an agreement that met their interests. As the *Globe and Mail* reported, The North West Company "instead of simply dropping into the community—as it did in the past—it must bargain the terms of its continued presence . . . the band took out a $1.5 million mortgage to finance the building, which is being leased back to the company. The band also receives a percentage of gross sales, amounting to $80,000 in the first year . . . the lease is for 50 years—a deal that spells more profit for the band."[49] Though this story shows the contours of local examples of Indigenous sovereignty, we want to underscore the extent to which the issue of very favourable lease conditions is important to Indigenous leadership across the North more broadly. For example, leases figured prominently during conversations we had with community leaders and members who identified HBC leases as research priorities in the archives.

Nutrition Upgrading Program

Acting in concert with the programs run by Indian Affairs to alter the diets of Indigenous peoples were the nutrition promotions run by the HBC as part of their broader advertising campaigns to increase sales. When corporations endorsed products under the guise of advocating what they regarded as healthier (read: white middle class) lifestyles, they did so because it benefitted their bottom line. Campaigns undertaken by the HBC/NSD were part of the broader assimilatory project intended to inculcate Indigenous peoples with European-Canadian foodways and culture, improving what they perceived to be deficits in Indigenous peoples' knowledge about nutrition and poor eating habits. Discussions about poor health in Indigenous communities drew on a deficit model that pathologized Indigenous bodies and elided the violent processes of settler colonialism that produced poverty and reduced access to land- and water-based foods, offering greater consumption of the "right" types of European-Canadian foods as the solution.

In 1978 the HBC employed a nutritionist, Marjorie Schurman, to develop nutrition campaigns and initiatives to be promoted by the company in Indigenous communities situated in present-day northern Canada. Schurman was responsible for developing the Company's Nutrition Upgrading Program and its associated marketing campaign.[50] In addition to educational programs, Schurman often served as a research coordinator for academics working with universities and helped to direct several nutrition studies carried out by post-secondary institutions, Indian Affairs, and the Department of Health and Welfare. As Krista Walters sketches out, the establishment of the Medical Services Branch (MSB) within the Department of Health and Welfare in 1962 included the expansion of nutrition education and programming.[51] Often this programming took place alongside initiatives undertaken by the HBC.

The intellectual origins of the HBC's Nutrition Upgrading Program were to be found in a series of conversations between Community Health Workers (also called Community Health Representatives or CHRs), who put forth a series of recommendations to the Medical Services Branch to address food insecurity in the North. CHRs were local people trained to deliver public health education and nutrition services to members of their community.[52] These positions were created as part of a larger reorganization of health services for Indigenous peoples in 1962, which saw the creation of the Medical Services Branch out of the merger of Indian Health Services, Northern Health Services, and five related federal health programs.[53] Several of the recommendations included suggestions about making nutrition information more accessible to community members by colour-coding foods, especially in instances where people's first language was not English.[54] The HBC used the CHRs recommendations to create a market-based campaign that benefitted their bottom line. The program at the store would be run in concert with federal, provincial, and territorial bodies and be shared at the local grocery store and nursing station.[55] The colour-coding program was so well-known and widespread that when the celebrated television show *North of 60* was shooting on location in the Mackenzie area, they wanted to include the NSD's Nutrition Upgrading Program in an effort to ensure the show's realism. Schurman saw this as an ideal opportunity for growing awareness of the program and sent out letters to stores in the region asking managers to ensure that "the coloured coding markers [were] visible and in the correct places; the basic food group posters have the appropriate traditional animals and [were] hung in a conspicuous location; nutritious snacks are available and visible at the checkout. If you do not have any of the snacks in the list mentioned above near the checkout, please incorporate some behind the cashier, i.e. meat sticks; small packs of nuts, raisins; cheese 'n' crackers are all easily incorporated and should also display the appropriate shelf markers."[56]

The Nutrition Upgrading Program consisted of shelf labels that matched the colours of Canada's Food Guide, a series of posters drawn by Indigenous artists to popularize the colour-coded food labels, nutrition fact sheets, signs translated into the local Indigenous language using bright colours and symbols, and newsletters. Schurman hired an Inuk artist, Allotook Ipellie, to create a cartoon character for the program called Nukilik, which was intended to mean "the one with strong muscles" in Inuktitut.[57] Nukilik was included on posters and slide presentations to be used by local teachers and health workers.

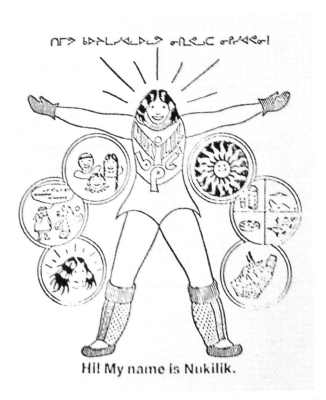

Figure 11. Nukilik was the cartoon character for the HBC's Nutrition Upgrading Program created by Inuk artist Allotook Ipellie. Credit: HBCA, RG 7, H2-273-5-2, Northern Stores Public Affairs Manager Correspondence and Subject Files, Nutrition 1977–1981, Newsletter, "News from Nukilik," Number 1, 1980, 2.

The newsletter served as both an important piece of propaganda and a marketing tool. It included scripts for radio advertisements, recipes, and advice for community members that always recommended people purchase food at the local store by connecting all community nutrition programming with monthly store themes.[58] For instance, the program was launched under the theme, "When You Choose Foods, Balance the Colours," to inspire shoppers to purchase foods from those colours representing the four basic food groups.[59] The food groups for Indigenous peoples mirrored Canada's Food Guide but were simplified and colour-coded so that people could easily spot them on store shelves and shape their purchasing decisions accordingly. Red was the colour for "Meat type foods for strong muscles and blood, Blue [was] for Milk type foods for strong bones and teeth, Green [was] for Fruits and Vegetables for good eyes and a healthy body, and Orange (or Yellow) [was] for Breads and Cereals for energy to work and play. Wise eating means eating from <u>each</u> colour group, <u>every</u> day."[60] Every month the newsletter featured a new food group and instructions to be read on the radio to inform parents that purchasing such foods would ensure their children grew up with strong muscles and blood, mimicking similar nutritional education messages employed among the non-Indigenous population. The newsletters were accompanied by colouring sheets to be handed out by CHRs, teachers, and at the local grocery store. A primary goal of the newsletter was to serve as an early childhood intervention to ensure that children were raised according to current European-Canadian knowledge and attitudes towards food.[61] Teachers were encouraged to include these lessons in their classes during language lessons, teaching Indigenous children how to speak English through words about food. There was also information about which store foods could be substituted for land- and water-based foods, for instance: "if you are not cooking country food, pick a food shown with a RED marker in the store such as canned chicken, beef or fish. Add this to cook with the quick meal you are making such as macaroni or rice and serve. It is easy and tastes good."[62]

One newsletter identified store-based and land-based foods as important ways to stay healthy and encouraged customers to purchase items within the colour-coded groups. Including land-based foods within the colour coding program was less about being inclusive and more about enclosing Indigenous foods within a western capitalist consumer framework. These foods, although they kept Indigenous peoples healthy for generations, could now be known as healthy within a European-Canadian framework, and it made the land-based foods part of a consumer diet.

These newsletters were sent to members of the Territorial Education Committee, the local principal, teachers, teaching assistants, Community Health Representatives, and members of the Settlement Council. The distribution of nutrition newsletters/packages by NWT Council gave them an air of authority—similar to messages issued earlier by doctors, Indian agents, and at nursing stations. Local nurses were asked to prominently display the newsletters and posters advertising the HBC's nutrition campaign to ensure that the message of "Balance the Colours" was passed on both in the community and the schools "as a tool to help people in the Store ... greatly assist in getting the message across to the community."[63] Radio messages urged: "Teenagers: Do yourself a favour. Try a new flavor. Try meat sticks or peanuts or walnuts or an egg for an easy, tasty snack. These are foods that belong to the Red Group: the Meat and Fish group—foods that are good to eat."[64] The announcements contained in the newsletters provided nutritional information that was condescending. It told community members how good it was to eat meat and that people should eat a variety of foods every day with catchy sayings like: "RED IS FOR STRENGTH. The group that makes you strong."[65]

The newsletter also offered helpful suggestions like taking local students on field trips to the Bay store to learn about proper nutrition.[66] Such advice drew clear connections between nutrition education and consuming products which were to be purchased at the local NSD. The recipes included in the newsletter drew on European-Canadian foods and offered suggestions on how to replace Indigenous foods. Elyse Amend observes that "the food guide, here, places accountability for eating well onto the individual: it works to 'solve' nutrition problems by simply providing citizens more information and then calling on them to educate themselves to make responsible choices, even though the food environments they are surrounded by present serious obstacles to healthy eating."[67]

Schurman's annual report to the Company identified the store as "in an excellent position to favourably influence the nutrition status of its customers, and thereby reap the benefits of releasing their productive potential."[68] In other words, improving the nutritional status of Indigenous peoples would mean that the store would benefit from decisions made by customers to consume food, and the NSD was ideally situated to assist customers in making those choices. In doing so, the HBC would improve the "mental capability, learning, and productive capacity" of its Indigenous customers, and thus they would be inclined to work harder, earn more money, and buy more stuff.[69] The newsletters were a poor attempt at appearing to package nutritional information rooted in European-Canadian culture as culturally sensitive to Indigenous peoples. Towards this end, the newsletter included phrases written in Inuktitut alongside familiar pictures of smiling Inuit. Despite Schurman's claims that she made newsletters accessible, they remained largely in English.

The Nutrition Upgrading Program was built on, to use the HBC's own words, the "philosophies of cultural appropriateness, constantly available non-verbal messages, a multi-approach within the community, and on positive activities to encourage children in new attitudes" (read non-Indigenous habits).[70] The program was based on Canada's Food Guide but with a northern twist and some translation into Inuktitut. This program also included fortified foods like calcium-fortified flour packaged under the Bay brand. Initially developed for Inuit communities, the goal was to extend this program to all Indigenous communities across northern Canada. Its similarities with Canada's Food Guide gave this Nutrition Upgrading Program additional legitimacy and obscured the fact that it was a neatly packaged marketing scheme. Indeed, the annual report drew on the results of the National Nutrition Survey conducted by the federal government in 1972 to lend urgency and value to implementing the program. Indian Affairs also recognized the value of using the HBC "programs such as the one initiated by The Bay for exerting a positive influence on native food consumption patterns."[71] The program was well situated within contemporary marketing practices: "repeated consistent messages, increased availability, convenience and visibility of nutritious food choices, and association of desirable outcomes with the suggested behaviours."[72] Again, Indigenous peoples were not passive recipients of state and corporate nutrition campaigns. In the annual report Schurman provided on the Nutrition Upgrading Program in February of 1978, she complained that people wanted to control this programming themselves.[73] Schurman bemoaned the fact that CHRs wanted to control the messages delivered as part of the Nutrition Upgrading Program.

We cannot look at nutrition education programs as merely about getting people to eat "good food." What constitutes good food is a cultural concept that is fluid and changes over time. As Franca Iacovetta has shown in her work on food, recipes, and immigrants, we must acknowledge how food procurement and preparation are deeply embedded in cultural understandings. The efforts of immigrant and settlement officials after the Second World War demonstrate how important food was to "Canadianizing" immigrants.[74] This same practice took place in residential schools and other government-run programs.[75] Fundamentally, nutrition programs were about changing the behaviour of the groups being "educated" beyond eating good food—because those notions are cultural. The Nutrition Upgrading Program was intended to "promot[e the] rational consumption of available foods: i.e. amount, frequency of intake, relation to other foods, distribution within the family, preparation, storage, cleanliness; modification of behaviour: breast-feeding; use of marketing techniques to modify consumer behaviour (i.e., food product display, promotion)."[76]

The company believed it was better situated to carry out effective nutrition education than the federal government because of its "vast network of Northern Stores," which put it in "a position to successfully exert a tremendous positive influence on dietary habits."[77] In this capacity, the HBC noted that a "joint attack on this problem would be innovative, will improve our public image, and in the long run will be profitable."[78] As Alan R. Marcus explains in *Relocating Eden*, postwar Canadian culture was introduced to the notion of northern starvation, hardship, and desperation via the popularity of Farley Mowat's *People of the Deer*, which followed the struggles of an Inuit community set against the precarious food availability of the far North.[79] The image of the Canadian government was also called into question by popular depictions of northern starvation; thus, the collaboration with the HBC and the bolstering of each party's image as making modernity possible in the North had significant public relations benefits for both state and corporate actors.

Conclusion

The Northern Stores Department of the HBC operated in First Nations and Inuit communities across northern Canada with very little retail competition. The largely unchallenged position that the HBC held and continues to hold as the North West Company was not a natural process and was the result of a long settler colonial history in which the retailer received significant benefits from the federal government. The HBC in the post–Second World War period, much as it had in the late nineteenth and early twentieth centuries, carried out roles and services normally delivered by the state. The company's position has enabled the corporation to obscure its singular purpose of profit-seeking; this is especially true when promotional campaigns and corporate propaganda espouse concern for the health and well-being of its customer base. Nan Enstad's work on corporate imperialism is important here because it cautions us to remember that the primary reason for a corporation's existence is to make money for its stakeholders and board of directors; everything else is "part of the cost doing business."[80] Thus, when the NSD promoted Canada's Food Guide or undertook similar promotional efforts, it was not done out of a sense of altruism but rather because the Company would make more money by investing in nutritional programming that would result in the purchase of more market-based foods.

In her work on the rise of department stores in Canada, historian Donica Belisle observed that as companies like the HBC "transformed themselves into large, anonymous corporations at the turn of the twentieth century, they drew upon their paternalist traditions in order to appear righteous and benevolent."[81] The HBC positioned itself with the assistance of the state as performing a service for remote, largely Indigenous communities located in Canada's North. Within the Canadian imaginary, shopping at the HBC was the embodiment of democratic white middle-class values. In reality, this process whereby postwar Canadian market culture was sutured onto northern life was always incomplete and fraught with complications. As colonial policies of assimilation were applied, tensions over the feasibility of that assimilation encouraged the rise of surveillance measures, education initiatives, and other tactics or modifications meant to make European-Canadian postwar life possible in the far North. In our next chapter, we focus on what is perhaps the most significant attempt by the settler state to constitute northern Indigenous communities as consumers of southern goods: the Food Mail Program.

CHAPTER 5

"PREFERRED PERISHABLE FOODS":
Origins and Outcomes of the Food Mail Program

Building on the discussion in Chapter 3 about the role played by purchasing lists under the Family Allowance Program, this chapter explores the ways in which transportation subsidies under the Northern Air Stage Program for "preferred perishables" and select goods were used by the federal government for very similar purposes. Tracing the early history and origins of the Northern Air Stage Program is challenging. While there is a plethora of archival materials and grey literature produced by the program after it was transferred to Indian Affairs in 1991, the origins of the Northern Air Stage Program remain somewhat obscure. The creation and expansion of the program seem to have coincided with the growing presence of resource extraction industries, the state, and medical services in the North after the Second World War, but beyond that, there is little detail. Built on top of the pre-existing Northern Air Stage System run by Canada Post, the Northern Air Stage Program, popularly known as the Food Mail Program (FMP), was a transportation subsidy applied to perishable food and some goods shipped into northern and fly-in communities.[1] Beginning in northern Quebec and northern Ontario in the late 1960s, the program expanded in an ad hoc fashion to include communities in northern Saskatchewan and select communities in other rural and northern regions and territories.[2] Ostensibly, the program's objective was to reduce the cost of food and goods. However, in practice, the program took up earlier efforts by the state to transform the foodways of Indigenous peoples and resolve poverty through a market-driven solution. In short, the FMP was premised on the notion that Indigenous foodways could be easily replaced by an infrastructure of transport and retail operations that made it possible for northern communities to live more like settlers in southern locales.

The FMP figured prominently in federal food policy in northern Indigenous communities, especially after it became housed within the Department of Indian Affairs and Northern Development (DIAND) in 1991. Under this iteration, the FMP subsidized transporting nutritious perishable foods, some non-perishable food, and essential non-food items to communities that did not have year-round surface transportation. Foods considered to be of little nutritional value were not eligible for the subsidy. Under the management of Indian Affairs, the FMP employed many of the same assimilatory policies and practices as the Family Allowance Program in the 1940s. However, in this iteration, the language of science and nutrition, alongside the appearance of community consultation, obscured the more coercive elements of the FMP.

DIAND nutritionists and employees created lists of preferred foods and goods and these items received higher subsidy rates. The foods included on the list were identified as "healthier" and conformed to European-Canadian food preferences and norms. Following the advice of nutritionists and FMP literature, Indigenous peoples were expected to make "good choices" about food which meant eschewing junk foods. Food described as junk food (read perceived as less healthy because of high sugar, fat, and caloric density) was loaded with moral judgements and the people who made these "bad choic-es" were characterized as "thoughtless" or "unable to make decisions for themselves."[3] The FMP followed a long settler colonial history wherein the Canadian state and so-called experts sought to determine "good" and "bad" food choices for Indigenous peoples and their northern lifestyles. Thus, these lists served as another assimilatory tool designed to "educate" Indigenous peoples about the "right" types of foods to eat. As Krista Walters illustrates in her work on the history of food and nutrition in Indigenous communities in Canada, "Indigenous peoples were viewed as problematic for 'modernizing' the wrong way by adopting a diet that incorporated what were seen as poor choices from packaged western foods shipped into remote northern and rural communities, particularly foods high in fats and sugars."[4] The advice regard-ing prepackaged foods several decades earlier contradicted "new" nutritional recommendations that favoured fresh fruits and vegetables. Such shifts in advice and policy initiatives are illustrative of the contradictory and inconsistent nature of both federal Indian policy and nutritional science advice.

The government employees who operated the FMP also generated a food costing tool to track food costs in the North, and in order to measure the impact that lower food costs had on Indigenous communities, the Food Mail Program also collected information on nutrient intakes and eating habits. These evaluation tools were predicated on European-Canadian beliefs about nutrition, health, and well-being. What resulted over the two decades the FMP operated was the collection of copious amounts of household and personal data about food and lifestyle choices and nutrient intake that created a repository of bodily knowledge used to demonstrate the need for outside intervention into Indigenous communities and households believed to be in desperate need of "fixing." According to Elyse Amend, dominant discourses about nutrition are used to present "oversimplified ideas about eating healthy that, while often presented as common sense, marginalize and exclude complex economic, political, ethical, and sociocultural issues tied to food."[5] In the gathering of data, the FMP encouraged increased surveillance of Indigenous peoples by health and social service authorities and retailers. Knowledge about Indigenous bodies, their communities, and supposedly unhealthy lifestyle choices further justified increased intervention and surveillance by health authorities and the state. What follows in this chapter is an overview of the program and the 1991 reorganization, an examination of the evaluation tools and projects employed by the FMP, and how this work was premised on the assumption that obesity was a moral problem in northern communities and that Indigenous bodies were "abnormal," unhealthy, and in need of correction.[6]

FMP: Program Review and Reorganization

In its early decades, the FMP was a slipshod program that expanded with little guidance and no operating budget. Originally housed within the Post Office Department and funded through an annual appropriation from Parliament, program eligibility seemed largely to be determined on a case-by-case basis and dependent on the lobbying efforts of individual communities, retailers, and people.[7] A report released in 1991 reviewing the effectiveness of the Northern Air Stage Subsidy stated that it could find no justification or rationale as to why some communities and/or regions were eligible and others were not. Access to the FMP was frozen in the early 1980s with the goal of gradually phasing out the program. Further cost containment measures were introduced in 1986 when the program budget was fixed at nineteen million with the expectation that the budget would decrease by one million each subsequent year.[8]

In 1989, the federal government announced that postal rates for northern and remote communities under FMP were to increase by an exorbitant 30 percent.[9] Unsurprisingly, this announcement was met with significant opposition from Indigenous organizations and northern politicians who called for a moratorium on rate increases and a meeting with government officials. In response, Canada Post and DIAND held a series of "consultative meetings with commercial shippers, retailers, interested northerners, [Indigenous] organizations, and elected officials" to manage public opposition. This same strategy was repeated from 2009 to 2010 when the federal government announced the replacement of the FMP with Nutrition North Canada (NNC) and then proceeded with its original plans anyway.[10]

Following stakeholder meetings, Canada Post agreed to raise postal rates by *only* 25 percent (compared to the original 30 percent), with the new rates going into effect on 19 January 1990. To add weight to the fiction of addressing the high cost of market-based foods in northern communities, the federal government established a committee to study the impact further increases to postal rates would have on the cost of food and the health of people living in the North (as if the answer to this question was not already apparent). Chaired by DIAND, the interdepartmental committee included representatives from Health and Welfare Canada (HWC), Agriculture Canada, Transport Canada, the National Transportation Agency of Canada, the Treasury Board, and Canada Post. The committee's role was to provide direction for the "core study team composed of two DIAND officials, a nutritional expert representing HWC, and senior observer from Canada Post."[11]

Over the course of the program review, the committee's study team visited over twenty communities and held meetings, conducted one-on-one interviews, carried out food costing surveys, and received written submissions from a variety of stakeholders, including Indigenous political organizations, tribal councils, retailers, local governments, and regional health authorities. Community visits were described in the report as consisting of the following: "an open meeting with the band or town council and other interested members of the reserve or community. An explanation of the subsidy was provided by the study team, individuals sometimes made presentations to the study team (some of them very graphically)."[12] What was meant by a "very graphic" presentation is unclear, nor did the report elaborate. Examining the performative role played by public consultations in the generation of government policy, Sunera Thobani aptly observes that ultimately the goal of such events is designed to give the façade of meaningful input while the "prior identification of the issues for discussion meant that the specific 'problems' [were already] pre-determined by the state" and thus, the outcome was a foregone conclusion.[13] Perhaps the "graphic portion" of the community consultations represented those moments when community members went off-script to address those concerns most relevant to them, making members of the study team uncomfortable. One-on-one interviews were conducted with local medical staff, social workers, teachers, and retail managers.

Conversations about the program and its importance seem to have been largely dominated by non-Indigenous peoples whose presence in the region had long represented the assimilatory work of the state. Although present, Indigenous perspectives and voices remained peripheral at best and, at worst, were described as "graphic." In this manner, the FMP and its value in the region were defined by non-Indigenous peoples and viewed largely through frameworks that favoured market-based solutions and used biomedical/ nutritional science and individual responsibility as measures of health and well-being. The weight given to the voices and perspectives of retailers re-flected the NWC's dominance in the region and its influence on government policy for almost a century.

In addition, the program review also led to the adoption of a series of recommendations that shaped the direction of the FMP for the next several decades, establishing governance structures within the program, until it was replaced by NNC in 2011. When the management of the FMP was trans-ferred from Canada Post to DIAND in 1991 with a budget of fifteen million, DIAND became responsible for establishing program objectives and iden-tifying measures for quality assurance and program impact.[14] Given that the long-term objective of Indian Affairs was the erasure of Indigenous peoples, it is not surprising that the continued imposition of European-Canadian norms and standards endured despite acknowledgement from FMP nutri-tionists and employees related to the nutritional value of Indigenous foods and poverty in Indigenous communities that it was difficult for people to purchase expensive food at the store. The transfer of the FMP from Canada Post to DIAND both signified and solidified the role of the FMP in the assimilatory project. Canada Post remained involved to provide the logistics for transporting food and goods.[15]

Although the FMP took on additional responsibilities and expectations during this period, staffing for the program remained minimal and never exceeded more than four people. A program manager was hired in 1991 to oversee these changes. The operating budget for the program also remained nominal despite increased reporting and oversight requirements and the enormous geographical area served by the FMP. For instance, from 2007 to 2008, there were only two staff members—the program manager and one other person—and the operations and maintenance budget of $65,000 was used largely to pay for price surveys and spot checks carried out by staff borrowed from other departments or locales.[16] The systemic under-resourcing of a program intended to address food insecurity in northern Indigenous communities ensured the FMP could never achieve its stated objectives. Instead, the program helped make invisible the context in which food insecurity in northern Indigenous communities had been manufactured. Bradley Hiebert and Elaine Power's work on media representations of food insecurity in Nunavut found that the characterization of Inuit as powerless to address food insecurity in their communities allowed the federal government to represent itself as a benefactor in the North while simultaneously enabling settlers to distance themselves from the context and consequences of settler colonialism.[17]

For most of its existence and increasingly so after 1981, precarity was the most defining feature of the FMP. Indeed, its precarity is indicative of federal Indian policy generally where the stated purpose of the program is to "improve the lives of Indigenous peoples," but the actual objective remains assimilation and erasure. As we illustrated in previous chapters, where mothers who failed to conform to European-Canadian standards in impossible circumstances were constructed as the root cause of their families' ill health, similar strategies were operative here. Focusing on Indigenous peoples and their food purchasing patterns as the supposed problem allowed the problematic nature of the program to be obscured, ultimately subsidizing retailers' profits. It should be noted here that the Northern Air Stage Program was never a large program and, even at its height, only cost about one cent a week for every Canadian over the age of eighteen.[18]

After 1991, program eligibility was extended to all northern fly-in communities; FMP nutritionists also created a list of preferred perishable foods that were identified as more nutritious or "healthier" and thus received higher subsidy rates. Foods considered less nutritious or "junk food" either received lower subsidy rates or no subsidy at all. The differential subsidy rates were intended to encourage the purchase of nutritious and fresh foods and the use of the "sealift for non-perishable food, foods of little nutritional value and non-food items."[19] However, planning ahead to purchase certain items in bulk required households to possess enough flexible income that they could make bulk orders when necessary (not to mention the physical space to store these provisions, where housing in northern communities is often precarious and overcrowded). The program also adjusted rates according to community location so that shipping rates across the North were uniform. The implementation of differential subsidy rates meant that as soon as the service became available across the North in October of 1991, shipping rates in regions like Nunavut (Baffin Island) and the territories immediately went down while the provincial norths saw their rates increase.[20]

In response to the increased provincial shipping rates, the North West Company (NWC), formerly the Northern Stores Department of the HBC, switched from the Air Stage Network to charter or regular air cargo because the company was able to obtain better shipping rates privately for the provincial norths. As we discuss in the next chapter, this shift encouraged the NWC to further develop its own shipping system, which culminated in the purchase of its own airline in 2017. As the "retail trade in most air stage communities [was] dominated by the North West Company" this company benefitted enormously from the high cost of food and any changes that subsidized the cost of shipping in their favour as it did in Nunavut, the NWT, and the Yukon.[21]

While the FMP was intended to alter the diets of Indigenous peoples living in the North by making market-based European-Canadians foods more affordable, for much of its early existence, the program was used largely by northern retailers like the HBC/NWC and non-Indigenous peoples. The lack of use by Indigenous peoples, except indirectly through food purchased at the NWC or Arctic Co-operatives, was due to the program's lack of visibility in the region as well as the general perception that in order to access the subsidy, a Canada Post service centre had to be located in the community.[22] As a result, the perception (and often the de facto reality) was that the FMP was primarily a service used by "white people" from the south who came to live in the community temporarily, such as nurses, teachers, and police.[23] Even after the FMP was transferred to Indian Affairs, it remained a relatively unknown program and was described by community members as "flying under the radar" or "invisible."[24] The critique that the program was designed to serve the HBC/NWC more than benefit community members is bolstered when taking into account its relative obscurity on a community level.

Navigating the FMP bureaucracy in order to place personal orders was challenging, and the requirements precluded its use by many Indigenous peoples. Community consultations revealed that placing personal orders was not an easy task because it required a personal credit card, a vehicle to pick up the order when it arrived, "extensive paperwork," and services were only offered in English or French.[25] Even after language and paperwork requirements were met, poverty remained a significant challenge in accessing the program directly. In First Nations and Inuit settlements, where settler colonialism and the violence of resource extraction ensured disproportionate rates of poverty, purchasing market-based foods through personal orders was next to impossible. This meant that when Indigenous peoples purchased market-based foods, they did so through the only retailer in the community, which was most often the HBC/NWC. That the employees of the FMP described the program as easy to use overlooked the structural barriers embedded in the program that were functionally exclusive and therefore racist.[26] As a result, personal orders amounted to only about 5 percent of the program, and users remained primarily non-Indigenous peoples.[27] Because the HBC/NWC sold subsidized foods and other goods at marked-up prices to ensure profitable operations, there was no motive or incentive for the retailer to communicate to potential customers that individual orders were even a possibility.

FMP: Food Costing and Data Collection

The study team, supervised by the interdepartmental committee established to evaluate the FMP program, also developed a survey tool that would be used by the FMP and other government agencies and organizations with minor revisions to monitor food costs and food availability in the North over the next couple of decades. It is in the creation of these tools where the vast differences between retail spaces in northern and southern Canada and the erasure of Indigenous foods become most apparent. Known as the Northern Food Basket (NFB), this survey tool was used for several decades before being replaced by a very similar one called the Revised Northern Food Basket (RNFB) in 2007. The survey tool was based on a pre-existing price monitoring tool developed by Agriculture Canada in 1974 called the Thrifty Nutritious Food Basket and contained only market-based foods. The Thrifty Nutritious Basket included sixty market-based foods that were intended to reflect the spending patterns of low-income Canadians living in southern Canada and included recommendations from the 1990 Recommended Nutrient Intakes for Canadians and Canada's Food Guide.[28]

In consultation with the Medical Services Branch, Health and Welfare Canada, and Agriculture Canada, the study team modified the existing Thrifty Nutritious Basket to create the NFB.[29] Instead of sixty items, the NFB contained only forty-five foods that were chosen based on their availability in northern communities and existing retail consumption patterns.[30] The NFB included significantly fewer fresh and perishable foods in comparison to the Thrifty Nutritious Food Basket—more than a third. While this disparity between the baskets was a function of the lack of availability and variety of many European-Canadian fresh and perishable foods in northern and fly-in communities, the amount of prepackaged and prepared foods consumed by Indigenous peoples living in northern communities was and remains a frequent critique used to describe the supposedly poor eating habits of Indigenous peoples. The NFB also "overestimated the consumption of dairy products and carbohydrate foods, while underestimating the consumption of meats, poultry, and fish."[31] Those introduced foods that would most resemble a traditional diet were identified as too costly and, therefore, were not included in the survey tool.[32] Indeed, Indigenous foods remained notably absent from the NFB.

Further revisions to the NFB were proposed in 1998 to incorporate the results of surveys measuring nutrient intakes, especially among pregnant and breastfeeding Indigenous women, that were carried out in a limited number of northern communities during the 1990s. Changing perceptions about the nutritional value of certain foods and what constituted "junk food" guaranteed the list of preferred perishable foods was regularly amended to reflect the current state of "scientific" knowledge. For instance, in August of 1996, convenience perishable foods like fried chicken were removed, and in January of 2004, fruit drinks and sweetened juices were eliminated. The formal adoption of the new basket, the Revised Northern Food Basket (RNFB), occurred in 2007 following the release of the new Dietary Reference Intakes, the newest version of Canada's Food Guide in February of 2007, and the First Nations, Inuit, and Métis version of the Food Guide in April of 2007.[33] This new basket differed from the previous NFB in the following ways: it included sixty-seven foods rather than forty-six; the proportion of the perishable foods increased; and it was "designed to meet the energy requirements of people whose activity level lay within the 'low-active' range, the minimum level of activity recommended for good health."[34] It is important to note here that foods considered appropriate for weight loss and a healthy lifestyle change regularly. As Barbara Parker aptly observes, "ideas about healthy eating and good food are contested within a framing of food that promotes individualized responsibility rather than acknowledgement that it is social structures that create and maintain structural inequalities and barriers to eating right."[35] The foods included in the revised basket were:

- More yogurt and cheese, less evaporated milk, 2% instead of whole evaporated milk, and more fluid 2% milk;
- Mozzarella cheese replaces cheddar cheese, since mozzarella is more popular;
- More fruit and vegetables, but less canned vegetables, especially corn;
- A greater variety of fresh and frozen fruit and vegetables;
- Inclusion of instant mashed potatoes;
- More meat to make the basket more consistent with northern Aboriginal food preferences, and greater variety of meat alternatives;
- Chicken drumsticks replaced chicken legs without backs;
- Lean ground beef replaced regular ground beef;
- More fish;
- Inclusion of white wheat bread to improve fibre intake;
- Parboiled rice replaced long-grain white rice;
- Less sugar, eggs, lard, and butter, and more margarine and oil;
- Canola oil replaces corn oil, and non-hydrogenated margarine replaces regular soft margarine; and
- No fruit drink crystals or soda crackers in the RNFB.[36]

The RNFB was revised to include the "most recent scientific evidence on the intakes necessary to prevent deficiency diseases and chronic diseases."[37] Elyse Amend argues that when "scientific experts" are positioned by nutrition discourse as "those who know the 'truth' about nutrition and body weight, and thus possess the authority to advise non-experts on how to live in order to avoid obesity," such discussions have failed to reduce obesity rates and instead have served to increase the "number of people who self-identify as 'abnormal' and 'irresponsible' fat subjects."[38] Discourses of "abnormal" and "irresponsible" have long been used to describe Indigenous peoples, particularly women. As outlined in earlier chapters, Indigenous women who purchased and prepared those foods identified as healthy were perceived as conforming to European-Canadian standards and ideals and as moving towards "whiteness" through those "developmental stages" that included the adoption of neoliberal consumption practices and so-called proper eating habits.

The decentring of Indigenous foods within food costing and nutrition studies is representative of the assimilatory process. While the absence of Indigenous foods within the NFB is acknowledged as a limitation, steps are not taken to rectify this erasure. Significantly, when Indigenous foods were mentioned in the 1991 program review, their absence was assigned to the difficulties peoples faced in continuing to pursue land- and water-based activities, environmental contamination, cost, and a growing preference "among the younger generation" for market-based foods, especially those foods characterized as "junk food" or unhealthy.[39] In this context, Indigenous foods were increasingly represented as beyond reach and no longer a viable choice for many Indigenous peoples. Significantly, by acknowledging the declining reliance on Indigenous foods, the historical and ongoing processes of settler colonialism that produced the current situation remain unvoiced. As Krista Walters's work on the history of food and nutrition in Indigenous communities demonstrates, even though the importance of Indigenous foods was increasingly acknowledged by nutritionists and people within FMP and the Medical Services Branch more broadly after the 1980s, it was done so within a context where "Indigenous foods were treated as limited and supplementary, rather than as normative, legitimate dietary choices with adequate nutritional composition and consumed on a regular basis."[40] In this frame, land-based food procurement strategies were decentralized and demoted from a primary source of food to a tangential recreational activity meant only to supplement grocery store–style shopping habits, which further eroded the relationships of Indigenous peoples with land and food as medicine.[41]

The survey tools were based on European-Canadian standards and values. Examining the program evaluation tools developed to measure the success of the food subsidy is important because these food-costing tools and nutrient measurements continued to be employed by the FMP and other entities in northern Canada for the next several decades. It is also important to understand the generation of these food-costing tools and the imposition of European-Canadian nutritional standards and concepts alongside educational initiatives as a part of the architecture of settler colonialism. That Indigenous foods were absent from the NFB was not happenstance; rather, it was part of an ongoing process of violence that ignores Indigenous perspectives on food and culture, especially place-based Indigenous understandings of health and well-being. Indeed, given that all relationships between Indigenous peoples and settlers and the state are premised upon racist policies that seek to destroy and replace Indigenous cultures, how can any tool generated by European-Canadians/non-Indigenous peoples appropriately address food insecurity? Thinking about food security in ways that acknowledge and centre Indigenous culture and understandings of well-being as supported by "traditional food activities such as hunting, gathering, fishing, cooking, and feasting, which help provide a diet rich in culture food [and] also work as social networks bringing people and place together" is important and not part of the ways in which these so-called evaluation tools were developed.[42] Within a European-Canadian world view, food-costing tools and measuring nutrients through instruments like 24-hour dietary recalls reduce health and well-being to quantifiable categories located within individual bodies that make good or bad lifestyle choices. Biomedical understandings of health and well-being situate health within discrete bodies, genetic predispositions, or personal choices identified "through physical health disparities and the prevalence of chronic disease experiences."[43]

Programs like Family Allowance and FMP merely continued earlier rationing practices, though instead of directly providing food, wages and cash were exchanged. As Tim Rowse observes, rationing by the state was more than just the passage of goods: it also included expectations of instruction and facilitated practices of governance, and it is important to acknowledge that such "governing [always] generates knowledges of those that are governed."[44] Throughout the 1990s and the early 2000s, FMP collected a broad range of data from Indigenous communities, ostensibly to evaluate the value of the FMP and its impact on health and well-being in the North. Indigenous bodies were measured and mapped using 24-hour dietary recall and food frequency questionnaires; socio-demographic and health and lifestyle questionnaires; and fat, energy, protein, carbohydrates, vitamin mineral, and cholesterol and caffeine intakes. Of course, all this information was further tabulated and categorized according to gender, age, and reproductive status. For instance, in 1992 and 1993, the Food Mail Program carried out more than 800 nutrition surveys with Indigenous women of childbearing age (15 to 44) in five communities in Nunavut, two communities in Labrador, and one in northern Ontario. In 1997, these surveys were repeated again in two of the original Nunavut communities. An updated analysis of the nutrient values was published in 2002 to include some land-based foods like goose and Arctic char and the updated Dietary Reference Intakes (DRI)[45] so that information collected always reflected the most current state of scientific knowledge regarding nutrient requirements.

Food Mail Pilot Project

Between December 2001 and January 2003, a Food Mail Pilot Project was held in three Indigenous communities: in Kugaaruk (Nunavut), Kangiqsujuaq (Nunavik), and Fort Severn First Nation (Ontario). These case studies were designed to incorporate a more focused approach to measure the impact that lower shipping rates would have on the cost of food and, in turn, people's abilities to purchase a broader range of fresh fruits and vegetables. Each community received a greater reduction in shipping rates for the following priority perishables: milk, yogurt, cheese, eggs, frozen apple and orange juice, oranges, apples, bananas, grapes, potatoes, carrots, onions, cabbage, turnips, and a variety of frozen vegetables.[46] It should be noted here, as in previous chapters, that dairy and its various iterations remained a well subsidized and highly touted preferred perishable food. Additionally, the Food Mail Pilot Project included a significant educational component, and a part-time local Food Mail Pilot Project coordinator was hired in each community to deliver the nutritional education programming. The local coordinator received training and ongoing support from a nutrition specialist.[47] The pilot coordinator was responsible for "consumer education," which included taste testing at the local grocery store, cooking classes, healthy snacks, and nutrition activities at mother and child clinics, and a "healthy foods" poster contest at the local school.[48] Canada's Food Guide remained at the centre of the consumer education with school visits and monthly radio messages that promoted the

Guide and message of "healthy eating."[49] This program seemed very similar to the Nutrition Upgrading Program and marketing campaign used by the Northern Stores Department only a few decades earlier.

Local retailers also participated in the Pilot Project by agreeing to stock the preferred perishable foods; to pass savings on to customers; and to display food prices and the promotional materials designed by DIAND to increase awareness about the FMP and identify for customers which items were preferred perishable foods in "order to help [shoppers] make better choices."[50] Participating communities had to commit to eighteen months in order to ensure that there was "adequate time for all components to be fully implemented, for behavioural changes to occur, and for an adequate evaluation of their impact."[51] This implies that if people followed these rules, changed their food choices, and better managed their money, then food insecurity in Indigenous communities would be ameliorated (at least according to the education messages of the FMP). What the so-called education components of these projects ignored and often obscured was that poverty and settler colonial violence cannot be resolved through kids' poster contests, better knowledge of Canada's Food Guide, and taste-testing opportunities at the local grocery store. The suggestion that such activities could begin to address the systemic challenges facing Indigenous peoples is quite ludicrous. Indeed, the report from the Pilot Project concluded that even with the subsidy, people still could not afford a nutritious diet. While the report's conclusion stated that without the subsidies, the preferred perishable foods in the NFB would not be affordable in the three participating communities, it also noted that even with the subsidy, the after-shelter income of households remained in deficit anywhere from $120 to $373 every month.[52] The FMP report failed to note that northern retailers benefitted greatly from the continued transportation subsidy provided by the federal government.

The histories of the food baskets and dietary guidelines and educational resources like Canada's Food Guide must also be considered, as Ian Mosby's *Food Will Win the War: The Politics, Cultures, and Science of Food on Canada's Home Front* illustrates well. They were not generated in a vacuum, and they represented the social, economic, and political interests of both the dominant culture and the food industry. Work in critical dietetics illustrates how food guides serve as texts to be read above and beyond the good food/ bad food dichotomy messages they present to include hegemonic nutrition discourses that ignore the contexts in which food choices can be made.[53] These messages—alongside the educational initiatives carried out by the state and the appearance of benevolence that the FMP provided—allowed the blame to be placed squarely on Indigenous peoples and their so-called poor personal choices when such activities failed to "fix" food insecurity in northern communities. Nutrition education cannot change poverty or dismantle the structures and systems of settler colonialism. Instead, what these kinds of initiatives do is obscure their violence as well as their endurance.

Manufacturing Food (In)Security and the Contradictions of Federal Policy

In addition to the program changes and the growing efforts to measure and evaluate the success of the FMP as outlined above, the FMP witnessed a shift in how it talked about hunger and food access in Indigenous communities. While the reports generated by the Food Mail Program continued to centre discussions of health and well-being largely within biomedical discourses, it was increasingly placed alongside conversations about food insecurity. These shifts were also reflected in the research and program evaluation activities carried out by the Food Mail Program during the 1990s and early 2000s. Most often, the people who operated the FMP followed broader patterns in the intellectual community, not-for-profit organizations, state actors, and government institutions. Food insecurity measured hunger at the household level and moved away from examining hunger solely as a function of the absence of food to include larger systemic and social processes that considered food availability, accessibility, utilization, and stability.[54] In this context, the larger socio-economic circumstances that produced a lack of food access and availability in northern communities were acknowledged, but the roots of these problems remained largely unexplored. While First Nations and Inuit communities were described as experiencing high rates of food insecurity and poverty, discussions about settler colonialism remained notably absent. Significantly, nutrition education and the development of budgeting and money management skills and knowledge about how to cook market-based foods were posited as a solution to food insecurity and these supposed deficits were identified as important education tools because they had not existed in previous "hunter-gatherer societies" that were now undergoing rapid transitions.[55] In other words, assimilation was situated in the reports generated by the FMP as the current and most viable solution to food insecurity in

Indigenous communities, and the illusion of choice created within these contexts remained ever-present. Northern food insecurity, in this framing, would be resolved to the extent that Indigenous peoples accepted instruction on how to make good choices at the grocery store check-out. Thus, impossible situations were created in which the benevolent guise of these state-run projects obscured how deeply embedded they were in the architecture of settler colonialism.

In recognition of the high costs of living in northern parts of Canada, provincial, federal, and territorial governments heavily subsidized the living expenses of people who came from outside of the region to live and work in northern parts of the country. These subsidies were designed to offset the higher costs of foods, goods, and services in the North. All federal and territorial government employees received a monthly cash payment called Isolated Post Allowance or a Settlement Allowance, respectively. In Quebec, government employees received both a living allowance and a cargo allowance to "cover the air cargo or postage costs for food purchased directly from southern suppliers."[56] It is interesting that these individuals received additional financial support and not the same educational directives regarding budgeting and proper food choices in order to assist them in living in the North in an economical and healthy fashion. Indeed, the tone deafness is further compounded by those same employees who received these higher incomes and "isolation allowances" identifying the three most important barriers to food security and health and well-being for Indigenous peoples as a "lack of knowledge and skills regarding food budgeting, nutrition, and preparation of southern foods, followed by the loss of traditional values and the transition to a wage economy."[57]

Community consultations undertaken by the people who ran the FMP frequently included questions which asked people what they would do if the program was cancelled, and more troubling, what they would be willing to give up in order to keep the bare minimum of the program. During these conversations, and in the context of eliminating or reducing the transportation subsidy, people were asked to choose those food items that were more "valuable." Such a conversation took place in late 1995 to 1996, and it was reported that the preferred option identified by community members for managing the subsidy was the "elimination of some non-essential non-food items and a lower rate for nutritious perishable foods."[58] In other words, according to the 1996 report, people chose food over entertainment and recreational equipment and supplies and hardware; all of which were pro-hibitively expensive in fly-in communities. As noted earlier, the outcome of these kinds of conversations was already decided by the government body that initiated them, and thus the role these discussions performed was to give the appearance of consultation and permission from the people they would most impact. Requiring people to make such choices is unnecessarily cruel and would not be expected in any other context where non-Indigenous peoples were talking about access to food and essential goods. The creation of lists that identify preferred, essential, and non-essential items set false dichotomies and predetermined a situation wherein any choice made outside of these already established parameters of "preferred perishable" foods and appropriate retail choices was perceived as poor. Focusing on junk food is a red herring and diverts attention from larger structural problems that are supported and perpetuated by the state and the major retailer in the region. Indeed, the shift to prioritizing "healthy eating habits" in a period when the state and corporate entities are increasingly coming under fire from Indigenous community members and political organizations for their role in producing food insecurity in the North is a distraction, especially when there is lots of money being made by retailers.

Conclusion

The FMP expanded existing government food policies and practices in the North. The adoption of food insecurity discourse, the employment of food costing tools, and the measurement of dietary intakes diverted attention from larger structural problems that allowed retailers like the HBC/NWC to continue to make enormous profits and the government to identify Indigenous bodies and people's supposedly poor choices as the problem. It is clear that the more important question becomes who is permitted to eat well and live well within the larger structural processes of settler colonialism, especially when these methods take on the appearance of benevolence within a neoliberal framework.[59]

The Food Mail Pilot Project that partnered with local retailers like the HBC/NWC to facilitate nutrition education delivery is emblematic of the deeply flawed nature of government food policy in the North for the past century. The state helped to produce the conditions in which a retailer like the NWC/HBC was positioned as the most "reasonable" option to work with to resolve access to food, even though the HBC/NWC was in a clear conflict of interest. HBC/NWC profited from the high costs of foods in the North, which is emblematic of a larger mind-numbing problem that seeks to frame Indigenous sovereignties within the limited context of market-based solutions. As we illustrate in subsequent chapters, the NWC benefitted enormously from the situation in northern First Nations and Inuit communities and, with the help of the federal government, continues to do so. A community that is dependent on social support from the federal government and purchases market-based foods is a preferable entity for the NWC, whose annual reports often boast that "our customers are more dependent than most Canadians on government spending programs."[60]

While there were people working within the FMP who tried their best to address food insecurity in northern Indigenous communities by calling stores when price gouging was reported,[61] the FMP operated within a larger settler colonial system where the outcomes prevented or inhibited participation in land- and water-based activities and ensured Indigenous dependence. While government reports noted the high costs of food, that these costs were prohibitive, and that the ability to eat a healthy and nutritious diet based on market foods was functionally impossible for many community members, government reports and discourses continued to cite nutrition education as an important factor in reducing nutrition-related illnesses. Reports also described a need for Indigenous peoples to learn to adapt to a cash economy—all stereotypes that place Indigenous people as part of the past and poorly prepared for modern (read: white) life.[62] The next chapter, which explores the role played by the Northern Stores Department after its sale and transformation into the North West Company in 1987, will demonstrate in closer detail the way in which the NWC was able to capitalize on these colonial relations and successfully expand their business operations, profits, and relationship with the federal government.

CHAPTER 6

"WE BLANKET THE NORTH":
The Expansion of the North West Company, 1987–2007

In 1987, amidst efforts by the federal government to contain what they perceived to be the escalating costs of the Food Mail Program (FMP), the Hudson's Bay Company (HBC) sold their Northern Stores Department (NSD).[1] This sale initiated a series of changes to northern retailing that fuelled the Northern Stores Department's (also referred to in some sources as the Northern Stores Division) transformation into an international corporation that specialized in "serving" hard-to-reach locations in rural and remote areas occupied largely by Indigenous and low-income populations. Drawing on the praxis of working with Indigenous communities located in present-day northern Canada developed by the HBC over centuries, the NWC refined many of those business practices that positioned the Company as best situated to "take care of" Indigenous peoples by selling them food and goods and providing limited health services that returned vast gains to the company. Much like the HBC, the NWC represented themselves as performing a service to Indigenous peoples in the North, offering market-based solutions to food insecurity and a lack of essential services in northern communities. What is obscured in the discourses and practices employed by the HBC, and later the NWC, is the enormous profit that was to be made from communities with limited food options and disproportionately poorer access to health care and other necessary services. Thus, we borrow our chapter's title from the 2001 annual report as we bring attention to the ways in which the NWC came to "blanket the north."

Figure 12. The Northern Store. Credit: Mandi Chan Peters.

The NWC did not achieve retail dominance in the North as a result of their self-prescribed enterprising frontier spirit; rather, it was through avaricious corporate practices that were predicated on a solid foundation of more than a century of settler state interventions in the North. The NWC also refined and honed a particular strategy of tailoring their retail operations to avoid expensive or high-quality items that low-income communities could not afford. As we illustrated in previous chapters, the HBC often served as a stand-in for the settler state in many First Nations and Inuit communities, and the NWC has benefitted from these longstanding relationships and the state's continued support. The annual reports of the NWC offer a useful text through which to understand how the company imagined its roles and responsibilities in the North and, in particular, how the Company situated itself in relation to Indigenous peoples. Importantly, the reports allow us to see how the Company represents itself as performing a service to the North and its residents, thereby enacting a form of self-sanctification that belies their relentless pursuit of profits and the diversion of state resources earmarked to assist with northern food insecurity. This chapter outlines the continuities and departures of the NWC from its HBC past, the ways in which the company constructed itself as a frontier merchant, and how the company employed nutrition discourse to market particular lifestyles and foodways. Importantly, this chapter notes how the NWC leveraged their existing knowledge of northern operations in Canada into a transnational retailing empire that targets Indigenous and rural communities outside of the geographical area that came to be known as Canada.

From Acquisition to the "Enterprise '95" Plan: 1987–1992

On 31 March 1987, the NSD was sold for $180 million dollars.[2] The sale was part of an effort within the company to reduce the $2.5 billion debt accrued during the global recession of the early 1980s. It was also a calculated move by company executives to liberate the NSD from a debt-ridden and moribund HBC. HBC executive vice-president Iain Ronald was the mastermind behind the deal, as well as the architect of the HBC's current austerity measures. Ronald approached Raymond Dore and Ian Sutherland, president and executive vice president of Mutual Trust Company, respectively, with the idea. Sutherland's father had worked as a senior vice-president of the Northern Stores Department and was familiar with the department and its activities.[3] Shortly thereafter, the NSD was purchased by Hudson's Bay Northern Stores Incorporated. The newly formed company was comprised of the Mutual Trust Company of Toronto, existing upper-level management of the NSD, the Hudson's Bay Company itself, and several financial institutions made up of two major pension funds and life insurance companies.[4] Under the terms of sale, the new company retained the use of the name "Hudson's Bay Northern Stores Inc." for a period of two years.

NSD executives greeted the sale of its division with enthusiasm because the austerity measures enacted by the HBC to service the Company's crippling debt for the better part of a decade had ensured there was little support and space for expansion within the NSD. While a commissioned store history published in 1999 described the response of NSD employees and executives to the sale as "thunderstruck" and unanticipated given the financial problems experienced by the HBC, the sale seems largely to have been an inside job demonstrated by the extent of collusion between the Company's executive elements, who were very familiar with the NSD and its potential for growth and profit. Indeed, several high-ranking executives within the HBC departed in order to partake in the opportunities presented by the new company. For instance, Marvin Tiller, chief operating officer of HBC's Northern Stores Department, became the new president of Hudson's Bay Northern Stores Inc. Though there is always risk involved in any such market investment and activity, senior and experienced members of the HBC executive viewed the acquisition as sufficiently secure to warrant a career move, which speaks volumes about their certainty of profitable operations.

During the first couple of years following the sale, the Company focused on renovating outdated stores and upgrading company infrastructure and merchandising systems. Such efforts mirrored the modernization process undertaken by R.H. Chesshire in the 1950s when the HBC decided to grow its retail presence in the North. The goal of these early years was to identify "opportunities to solidify [the Company's] position in the market place and maximize [its] returns."[5] In 1988, the Board made further investments in computerizing merchandising and retailing inventories; for example, new cash registers were purchased and shipped north in order to facilitate the generation of financial data and monitor point of sales information.[6] The accumulation of such information enabled the company to understand where and how the greatest profit could be made. Although food had come to comprise a significant share of the Northern Store Department's sales, especially in the wake of the Family Allowance and Food Mail Programs after the Second World War, it was in the late 1980s and early 1990s when the newly purchased company decided to adopt a business model wherein food would be the primary driver behind the company's growth and profits. While the annual reports in the years immediately following the sale included very little information about food sales, what is available reveals that during its first full year of fiscal operation, Hudson's Bay Northern Stores Inc. reported earnings of $10.08 million.[7] Data on what fraction of the Company's sales came from food sales were unreported. In 1989, the company posted earnings of $12.02 million, with 46.4 percent of sales coming from food.[8] As a point of reference, in the year 2000, food sales constituted more than two-thirds of NWC sales and earnings were in excess of $28 million.

The early 1990s witnessed significant changes within the Company, including a rebranding campaign that sought to distinguish the current iteration of Hudson's Bay Northern Stores Inc. from its HBC past. With the expiration of the two-year grace period, the company was renamed the North West Company; over the next decade, the Company launched a series of strategic plans that positioned food as the profit generator for the company and its building block of expansion. Each strategy was identified by an exciting name that conjured up a sense of innovation, energy, and forward thinking. The first scheme, called Enterprise '95, was designed to improve the Company's bottom line by eliminating those aspects of the current retail platform that were not performing well, like apparel, Christmas items, and big-ticket merchandise.[9] In other words, those goods considered to be luxury items and beyond the reach of communities with limited disposable income were to be decentred in retailing operations. The NWC also announced their intention to "sell twenty-six junior department stores [located in more southern locales] in order to concentrate on core retail operations in the Canadian north."[10] In the same fiscal year, five new Northern stores were constructed as part of an "aggressive effort to increase market share in several key locations."[11] Enterprise '95 set the stage for the company's long-term business plan, wherein food sales drove the NWC's profits and expansion. The NWC understood well the profits to be made from food sales in Indigenous communities, and the company intended to secure food sales across multiple platforms throughout the North as a way of specializing within and targeting a niche market that included high barriers to entry.

In short, then, Enterprise '95 was not merely a plan to expand food sales over a five-year period: instead, it reflected a concerted, clear, and intentional effort to reorganize business operations in a way that generated surplus capital from the unique forms of socio-economic marginalization faced by First Nations and Inuit communities through the sale of the necessities of life. Settler colonialism operated in such a way in the North that NWC was now allowed to operate with minimal oversight amongst a population that had very limited options when it came to the purchase of food and other general merchandise. In this context, food becomes the ideal foundation upon which to cultivate the Company's profit-seeking.

Fast Food and Filtered Water: 1992–1997

Rather quickly, the focus on food sales produced dramatic results for the NWC. In 1991, food sales represented 58.4 percent of the NWC's total revenues, which was an 8.1 percent increase from the previous year.[12] The board of directors described the success of the new business model in the following terms: "our recent performance is evidence that our business is less cyclical than other retailers and that our niche strategy of concentrating on small, northern communities is working."[13] The annual reports frequently noted that "nearly three-quarters of the NWC's customers were of aboriginal origin (Indian, Metis and Inuit)" and that "our customers are more dependent than most Canadians on government spending programs."[14] While Indigenous peoples living in the provincial and far norths (especially on-reserve) may have faced disproportionate rates of poverty and unemployment, and thus had limited disposable income to purchase luxury items, the sale of food was not restricted by these factors. Discussions about the socio-economic and legal status of Indigenous peoples in northern Canada were included in all annual reports after 1990 as a matter of formula, illustrating an intentionality and awareness on the part of the Board of Directors that the Company's profits were largely dependent on the colonial power relationships that make up material conditions in the provincial and far norths. Indeed, this predatory practice of targeting colonized communities was made crystal clear when long-term NWC President and CEO Edward Kennedy noted in his annual message to shareholders: "we benefited from spending tied to resource development projects in the North, higher oil-generated Permanent Fund Dividends in Alaska, and *the payment of Indian Residential School Survivor settlements in Canada.*"[15]

The NWC made more aggressive gains in the northern market in 1992, which translated into further accumulation of capital and fuelled subsequent corporate expansion. In that same year, the NWC acquired the Alaska Commercial Company (ACC), a retailer of food and general merchandise that continues to service remote communities in Alaska today. As part of Enterprise '95, the NWC also introduced the "Tomorrow Store" initiative in 1992, echoing the strategy's characterization of store expansion and the new Northern store brand as signalling that the future of retail in the North was a labour-saving one-stop shopping experience for northerners.[16] The Tomorrow Store was characterized as more modern and efficient, including additional space for "butcher shops, bakeries, delicatessens, small post offices, pharmacies or banking facilities," which the company made plans to acquire.[17] Financial services were not a new activity for the NWC but an extension of a historical pattern that encouraged, maintained, and perpetuated the financial dependency of Indigenous communities. By 2002, the NWC had its own credit card and reported that "financial services, including our credit card operations and cash services, [have] grown at a compound rate of forty-six percent over the last three years and now represent thirteen percent of our trading profit."[18] The goal of the Tomorrow Stores was to provide the NWC with a virtual monopoly over retail and financial activities in northern communities that would not be susceptible to economic vagaries.

The NWC's strategy of cornering financial services in the North has been very successful, targeting particularly vulnerable people who do not have many options; it should be noted here that fly-in First Nations do not have financial institutions on-reserve, and therefore community members have little to no choice regarding where and how they can carry out financial transactions. For example, a contemporary iteration of in-store financial services at the Northern is the WE Financial line. It allows customers to directly deposit any Canadian Revenue Agency payments, COVID-19 relief payments, GST/HST credit payments, Canada Child Benefit payments, Income Tax refunds, working income tax benefit payments, and Ontario Trillium Benefits onto a WE prepaid Visa Card.[19] The WE Card was preceded by the Benefits Card,[20] where "no fees for loads or purchases and as an added bonus, [the NWC] waiv[ed] the cheque cashing fee when you load[ed] your cheque to the card."[21] Community members could only use the Benefits Card at the Northern, NorthMart, and Value Lots. During several community conversations, we were asked questions about the Benefits Card, and the financial services of the NWC more broadly, because a general perception existed that people were expected to deposit all of their monies on the card in order to shop at the store.[22] The similarities and continuities in practices that have persisted across time between the credit customs of the HBC and the financial services offered by a contemporary version of the NWC are deeply concerning.

The NWC also began to heavily invest in introducing fast food outlets to northern communities in 1992. Between 1992 and 1996, more than fifty Kentucky Fried Chicken (KFC) stores in NWC-owned retail outlets were opened. Two Pizza Hut outlets were built in 1993 and that year's annual report described them as "very successful."[23] In 1994, the NWC added seventeen KFCs, nineteen Pizza Huts, and one A&W and Burger King to their Quickstop brand.[24] The appearance of fast food outlets in northern communities coincided with the removal of those foods that had been identified as "junk food" and their elimination from the Food Mail Program (FMP) subsidy. In particular, high-fat convenience perishable foods like frozen fried chicken were removed from eligibility for subsidy in this period.[25] To be clear, we strongly affirm the right of Indigenous peoples to make whatever food choices they want, including fast food and so-called junk food. However,

Fees	Standard (Pay as you go)	Preferred (Direct Deposit)
Initial sign-up (new card)	Free	Free
Card Maintenance	$3.00	$3.00
POS Purchase	$0.50	Free
ATM Cash Withdrawal	$2.50	$2.50 One Free per month
Direct Deposit (ACH) Value Reload	Free	Free
Value Reload	$3.00	$3.00
Card to Card Transfer	$3.00	$3.00
Additional Card	$5.00	Free
Card Replacement	$5.00	$5.00
Automated Phone Service Call	$1.00	$1.00
Agent Customer Service Call	$2.50	$2.50
Email Alerts	Free	Free
SMS Text Alerts	Free	Free
Foreign Currency Transaction	2.50%	2.50%

We Financial™ Visa Prepaid card

Schedule of Fees and Limits
Effective as of September 30th, 2015*

(1) The Card Maintenance fee is deducted on the first day of every month.
(2) Some ATM operators may charge an additional fee. This should be posted on the ATM or yo will be asked to agree to it during the transaction.
(3) If after 3 months you have not received a Direct Deposit load on your card, the fees applied will revert to "Standard".
(4) Fee is to the recipient of the transfer.

Figure 13. Notice to customers of fee increases to the prepaid credit card offered by WE Financial, the North West Company's financial services, September 2015.

it is important to understand the context in which successful fast-food operations in the North were produced after almost a century of eroding Indigenous food sovereignties and the introduction of prohibitively expensive market-based foods. Thus, we are critiquing the creation of the conditions in which eating fast food becomes the most affordable, reasonable, and often the only option in a northern community. Food scholar and sociologist Andrea Freeman, though writing about food oppression against Black and Latinx communities in the United States, highlights these power relations: "government policies engendering food oppression range from providing public assistance insufficient to cover the cost of fresh food to collaboration with the fast food giants to ensure that their products dominate lunch-room counters and dinner tables. This state-sponsored racial inequality is obscured by the distinction between public and private spheres of action and is perpetuated by the myth of personal choice, even where a lack of options and resources severely limits the ability to exercise choice."[26]

Figure 14. A Northern Store location, including a partnership with KFC and Pizza Hut, February 2023. Credit: Mandi Chan Petters.

Both Enterprise '95 and the Tomorrow Store signalled significant and rapid growth in food sales for the NWC, and established the process through which the NWC accumulated further wealth in the North and invested it in purchasing a greater market share of food sales in hard-to-reach and impoverished settings. By 1993, the NWC operated under multiple banners across the North in Canada and the United States. First and foremost was its Northern chain, which included 156 stores across the Canadian North and accounted for 79.3 percent of the company's total revenue.[27] Next was the NWC's Alaska assets, where they ran twenty "Value Centres" under the Alaska Company brand.[28] The NWC also continued to run twenty retail outlets branded as Trading Posts. These outlets were generally in larger cities such as North Bay, Thompson, or Whitehorse, and were described in annual reports as "offering native crafts, furs and gift items." The Trading Posts were also described as having been "designed for communities in regional markets with potential for both increased tourist trade and procurement of wild fur."[29] The NorthMart brand was launched in 1994 and serviced semi-remote regions and focused on "fresh food, instore-licenses, branded fast-food restaurants and a focus on everyday non-food shopping needs such as basic apparel, housewares, cards, stationery, and health related products and services."[30]

The annual report for 1994 included descriptions about the success of the Enterprise '95 plan as well as considerable information on the Company's growth in food sales since 1990, which had risen from 54 percent to 60 percent of the company's total revenue.[31] Operations from the Northern stores constituted 78.7 percent of the NWC's total profits.[32] Thus, while the company expanded into different markets and areas of service provision, food sales across the Canadian North became the foundational market upon which this growth was built. Thus, what was suggested in the early nineties became, by 1995, a clear and stated strategy to target low-income communities that disproportionately relied on various forms of state-based assistance, had high barriers to entry, and rarely purchased luxury or big-ticket items. While previous annual reports discussed social assistance payments and highlighted Indigenous political issues as a matter of format, the inclusion of data on the spending increase projections of the Department of Indian and Northern Affairs in the 1995 annual report is a powerful sign of the extent to which the NWC gathered data on the colonial administration of First Nations and Inuit poverty:

> Many of our Canadian aboriginal customers are dependent on the continuation of basic social support programs provided by the Canadian government. While we anticipate that all Canadians will share in deficit reduction initiatives, we believe that many of the statutory obligations, especially to the more needy, will be maintained. Latest government spending forecasts for the Department of Indian and Northern Affairs predict spending increases at 3% per year over the next four years. . . . While some cutbacks may occur, there will likely be other compensating payments in the areas of child tax benefits. Further settlements of land, hydro and user tax claims along with the move towards self-government are positive trends in our market.[33]

The final initiative of note in this period was "Enterprise '98," which was announced in 1995 as a follow-up to the highly successful Enterprise '95. Enterprise '98 was described as: "aggressively build[ing] on The North West Company's strength and market dominance in northern Canadian markets. . . . We will continue to expand our fresh and frozen food departments, branded fast food business and services such as post offices, banking, one-hour photo development, and pharmacies."[34]

From 1990 to 1995, the NWC slowly but surely grew its capacity and market share of northern food sales and increasingly used the capital generated from these and other business operations to expand into other northern markets (both in Canada and Alaska) as well as other forms of service provision (such as medical, financial, and postal). Throughout this period, the company intentionally monitored the socio-economic and legal factors that informed material conditions for Indigenous peoples as a means of adjusting business operations to ensure profitability. Significantly, at least based on the company's annual reports, store managers continued to exercise extraordinary power over their customer base: "Northern Stores often operate in communities without banking facilities, and managers must make sensitive credit-granting decisions about customers who may well be their neighbours."[35] The NWC in general, and the Northern chain in particular, specialized in administering poverty in Indigenous communities and regulating food purchases in a manner that increased profits for the company and made individuals and families beholden to the NWC, continuing many of the same practices begun by the HBC where factors and post managers made decisions about credit based on their perception of the individual's "character." In these decades, the NWC both maintained and acquired new power in these communities as often the sole provider of not only commercial food, but of medicine, financial credit, and access to the outside world.

From the Creation of the Company Fund to the Giant Tiger Deal: 1997–2002

From 1997 to 2002, the NWC followed the same trajectory of aggressive growth and expansion set in the first half of the decade. Northern sales grew by 4.2 percent in 1996 and contributed to 78.9 percent of the company's total annual revenue. Food retailing represented 62.9 percent of NWC's total sales, which included Alaskan operations and Trading Post outlets in addition to Northern stores and NorthMarts in Canada.[36] In March 1997, the Company created the North West Fund to maximize shareholders' profits. The Fund allowed investors to exchange their shares in the company for "units" in the company fund (a move that allowed the company to pay out dividends from a source other than company earnings, thereby avoiding income tax on returns).[37] The same month that the NWC Fund was created saw Edward

Kennedy became the president and CEO of the NWC, following a two-year stint as the CEO of Alaskan operations. Kennedy remained the CEO of the NWC until August 2021. For that reason, he is a key architect of northern food economies in Canada.

Shortly after becoming CEO, Kennedy reassured shareholders in an interview that his plan was to respond to the problems faced by the Company through a strategy of "leveraging activities in Canada" and "reposition[ing] our stores to be dominant in foods, emphasizing perishables and home meal replacement [read: fast-food/frozen foods], apparel and lower-priced home and outdoor living categories."[38] In short, Kennedy was a CEO who understood that the sale of frozen and fast food would return immense profits. Family funds not consumed by the grocery bill would most likely go towards purchasing clothes and merchandise he characterized as "low-priced home and outdoor living" goods. Though the company was already headed in this direction when Kennedy took office on 21 March 1997, he hastened the shift in corporate strategy by exploiting the sale of food and low-priced merchandise in northern communities as the core of NWC business operations.

Significantly, the 1997 annual report of the NWC revealed that the decision to reorganize the company into a fund with units rather than the original shareholder structure was not simply to increase payouts to investors but to ensure that "cash flows [were] sufficient for expansion and/or acquisitions."[39] The report also clearly described the company's strategy to leverage food sales across the Canadian North for aggressive expansion. The Canadian North was described as a market with "tremendous, untapped potential": "Within NWC's redefined core business, our first goal is to capture a higher share of spending on products and services which are most valued by our customers and can earn the greatest return. This means further enhancement of our food and basic general merchandise assortments and less in-store emphasis on fashion apparel and big-ticket durables, which represent about 10% of our sales base."[40] In terms of settler colonial power relations and regulatory regimes, the NWC specialized in servicing Indigenous communities with very few retail options and disproportionately high rates of poverty. The NWC is a corporation whose sole objective was and is to invest in fixed-capital expenditures that earned the greatest returns. Through this process, access to necessary goods and services in Indigenous communities was not provided by the federal government and left to the cold profit-seeking and neoliberal logics of the NWC.

Ten Northern stores and three fur marketing branches were closed in 1998, "primarily in southern, former junior department store markets," in accordance with a new expansion strategy called "Vision +2000."[41] Vision +2000 once again concentrated on food sales and the further divestment of retail holdings outside northern locales. Like Enterprise '95, Vision +2000 appeared to be quite profitable. For example, in 1998, the Company's profits grew a staggering 29.7 percent to $27.3 million and more than two-thirds of all sales were derived from food.[42] Unsurprisingly, the 1999 report to shareholders explained that the NWC "expanded our offering of lower price-point merchandise to our largest and lowest income customer group," highlighting the Company's specialization in securing the business of Indigenous community members with limited income and few options to shop elsewhere.[43]

Drawing on the capital generated from northern food sales, the NWC boasted that "the greatest opportunity for growth is within the expanding communities we already serve in northern Canada and Alaska."[44] The Company opened two Giant Tiger discount test stores in 2001. Giant Tiger is a junior discount chain founded in Ottawa in 1961 that was in operation long before its partnership with the NWC. Giant Tiger specialized in low-end fashion and food sales and was therefore a perfect match for the NWC, which by 2001 had demonstrated a preference for servicing low-income communities across the Canadian North. The NWC described the partnership in its 2002 annual report: "by providing food distribution services to the Giant Tiger stores, we will be able to significantly drive down buying costs for our Northern and other stores."[45] Thus, given that Giant Tiger was a discount brand, the 2001 decision by the NWC to test operations in two stores can be understood as a trial run in determining whether or not the Company could conduct business operations that targeted low-income consumers in southern and western markets in addition to the North. Eventually, this developed into a broader retailing strategy of providing, as the NWC called it in 2005, "one-stop service to the small, independent retailer serving rural towns and inner cities."[46] As a point of reference, by 2017, forty-one Giant Tigers operated across Canada, selling discounted food, clothing, and household items to largely low-income families. The Giant Tiger project has therefore turned out to be very profitable for the NWC and allowed them to keep their surplus capital within Canada. However, because it targeted western and southern markets, we will leave

Giant Tiger behind in our analysis and return to the ways in which the NWC
acquired other essential services across the Canadian North.[47]

From Pharmaceuticals to the Cost-U-Less
Expansion: 2002–2007

By 2002, the share of food sales rose to 68 percent of NWC sales in northern
Canada and food represented 80 percent of sales in its Alaska operations.
The 2004 report showed that frozen food sales had witnessed a precipitous
50 percent increase.[48] The annual reports revealed that the Company's plan
was to use its market dominance in food sales across northern Canada and
Alaska to pave the way for expansion into other services that Indigenous
communities did not have, and that should have been provided through
other entities like the state. This plan was formulated with a close eye on
demographics and population trends in Indigenous communities:

> Considering the North's younger, larger families, food retailing is
> very, very attractive. We've known this for some time and that's
> why our strategy is to be the leading local food retailer in as many
> markets as possible. This means our food business has priority.
> . . . The results speak for themselves. Since 2000, *our same store
> food sales have grown at 3.5% to 5% per year, a higher rate than most
> North American food-only retailers.* . . . Once we've looked after
> our food potential, the next question we ask ourselves, on a mar-
> ket-by-market basis, is what other customer needs can we meet in
> this community? Where can we leverage our store presence and
> operating skills to offer more convenience and service at a lower
> local price? Can we shift selling space to a full hardware store
> product line-up? Can we add gasoline pumps or a quick service
> restaurant? What about a tax preparation service or a pharmacy?
> The challenge is to do this profitably and without compromising
> store management's ability to take care of the food side.[49]

The NWC continued to experience growth in food sales as well as profits
during a period in which the broader retailing and food sales market was
experiencing an industry-wide decline. This demonstrates the extent to
which the northern and remote locations of their retail outlets provided the
Company with a certain kind of security and insulation over and against wider market forces. More pressing, however, is the way in which the company

planned to use its grocery store monopoly to move into other avenues of business or service provision to which Indigenous communities in northern Canada and Alaska did not have access; this process is key to understanding the way in which necessities of life in Indigenous communities were abandoned to market-based solutions and a source of revenue for the NWC.

In its 2004 annual report, the NWC discussed how it was going to create "a liquid asset out of H_2O" by selling filtered water in more than half of its northern locations.[50] The sale of clean water to northern residents had begun as a test phase in 1992, when a partnership with the company Dyna-Pro placed water filtration outfits in some Northern Stores under a trademarked brand of Ultra-Pure. As the vice president of operations at Dyna-Pro reported in 2004, "Today more than half of all [Northern] stores offer our Ultra-Pure systems and water sales have been growing quickly. We hope to have systems in virtually all stores within the next year. It's the only product the stores sell that they also produce."[51] Thus, while a criminal lack of infrastructure and state support for clean water in Indigenous communities was producing boil water advisories and do not consume orders across the Canadian North, the NWC was able to turn that crisis situation into profit by obtaining its own means of selling purified water within the majority of communities where it operated.

Similarly, in its 2005 annual report, the NWC reported that it had acquired "a large in-store pharmacy business" that granted it a "base capability" in the provision of medical services in northern communities.[52] The provincial and far norths were and are disproportionately underserved when it comes to health care.[53] The report claimed that "this transaction brought knowledge into the North West related to remote pharmacy operations, telepharmacy and contract pharmacy services to northern hospitals."[54] In 2006, the NWC opened two pharmacies and one telepharmacy at their northern Canadian locations.[55] That same year, the NWC opened five Giant Tiger locations and struck a partnership with Bailey's Furniture to advance further into the home furniture market.[56] In other words, whether it was food, water, clothing, furniture, medicine, or financial services—if it could produce profit in the North, the NWC had a hand in it by 2006.

By 2007 the NWC was ready to extend its business model into the South Pacific and Caribbean. As the CEO explained: "We were attracted to the U.S. west coast gateway that the South Pacific shared with Alaska. We determined that the market characteristics were more similar than different compared to our existing store locations, including the predominance of indigenous cultures, second world infrastructure, high North American brand acceptance, unique regulatory barriers, relatively small population bases and weather challenges."[57] As is evident from the above description, the demographics of the South Pacific were "attractive" to the NWC because they included isolated Indigenous communities with high barriers to entry. Trying to explain why a company specializing in northern food sales and retail acquired the rights to business operations in the South Pacific and Caribbean, CEO Edward Kennedy stated in a news release dated 27 August 2007: "Cost-U-Less is an exciting new chapter in our growth. At first glance it may look different from what we do today but, in fact, it is an exceptional strategic fit with our capabilities in serving unique, physically distant markets. Similar to our own business, Cost-U-Less' success has depended upon a proven remote retail capability, the advantage of high competitive entry barriers and a disciplined geographic niche."[58] Clearly, the isolation of Indigenous communities in the South Pacific and Caribbean was seen by the NWC as the perfect opportunity for further profitability and made sense within their extant business model.

Constructing Race and Region: Normalizing High Prices

The annual reports of the NWC fabricated an image of the North as "frontier" space largely untouched by modernity and in need of "modernization." Within this space, the NWC was a pioneering enterprise that brought "the south" [read: modernity] to the North through "frontier merchandising." Building on this theme, the annual reports regularly included descriptions of the landscape as vast, isolated, and remote—a construction that served to paint their business operations as riskier than was really the case. Indeed, the ability of the NWC to bring food and goods into such a foreboding environment becomes part of a larger heroic narrative in which the Company bestows settler advantages on the deprived inhabitants of the region. As health historian Mary Jane Logan McCallum has observed, the construction of the North as remote and isolated has historically served to sanctify medical professionals who travelled to the region.[59] According to McCallum, medical professionals regarded themselves as "nation-builders who cared deeply about the country's future," a role the NWC also envisioned for itself.[60] In other words, the NWC saw themselves as the harbinger of "civilization" through the marketing of food and household goods. By operating on this so-called merchandising frontier, the NWC represented itself as linking isolated communities to the outside world and being responsible for bringing the modern world to the North. The annual reports contain descriptions like a "trip to the frozen food aisle allows northerners exposure to the outside world."[61] Reports also portray the company as bringing the conveniences and luxuries of an urban city to the region: "not every remote northern community has a restaurant. Therefore, a visit to the frozen food case at the Northern offers alternatives—14 varieties of frozen Chinese dinners."[62] The NWC clearly considered themselves to be providing a service for Indigenous peoples by selling food and merchandise, especially in such hard-to-reach spaces, at prohibitively expensive prices. Here, the conflation between Indigenous peoples and the North as isolated space shows how isolation became a "metonym for cultural difference,"[63] and that entry from the "south" was characterized as bringing civilization. Situated in the inhospitable North, according to the annual reports, the average northern community is "90% Aboriginal. Electricity is provided by a diesel generator, and water is supplied from holding tanks on a daily delivery system. Access to the community is a year-round gravel runway. In summer, a barge operates from Churchill, MB supplementing air services."[64] Nowhere in these accounts does the lack of infrastructure become a function of state neglect in a region where wealth is produced for people geographically distant through the dislocation of Indigenous peoples from their territories and the exploitation of Indigenous lands and resources. Instead, Indigenous peoples are constructed as inherently different and their communities as isolated and in need of intervention.

The supposedly primitive conditions of Indigenous communities were further emphasized by the terrain that the company had to navigate to serve as the North's "life line." Notions of difference were reinforced by accounts of the transportation barriers faced by the Company in pursuing their extremely heroic and difficult yet highly profitable enterprise. The NWC "deliver[ed] over 100 million pounds of goods to 240,000 customers in 150 remote communities across Canada by truck, ship, rail, aircraft, barge, helicopter, and sometimes snowmobile—across immense territories, through hazardous ice conditions and the harshest inhabited climate in the world. An early thaw resulting in a loss of winter roads over frozen rivers, lakes and muskegs can result in huge increases in transportation costs."[65] Such accounts highlight the Company's intrepid nature and herculean efforts to overcome enormous geographic challenges to ensure that a population supposedly in need of assistance was served through the benevolence of the NWC.

The annual reports created a vision for Company shareholders of a region desperately in need of "help" and the NWC as bringing food and goods that would otherwise be unavailable to northerners. In this discourse, the enormous profit to be made from operating as a retailer in the provincial and far norths is made invisible and the service aspect is highlighted and fetishized. The Company represented itself as offering a necessary intervention into the lives of Indigenous peoples—one that will ultimately help them bridge the chasm between "tradition" and "modernity." The annual report included quotations from very satisfied customers, such as "we enjoy a traditional lifestyle but thanks to the Northern, we have access to just about anything we want in this frontier community."[66] Another story related, "B's family enjoys a traditional lifestyle, with moose, caribou, and salmon serving as important dietary staples. But B relies on the Northern for just about everything else."[67] In this context, the NWC imagines itself as the bridge between two worlds—traditional and modern, which as we illustrated in Chapters 2 and 3, remained embodied by a consumer culture coded as European-Canadian. Without any trace of irony or acknowledgement of the role played by settler colonialism or their predatory retail practices, the NWC located itself as a generous benefactor for Indigenous peoples by assisting them in pursuing traditional lifestyles and "help[ing] provide a livelihood for northerners pursuing traditional lifestyles."[68] The NWC also delivered another service by bringing Inuit culture to the world by distributing it to "fine art galleries and boutiques world-wide."[69] The constructed dependence of northern communities on Company operations was regularly recast as a favour the NWC was doing *for* Indigenous peoples rather than an attack *on* the food sovereignties and security of those same communities for enormous profit.

A final and important discursive practice employed by the NWC was the representation of Indigenous peoples living in the North as largely impoverished and reliant on the largesse and goodwill of the federal government. Indeed, the NWC clearly and openly regards this situation as desirable for their business model and one that takes place within a protected market. In the annual report under a section entitled "Risks," the NWC provides nearly the exact same description of the socio-economic and legal status of Indigenous peoples in northern Canada after 1990 as a matter of formula:

"Our aboriginal customers are more dependent than most Canadians on the continuation of basic social support programs. While we expect to see a continued shift towards aboriginal self-government, this is not expected to significantly change the economic circumstances of aboriginals over the next decade, with the exception of the impending Nunavut land claim in the eastern Arctic."[70] Here, Indigenous peoples are constructed as dependent and thus different from the "average tax-paying Canadian" and in need of government aid and educational direction. If we consider how the NWC represented itself as a bridge between modern and traditional lifestyles, the NWC is (according to its own account of itself) ideally situated to assist Indigenous communities with navigating modernity. Indigenous peoples living in the North are largely characterized by the annual reports as dependent on the government for social assistance and welfare because "northern and remote communities . . . have few alternative sources of economic activity."[71] However, this state of affairs is not seen as a risk, even though the description is included under that section: "our customers are more dependent than most Canadians on government spending programs. While we do not foresee the curtailment of basic government social programs, our customers are affected by changes in levels of discretionary program spending."[72] Instead, such income sources were characterized as a source of reliable revenue: "the largest source of customer income is derived from government transfers. This consists of social assistance, family benefit payments, old age security, and income related to employment with local public services, such as schools, health facilities, municipal government and transportation."[73]

Unpacking these discourses is essential to dismantling the settler colonial systems operative in the region. Such language serves to make the high costs of food appear natural and neutral and divert the attention away from the retailer. According to Warwick Anderson, understanding the way in which constructions of healthy and unhealthy operate in geographical contexts is important because they show how these processes are "a discourse of racial adaptation and colonial settlement, a means of structuring and reforming."[74] It becomes about the environment producing ill health due to distance and isolation from modern centres of health and civilization. A favourite image employed by the NWC in the annual reports was to describe the far North as "very different view of the world: in late November the sun sets, not to rise again until early February."[75] In this way, difference and isolation are used to construct a population in need of assistance, and in the absence of the state, the NWC offers market-based solutions.

Healthy Living: NWC and Nutrition Education Programs

The broader pattern of relying on market-based solutions to resolve nutrition-related illnesses in northern communities like diabetes takes on added authority with the rebranded NWC. Under the NWC, many of the nutritional education initiatives carried out by the HBC, including health care provision and nutrition education, become a major component of the Company's business plan and, indeed, a huge source of profit. In addition to bringing the "south" to the North in order to make habitable a supposedly harsh geography, the NWC situates itself as making health available to Indigenous peoples—a population that has been largely pathologized as unhealthy. Mimicking patterns at grocery stores in the south, the NWC undertakes advertising campaigns that "sell healthier lifestyles" that are achievable through purchasing the right food and making the right choices. The healthy living campaign was premised on the belief that Indigenous peoples were pathologically unhealthy. The 2006 annual report noted "in the north, the demands for pharmacy and other healthcare products is growing at a rapid pace, triggered by a younger than average, but still aging population, and by the high incidence of related disease, most notably Type II diabetes. Our plans over the next five years are aimed at earning a distinct, trusted identity for North West as a local healthcare provider . . . this focus also gives us the foundation to grow other 'Healthy Living' programs through increased selling space dedicated to non-prescription medications, medical equipment and healthier food choices."[76] The subordination of northern service provision to the logic of NWC profitability is certainly on full display in this extended passage.

The Healthy Living campaign was intended to brand the NWC as a corporation that cared about the health and well-being of its customers. It was designed to appeal to northern contexts and provide a large corporation with the façade of being a local store. Twice a month, stores used issues identified as important in the community to draw connections with in-store products and in-store activities that promoted nutritional education and healthy dietary practices.[77] The Healthy Living program included easy-to-use shopping lists for people living with diabetes and "store training modules which give staff the basics of nutrition with an emphasis on northern health considerations."[78] The distillation of very complicated nutritional concepts related to metabolism as well as insulin sensitivity/resistance into marketable bits and bytes oversimplifies ideas about eating "well" and marginalizes the systemic, economic, political, and social issues that determine the contexts in which people are able to make choices about food.[79] According to the annual reports, the Healthy Living campaigns were part of the NWC's response to high rates of diabetes in Indigenous communities and their commitment to working with other health care professionals in "ensuring the availability of healthy foods and a labeling system to help the consumer identify healthy foods."[80] Such campaigns suggest that solutions to chronic, complex, and multifactorial diseases like diabetes can be easily resolved by adding a couple of "important" nutrients or foods to one's diet. Clearly, this strategy of the NWC is a reproduction of earlier attempts by the HBC to use colour-coded nutritional initiatives to guide northern consumers into purchasing the "right kinds" of European-Canadian food for a healthy diet.

The NWC's nutrition education programs persisted in various iterations and expanded to include collaboration and partnerships with community dietitians, nutritionists, and nurses; federal, provincial, and territorial health staff; coordinators of prenatal programs; and community health organization staff. The "Healthy Eating Initiative" consists of the following five elements:

1. An in-store component with signage, recipe cards, and cooking classes.

2. A monthly newsletter with nutrition information and coordinated recipes to go with foods that were on sale at the store.

3. A series of diabetes resources for health professionals to use with their clients.

4. Ongoing support for nutrition programs offered by the government, community, research, or school partners.

5. Donated space for health care providers to offer diabetes or other education classes.[81]

The current Northern/NorthMart iteration of the Healthy Eating Initiative was launched in 2017 and branded "Health Happy."[82] It is also designed to assist customers with "identifying healthier alternatives to the foods you usually buy" with easy-to-spot labels.[83]

The items identified as part of the Health Happy advertising campaign are: "products [that] have at least one of these nutritional attributes: low sodium, low sugar, low fat, low caffeine, based on guidelines from Health

Canada and the Canadian Food Inspection Agency (CFIA) . . . [with this disclaimer] Health Happy products are featured in store for information purposes only. Health Happy products are not intended to prescribe or treat any health conditions and should not be used as a substitute for consulting with a professional health care provider."[84] The Northern website offers a wide selection of recipes and lifestyle advice. Educational activities included guided school tours where a store employee introduced the students to the Health Happy program and showed the "program's signage, taught lessons on the benefits of the Health Happy products, and treated the students to a Health Happy snack."[85] Other in-store activities included taste tests.[86]

The use of language like "initiative" and evoking the state-sponsored nature of the information used to identify these products mask the influence of corporations on defining what is healthy. Particularly insidious is the failure to locate such programs more broadly within an advertising or marketing model. While ostensibly these foods may include a so-called nutrient or lack an element considered less desirable, stores undertake these marketing schemes because there is huge money to be made from selling a particular lifestyle and concept of health that is reductive to a single nutrient or specific type of food. Of note, such initiatives like Health Happy suggest that the main concern of a large corporation—whose primary responsibility is to shareholders and a board of directors—is the health and well-being of the very communities it is exploiting for profit. Such programs also help to mask the ways in which food and corporate practices, in partnership with the state, perpetuate and benefit from the current state of affairs in Indigenous communities. Settler colonialism and systemic conditions that ensured disproportionate rates of poverty in First Nations and Inuit communities were left unmentioned except when the company identified customer income sources. The selling of filtered water is a keynote example of how the deprivation of essential services in northern communities by the state creates fertile ground for the cultivation of NWC profits.

There continues to be an enormous profit to be made provisioning those programs run by local health authorities and Indigenous organizations to address food insecurity and health issues in northern Indigenous communities. For instance, interviews and community conversations revealed that school breakfast and dietary support programs for people living with diabetes all purchase their food from the NWC. The distribution of food vouchers— vouchers that are only redeemable at the Northern Store—by health centres for prenatal and breastfeeding women are also a boon for NWC profits.[87] Other not-for-profit organizations that run programs in the community also run much of their programming through NWC outlets, including the Northern Fruit and Vegetable Program administered by local public health districts and school boards. The Northern Fruit and Vegetable Program tries to ensure that school children get two servings of vegetables and fruit per week.[88] As we shall see in the chapter that follows, this state of affairs remains unchanged under Nutrition North Canada.

Conclusion: Settler Colonial Capitalism

The history of the NWC from 1987 to 2007 is a history of settler colonial accumulation of capital derived in its nascent stages from selling food to northern Indigenous communities. After a de facto monopoly on food sales was secured, the NWC expanded into other necessities of life and sold water and medicine to communities across northern Canada as well as Alaska. The NWC also monitored the structural contours of First Nations and Inuit poverty, going so far as to research Department of Indian Affairs budgets and counsel their store managers on how to "make sensitive credit-granting decisions about customers who may well be their neighbours." Throughout this entire period, Indigenous communities increasingly had their necessities of life subordinated to the market logic of the NWC, as food, water, and medicine became company assets.

We conclude this chapter by underscoring that the rise of the NWC was not the product of free market forces or a unique "enterprising" spirit on the part of the company—those are the narratives told and retold in commissioned company histories, annual reports, and media coverage to make invisible these violent processes. The "invisible hand" guiding the progress and expansion of the company was settler colonialism, as the federal government subsidized the shipping costs of the NWC's business operations in the Canadian North under the mandate of the Food Mail Program or negotiated lower than market value leases. In the next chapter, we look closely at the Nutrition North Canada program, the successor of Food Mail, both of which facilitated the profitability of the NWC. As we highlight in each chapter, the nutrition education components of these institutions and the programs they ran remained a major facet of the architecture of settler colonialism through the imposition of particular ways of viewing the world and adopting European-Canadian lifestyles. Though it was colonial collusion between corporate and state elements that constituted such conditions in northern communities, Indigenous peoples were perpetually targeted for assimilatory and educational initiatives as if their proper tutelage by settlers could undo the material realities of poverty, water pollution, and a lack of medical and financial services.

CHAPTER 7

"DIRECT, EFFECTIVE AND EFFICIENT":
Nutrition North Canada and the Restructuring of Federal Food Subsidy Programs, 2008–2017

Our final chapter takes us into the present in order to illustrate how the shape-shifting nature of settler colonialism preserves many of the same processes and systems put in place almost a century ago. While some of these systems may appear different or have adopted more outwardly compassionate appearances (e.g., federal food subsidy programs and nutrition education initiatives), the regulatory objectives of settler colonialism remain much the same. We have found that the subsidy programs and nutrition education initiatives undertaken by the state and corporations remain situated within the broader architecture of settler colonialism. Even though individuals working within these programs may have been well intentioned, these programs operated as a governing tool that both manufactured and maintained food insecurity and subsequently settler colonialism in Indigenous communities and the geographic area now known as Canada more broadly.

In 2011, despite significant opposition from Indigenous communities and political organizations, the Food Mail Program (FMP) was replaced by the Nutrition North Canada program (NNC).[1] The Conservative federal government under Stephen Harper declared the FMP to be too costly, and under the guise of efficiency, cuts were made wherever possible. Many foods and necessary non-perishable items were either eliminated or made ineligible for higher subsidies; the number of suppliers and retailers able to access the subsidy was greatly curtailed; the number of communities able to access the subsidy was vastly reduced; and a multi-tier system of community eligibility was imposed, wherein many First Nations across the provincial norths were suddenly ineligible for the NNC entirely or only eligible for the reduced subsidy of five cents per kilogram. However, what was most shocking was that instead of subsidizing the cost of shipping foods into the North, the NNC program provided payments directly to northern retailers for selling food with very little oversight. Northern community members were still required to spend exorbitant amounts of money for food and other necessities at the largest northern retailer, the North West Company (NWC), and corporate profits soared. Notably, nutrition instruction remained a cornerstone of the NNC program and funding for education initiatives continued to be made available through Health Canada.

Nutritional education, according to Alissa Overend, Meredith Bessey, Adele Hite, and Andrea Noriega, remains informed largely by "western, neoliberal culture, [wherein] 'eating right' has been rendered a healthist commodity disconnected from other social conditions ... [and] government documents, food labels, expert and lay advice alike conflate healthy eating with healthy outcomes—that is with the right ratio and quantity of micro and macro nutrients, immunity against chronic diseases is granted."[2] Gyorgy Scrinis refers to such practices as a "reductive focus on individual foods, whereby particular foods are analyzed and evaluated in isolation from other foods, diets, and broader contexts" and within this paradigm, foods come to be regarded as "good or bad" based entirely on their nutrient composition.[3] Within these conversations, the systems, both historical and contemporary, that produce hunger, lack of access to Indigenous foods, and poverty stay invisible. In their place, a supposed lack of money management skills and knowledge about "good foods," largely European-Canadian foods, became identified as the primary problem, and the acquisition of these abilities as the solution. This remained true even when conflicting evidence collected by the state illustrated no amount of money management acumen could resolve a clear monthly deficit in household income. For instance, the Food Mail Pilot Project that ran from December 2001 to January 2003 showed that even with higher subsidies for preferred perishables, the cost of the Revised Northern Food Basket remained well beyond the reach of most families, especially if shelter costs were considered an important part of monthly household expenses.[4] The study found that the cost of food and shelter exceeded the average income in the participating communities by at least two to three hundred dollars every month. While evidence of this shortfall was briefly acknowledged in the pilot project's final report, proposed solutions continued to suggest that personal choice and careful management of household finances would enable people to purchase healthier food and thus live better. Budgeting is not a solution to poverty, and while its suggestion as a possible remedy is quite ludicrous and insulting, these logics are hegemonic within a neoliberal framework that privileges market-based solutions and individual choices. In her examination of emergency food supports in the United States, Rebecca de Souza observes that in a "neoliberal era, the doctrine of *healthy citizenship* is deployed to control the bodies of the poor and food insecure" by using the language of "rights and duties to suggest that people need to take responsibility for their own bodies by eating good food and limiting harm to others through lifestyle changes."[5] Such discursive practices divorce food choices from larger structural inequalities and create the perception that people living in poverty are irresponsible. While food subsidies, or better yet price controls on food, alongside a guaranteed income are greatly needed in northern First Nations and Inuit settlements (as well as elsewhere), the benefits derived from food subsidies and supports should not be accrued almost entirely by corporations at the expense of the people who live in the North.

The introduction of the NNC in 2011 marked the entrenchment of market-based solutions to resolving food insecurity in Canada's North. The NNC highlights many of the contradictions in federal Indian policy that we have sought to underscore in previous chapters—programs that were established with the inevitability of failure and managed to accomplish very little except to pursue the state's assimilatory goals and to ensure that any blame was placed on Indigenous bodies for supposedly failing to make the "right" choices. In this chapter, we begin with an examination of The Dargo Report (2008), which called for the neoliberal restructuring of federal food subsidy programs and their defunding under the guise of making them more "efficient." We use this report to illustrate the NNC's intellectual origins. Next, we trace the somewhat bungled and highly publicized implementation of the NNC before speaking to the ways in which it affected relations between retailers, community members, and the federal government.[6]

The Dargo Report: The Entrenchment of Market-Based Solutions to Food Insecurity

The Conservative federal government under Stephen Harper hired Graeme Dargo of Dargo and Associates Consulting firm to audit the Food Mail Program. The report released by Dargo in 2008 illustrates the logic behind the NNC program and the false belief that if a free-market system was allowed to operate properly in the region, competition would "naturally" lower the cost of foods.[7] This reasoning ignored the reality that very little retail competition existed in most northern communities. As a point of reference, a 2017 article on retail experiences and competition in the North found that the NWC is the only full-service grocery store in 54 percent of the communities in which it operates in Canada (or 65 out of 120).[8] This picture becomes even more concerning when broken down for the provincial norths where Manitoba, Ontario, and Saskatchewan have the highest number of NWC stores, and the Company faces almost no competition. In northern Ontario, for instance, 91 percent of NWC stores located in fly-in northern First Nations face absolutely no retail competition; for Saskatchewan, it is 83 percent; and for Manitoba, 72 percent of communities are serviced only by an NWC store.[9] This retail dominance is also supported through data collected by NNC in 2015, showing that of the 131 of the NNC-eligible communities, two major retail chains operate in 97 of them—the NWC (67 stores), Arctic Co-op Ltd. (46); and independent retailers (18 stores).[10] Independent retailers are most often stores established either by the First Nation or a local community member. For instance, Kitchenuhmaykoosib Inninuwug (Trout Lake First Nation), an Oji-Cree community located in present-day northwestern Ontario, removed the NWC from its community in the mid-1990s and established its own grocery store.[11]

The Dargo Report had an enduring impact on federal food subsidy programs for northern communities. The perspectives of Northern retailers were given extraordinary weight during the consultation process. According to Dargo, retailers:

> share an interest with Canada to ensure that Northerners have dependable and affordable access to fresh foods. . . . The retailers want a direct relationship with Canada and are very eager to work collectively with Canada to develop a pan-northern partnership that would result in a direct subsidy at the till approach. The major

retailers have recently communicated their desire to develop a partnership with the Department. It is my opinion that when such noteworthy organizations come together to form a joint industry-wide approach their effort should command considerable attention. These retail organizations have outlets in most of the eligible communities and as they represent the largest users of the Program they should have a considerable say on the future of the Program.[12]

His bias towards retailers and the value of market-based remedies was obvious throughout the report especially given his suggestion that retailers "shar[ed] an interest similar to Canada to ensure that Northerners have dependable and affordable access to fresh foods." According to Dargo, retailers were far better equipped to ensure that the subsidy was properly applied and customers received its full benefits. By evoking the "dominant construction of economics as a realm of freedom [he was] deflect[ing] attention from the role of corporations in governance."[13] More troubling, however, was the description of retailers [read: the NWC] as a "noteworthy organization" and the claim that it ought to have a major say on the future of the program simply because it received the lion's share of subsidies under FMP—a prophetic statement made true under NNC.

Dargo's report also failed to account for the systemic barriers explored in previous chapters that prevented many community members, and Indigenous peoples in particular, from accessing personal orders through the FMP. Under Dargo's reasoning, an Indigenous woman who never used the FMP to place a personal order because she did not speak English or French, possess a credit card, or have adequate storage space was rendered less worthy of consultation or agency in the formulation of federal food policies than a corporation of considerable means whose shareholders and Board of Governors did not live in northern Canada. The privileging of white, largely male, and capitalist input in the design of policy governing Indigenous peoples' access to food has a long history on Turtle Island.[14] Without irony, Dargo noted that "allowing personal order shipments unintentionally benefits certain segments of the population and creates inequity."[15] He was extremely critical of personal orders because he viewed them as "encourage[ing] market disruption" and "at odds with the Minister's mandate of supporting northern economic development."[16] It should be noted that only certain forms of economic development were recognized—in other words, only economic development that took place within a particular European-Canadian framework was regarded as valuable. Sharing land- and water-based foods through community and family networks was not supported here. Nowhere in the report, of course, does Dargo acknowledge that the state providing subsidies was itself a form of market intervention that disproportionately benefitted the NWC and its shareholders at the expense of community members.

Particular food items were singled out for judgement, ignoring the lived realities of many communities that were and remain without potable water.[17] For instance, Dargo described the Food Mail Program as wrong-headed in applying subsidies to bottled water and in the report posed the following question: "bottled water remains on one of the Department's lists, a heavy item that is tremendously expensive to ship to places like Pond Inlet. Is quality of water the responsibility of the Program and is it nutritious?"[18] He failed to note that in many communities, the NWC was selling filtered water produced on-site at enormous profit. Dargo also made clear judgments about what should and should not be considered nutritious food and therefore eligible for subsidy: "In reviewing the perishable and non-perishable list of items I question the eligible inclusion of items such as frozen ready dinners, pizza and ice-cream. Although such items may contain some nutritional content they are near convenience foods and I do not believe that these are on the top of the list of nutritious foods that Canada wants to influence consumers to purchase."[19] Here Dargo's words evoke dominant discourses about nutrition that identify good and bad foods. By determining which foods get subsidies and which foods do not, Dargo was suggesting that he was better positioned to determine what people should eat, especially Indigenous peoples. Dargo's report also called for the Department to "review the eligible list of communities" and "refine the current list of items eligible under the Program." Sadly, Dargo's recommendations resulted in the elimination of the FMP and a gutting of the list of eligible foods, essential non-food items, and communities. All of these actions were undertaken under the pretense of making the program more efficient and cost effective so that those people who really needed it could benefit. Finally, and significantly, it should be noted that while Dargo declared he "had no vested interest in any organization, airline, or retail chain associated with this review,"[20] what remains unspoken throughout the report is that Dargo was employed by the North West Company for ten years.[21]

The Deepening of Corporate Welfare: Nutrition North Canada

On 21 May 2010, the federal government announced a "new" federal subsidy program would replace the FMP in April 2011. This announcement was faced with significant resistance from Indigenous communities, organizations, and politicians; indeed, the response was so vociferous that the NNC was delayed until November of that year. Unlike the FMP, the NNC operated at the retail level, and subsidies for a predetermined list of foods would now be paid directly to the retailers who were then expected to pass on savings to consumers at the point of sale.[22] Unlike the FMP program, which was closely monitored and carried out on-site surprise visits in approximately forty northern stores annually, including the collection of food costing data for the Revised Northern Food Basket (RNFB),[23] the NNC program included no mechanisms to ensure savings were passed on to the consumer. When the Auditor General of Canada, Michael Ferguson, audited the program in 2014, he expressed several concerns, including the inability to determine whether retailers were passing on the full subsidy to customers and the failure of the program more broadly to incorporate any evaluation tools or data-based metrics of success.[24]

Interviews with a former employee of the FMP expressed equal parts critique and puzzlement as to how such a policy change could be justified: "I don't know how departmental officials determine whether the savings are passed on really? Do they get this information mostly from the Northern Store? . . . I don't think it's a more effective means of delivering a transportation subsidy."[25] Another former employee was similarly confused: "the way they have it organized now . . . the subsidy goes directly to the retailer: well, that's the most ridiculous thing I've ever heard of. Who is going to look after the chickens when the foxes are there?"[26] They continued: "I don't see how the program can succeed when the subsidy goes to the retailer. . . . I just think it's an absolute misuse of public money and I don't believe it benefits the people at all. And that's probably one of the reasons the food prices are as high as they are up there now. . . . When you actually live in those communities and you see the price of food and the quality of food, you certainly wouldn't trust the retailers."[27] The Dargo Report's influence on the form the NNC took is remarkable. It was clear during the 2008 study that the perspective and wishes of northern retailers were given disproportionate weight, including their desire to administer the program through an "at-the-till approach." Dargo described the "at the till approach" as the most "direct, effective and efficient manner" of subsidy delivery that would result in "improved transparency, accountability, and recognition of Canada's investment."[28] One can discern here once more the neoliberal logic wherein corporations and capitalist entities are seen as the proper tools to solve social problems through a laissez-faire mentality where deregulation facilitates the growth of big business. During the 2013–2014 fiscal year, the NWC received the vast majority of the NNC subsidies at 59 percent, and the Arctic Co-operatives Ltd. was the second highest beneficiary of the NNC at 13 percent.[29] By 2018–2019, this distribution pattern had changed very little, with the NWC receiving 51 percent, Arctic Co-operatives Ltd. 17 percent, and Fédération des coopératives du nord du Québec getting 12 percent of the NNC subsidy.[30] The next highest was Les Consultants de l'Arctique at 5 percent. When customers and Indigenous organizations repeatedly expressed concerns about the program's lack of transparency, Bernard Valcourt, Minister of Aboriginal Affairs and Northern Development, announced after receiving the Nutrition North Canada Advisory Board's recommendation, that NNC savings would now be included on all receipts at the point of purchase.[31]

The use of and access to the NNC was strictly regulated through the imposition of a hierarchical ranking system for both eligible communities, food, and goods, constituting important practices of governmentality. Symbolically, eligibility served to moderate perceived rising program costs, allowing the federal government to appear to impose fiscal restraint on a population frequently characterized as "costing tax payers money." Severe cuts to its operational funding were made under the guise of creating more efficiency and preserving the program for those who needed it the most. In practice, however, the eligibility restrictions served to dramatically reduce access to the NNC for communities who desperately needed it and decreased the range of necessary food and goods that were subsidized. This eligibility structure was one of the primary tools used by the federal government to diminish its responsibility in providing access to the necessities of life like food, health care, and clean water. In place of health and social services frequently taken for granted by many Canadians, northern Indigenous communities "received" market-based alternatives offered through the ever-expanding business operations of the NWC. As a result, the group that most benefitted from the NNC was northern retailers and their company shareholders.

Tiers of community eligibility were created, and significant bureaucratic requirements were imposed on retailers and suppliers to use the NNC subsidy. Under FMP, any community without year-round surface transportation was eligible for the subsidy. In contrast, the NNC determined eligibility based on a community's use of the FMP between 1 April 2009 and 31 March 2010,[32] and introduced a tiered system of entitlement: full eligibility, partial eligibility, and no eligibility. In order to be eligible for the full subsidy, a community had to have received at least 15,000 kilograms of perishable foods through the FMP. The tonnage was calculated by combining the total volume of personal orders and retailers under the FMP. Partial subsidies were applied to those communities that received between one hundred and 14,999 kilograms. If eligible, a community was then subjected to a two-level system of subsidies based on their level of remoteness. For a fully eligible community, level one items (determined to be of high nutritious value) would receive a subsidy rate anywhere between $1.20 to $16.00 per kilogram; level two items in fully eligible communities were subsidized anywhere between five cents and $14.20 per kilogram. In partially eligible communities, there was no distinction between level one and two items and the subsidy rate was set at $0.05 per kilogram—a rate so low as to be almost non-existent.[33] The failure to recognize actual need versus program accessibility was also observed by the Auditor General of Canada (AG) in his 2014 report, which noted that "the Department has not established eligibility criteria that are fair and accessible" because "communities that had not used the previous program were determined to be ineligible."[34] The AG's audit found further "inconsistencies in the eligibility status of some communities . . . for example, two communities in northern Ontario are about 20km apart; they both lack year-round access and are about the same distance to the nearest town; however, one community is eligible for a full subsidy ($1.60/kilogram) while the other is eligible only for the partial subsidy ($0.05/kilogram)."[35] Failure to use a program that was not easily accessible for many residents of northern communities or broadly advertised was hardly evidence of a lack of need for food subsidies; rather, this was proof positive that the goal of the federal government was never really about substantively addressing food insecurity in Indigenous communities in the North in the first place. During the FMP, and especially during NNC, the goal was to keep northern food economies robust and healthy for settler corporations, even if it meant further compromising the food security of Indigenous peoples across the provincial and territorial norths.

The findings of the 2014 AG Report further demonstrated that community eligibility had been subordinated to market logic and tonnage rates.

Particularly problematic here is the fact that the NWC had routinely chosen *not* to use the Food Mail Program in the provincial norths, where the company was often able to find cheaper shipping rates through non-subsidized channels. This meant that First Nations located in the provincial norths that were now eligible for the full NNC subsidy based on past usage were only eligible because entities other than the NWC had been previously accessing the FMP. The Auditor General recommended that eligibility would have to be reorganized around need as opposed to things like tonnage and prior use. Shockingly, the report also detailed that while the "department [of Aboriginal and Northern Affairs] has committed to reviewing the community eligibility status for full or partial subsidies annually . . . it has not completed annual reviews."[36] In other words, between April 2011 (the start of NNC) and August 2014, there was no opportunity for ineligible communities to appeal their loss of access to the subsidy.

Further limitations on the so-called free market system operating in the North was the division of retailers into northern retailers and southern suppliers. The northern retailer category was fairly simple and included only food retailers currently operating in eligible NNC communities. However, the southern suppliers category was slightly more complicated and was identified as those "suppliers located in the south who s[old] food to northern retailers, eligible social institutions (schools, daycares), eligible commercial establishments, or individuals in eligible communities (direct or personal orders)." However, in order to become a southern supplier, organizations had to undertake a lengthy and bureaucratic application process that included providing evidence of an established customer base in the North and estimates of "monthly shipments of eligible foods by level subsidy and by eligible community for the upcoming fiscal year."[37] That an established northern customer base was a prerequisite within a closed retail system with high barriers to entry is ridiculous and doubly so in the context of neoliberal logics that purport to foster open competition. Even after southern suppliers/retailers were approved, the reporting and program requirements remained prohibitive, time consuming, and labour intensive.[38] Processing times for NNC applications are very long; one northern business had to wait ten months to be registered with NNC even after their application was approved.[39] An interview with several community members who operated a bi-weekly market that brought in perishable foods into a fly-in First Nation told us that they were unable to access the NNC directly because they did not have the capacity to undertake all of the paperwork and that the application processes and requirements were extremely onerous; notably, they did not have the capacity to provide sales receipts that included subsidy amounts for every sale.[40] If you recall, the inclusion of the NNC subsidy amount on all receipts at the point of purchase had been the federal government's belated response to critiques that the NNC lacked transparency. Taken together, these limitations created insurmountable barriers, especially for small independent retailers without the administrative capacity of large retailers like the NWC. The NNC operated in such a way that it limited access to the North for southern suppliers.

Additional practices of governmentality were imposed through the restriction of everyday necessities in the North; for example, medical devices (broadly defined), diapers, toothbrushes, toothpaste, shampoo, tampons, and cleaning products were made ineligible under NNC.[41] The restructurings of the NNC made it much harder and significantly more expensive to care for people across and between different stages of life. Providing care for the elderly and infants suddenly became even more prohibitively expensive. Further, individuals living with disabilities of any sort that required particular essential items experienced additional financial burdens due to the onset of the new subsidy structure. Personal hygiene became more expensive (particularly dental hygiene, given that toothbrushes and toothpaste were now ineligible for subsidy). Clearly, NNC was not designed to actually assist in healthy and affordable living in the North but rather to provide the appearance of making perishable and nutritious foods more affordable. Under NNC, "healthy living" was reduced to the consumption of select micro and macro nutrients and failed to account for the socio-cultural aspects of health and the lived realities of life in the North. This was a key difference and significant development in the way these subsidy structures were envisioned by the federal government. Though the impact of previous government programs, like the FMP, had always been patently colonial, there is some room for debate on the question of whether they were fully intended as the violent vectors of social policy they certainly became. In the case of NNC, however, there is less conceptual space for any generous interpretations of policy formation, given the extent to which essential items were fully dropped from subsidy eligibility.

A conversation held with a former employee of the FMP revealed vastly different attitudes towards subsidy eligibility, particularly in the area of non-perishable necessities:

> We had a list of ineligible non-food items . . . I felt that incomes
> in these communities are generally very low: most of the non-
> food items that people would be purchasing, most people would
> consider necessities. And rather than go through and try and come
> up with a list of everything that you might consider a necessity,
> it was better to identify things that that are not necessities and
> say well those are not eligible . . . in this last round of review [of
> Nutrition North Canada] there seemed to be a great deal of hos-
> tility [from non-northerners] towards the snowmobile parts, but
> I could never understand that.[42]

These comments illustrate that very different logics were employed when trying to determine what items were considered necessities. The example of bottled water here best illustrates this shift. Under NNC, bottled water lost its subsidy despite the high number of boil water advisories and do not consume orders across the Canadian North.[43] Its loss of eligibility was mentioned previously in the Dargo Report in 2008, wherein Dargo posed the ridiculous question regarding whether or not bottled water was "nutritious" and whether or not it was under the mandate of the federal food subsidy programs to deal with water problems. Evidently, the conclusion reached was that bottled water was not the responsibility of the state, as it was dropped in the revised eligibility list under NNC. Troublingly, the NWC was well-positioned to capitalize on the situation, as they had been investing in in-store water filtration outfits in Northern Stores since 1992. For example, a 2004 annual report of the NWC celebrated the fact that the company was "creating a liquid asset out of H_2O," as more than half of all Northern Stores were at that time selling Ultra-Pure™ water—a product that was a result of a partnership with a company named Dyna-Pro Environmental.[44]

Further restrictions on non-food items echoed earlier federal policy initiatives undertaken after the Second World War. Under NNC, items necessary to pursue land- and water-based activities (such as fishing nets, boat motor parts, ammunition, and gasoline) were removed from eligibility.[45] These prohibitions took place despite the federal government's avowed commitment to improving access to land- and water-based foods (referred to here as country foods). According to Greg Rickford, federal Member of Parliament for Kenora, Ontario, and Parliamentary Secretary to the Minister of Indian Affairs and Northern Development and Federal Interlocutor for Métis, and

Non-Status Indians, increasing access to country foods was a priority for the federal government. In a press release, Rickford stated: "Our Government remains committed to improving the well-being of Northerners. Having spent time living in the North, I realize the importance country foods have for Northerners from both a cultural and nutritional standpoint. That is why we have included subsidies for commercially produced country foods under Nutrition North Canada."[46]

The widely celebrated Country Foods Initiative (CFI), was intended to promote access to "meats commercially produced in northern Canada."[47] In other words, the initiative was designed to further regulate Indigenous food sovereignties and enfold Indigenous foodways within the capitalist system.[48] Under the CFI, if harvesters wanted to ship country food between eligible NNC communities, they had to have the meat certified by a country food processor/distributor. A country food processor/distributor was an "establishment that [was] registered, inspected and/or licensed by the government and produced food approved-for-export and [was] located in a community eligible for a subsidy under the program."[49] There are only three licensed food processing facilities in the North, and they are all located in the territories.[50] Thus, in order to use the NNC to ship land-based foods from one community to another, the food first had to be shipped to one of the federally regulated country food processors/distributors and then to the community in question. Under the CFI regulations, sharing informally between families and communities was ineligible under NNC. For provinces like northern Ontario, the CFI was utterly useless, and not one northern fly-in First Nation accessed the program. Such initiatives directly targeted the ability of Indigenous communities to exercise food sovereignty while operating under the false belief that the federal government supported access to land- and water-based foods.

In April 2020, the Government of Canada announced the Harvesters Support Grant, which according to the government of Canada website, was developed in "direct collaboration with Inuit partners to improve access to traditional foods and lower the high costs of hunting and harvesting [by] improv[ing] access to traditional foods and lower[ing] the cost of hunting and harvesting."[51] Administered through NNC, the Harvesters Support Grant was expanded to include the Community Food Programs Fund in June 2022. The Community Food Program is described as being co-designed with Indigenous partners to "support a variety of community food sharing activities that include locally grown, market and country food."[52] The stated intent of the program is to decrease reliance on "store bought foods" and support Indigenous harvest cultures and practices that include local food production and community food sharing.[53] The following activities are eligible for funding:

- Harvesting equipment, including maintenance and storage of equipment
- Maintenance of harvesting sites
- Transportation and fuel expenses
- Training, certification and education
- Safety and rescue equipment
- Food-related minor infrastructure, facilities, equipment and related maintenance
- Gardening and animal husbandry
- Food centres, hubs and community kitchens
- Local food programs, such as school food, Elders meals and local food banks
- Salaries and services required for the coordination of ordering, transport, or distribution of market foods within and outside of communities
- Buying clubs and revolving loan funds for bulk food purchasing
- Traditional decision making structures and community coordination
- Cultural ceremony and celebration
- Research and innovation.[54]

Only Indigenous organizations eligible for the NNC have access to the Harvesters Support Grant and Community Food Programs fund. These programs were created as part of the federal government's response to growing rates of food insecurity experienced by northern First Nations and Inuit communities during the COVID-19 global pandemic. Such programs build on the significant work undertaken by First Nations, Inuit councils, and tribal organizations to support hunters and trappers in their communities who recognized the growing cost of participating in land- and water-based food procurement activities and the continued socio-cultural importance of sharing foods within the community.[55] A 1987 study carried out by Indian and Northern Affairs Canada found that the cost of outfitting a full-time hunter in Arctic Bay exceeded $10,000,[56] and given inflation, we can only imagine that these costs have continued to increase. More work on the Harvesters Support Grant and Community Food Programs Fund offered by NNC is needed to ascertain its efficacy.

The Cheez Whiz Affair: Decreasing the Costs of NNC

When Minister of Aboriginal Affairs and Northern Development John Duncan described the NNC program to the general public in 2011, he pointed out that one of its principal benefits would be that "taxpayers w[ould] no longer [have to] fork out funds to ship Cheez Whiz, tires and snowmobile parts to Canada's North under the federal government's new market-driven food-delivery program."[57] Such racist comments provided the context in which food eligibility under the NNC was determined and illustrated a remarkable lack of understanding and knowledge about the experiences of Indigenous peoples. Significantly, such comments, especially those made by figures in Canadian society that are perceived to hold knowledge/expertise and exercise a great deal of power over the terrain of Indigenous peoples' lives, feed into incredibly racists stereotypes about Indigenous peoples that construct them as lazy and reliant on handouts from taxpayers who are positioned in these discourses as the "real Canadians."

Changes to food subsidies began in the months preceding the official start date of the NNC. Swift increases in the cost of everyday products began as early as the fall of 2010 and received immediate and harsh responses from northern Indigenous leaders and community members. Well-known Inuk politician Jose Kusugak testified before parliament in November of 2010 and pointed out the kinds of problems the confusing and complex nature of the implementation process promised to produce: "Inuit must not suffer because of price increases resulting from NNC. There is a real possibility that the prices of many items will increase dramatically in the coming months. Because of sealift timing, storage, and other issues, retailers have not necessarily adequately stocked newly non-eligible items through other transportation methods."[58] Kusugak identified what would become a material reality and potential crisis: with insufficient notice, northern retailers had no time (and really no mandate) to take advantage of the still available subsidies for non-perishables under the Food Mail Program. Speaking to a former nutritionist employed by the NWC, the amount of long-term logistical planning was explained to us: "it's quite a process to do that . . . if you're yeah if you're gonna be doing a sea-lift order or a large order or something like that then you need to give yourself you know time and not wait until the last minute."[59] Accordingly, as Kusugak envisioned, many non-perishables previously subsidized became profoundly and predictably expensive across the Canadian North. Indeed, an analysis of Nunavut households before and after the introduction of NNC found that rates of food insecurity increased. The authors suggest that the exclusion of most non-perishable foods and all non-food items from the subsidy "prevented households from improving their access to food and, in some cases, worsened their access to food as the prices of common non-perishable foods and essential items rose."[60]

In February of 2011, Cheez Whiz spread in an Arctic Bay store in Nunavut reached an unprecedented price tag of twenty-nine dollars.[61] Photographs of the price tag taken by community members were picked up by Canadian news outlets, who then shared pictures of other outrageous examples, such as a bag of frozen breaded chicken retailing for seventy-seven dollars.[62] Questions of how this was possible perplexed southern Canadian and non-Indigenous residents; however, for northern Indigenous communities, the Cheez Whiz affair was representative of the dysfunctional schema the Conservative government was setting up under NNC. The Cheez Whiz controversy was also a stark reminder that access to food in the Canadian North was very much at the mercy of the federal government's whims and party politics.

When the NNC was fully implemented in November of 2011, despite concerted community protest, which delayed but did not divert its implementation, food was further subjected to the cold market logic and neoliberal influence of the Dargo Report. Disconnects between policy and community life became readily apparent. For example, tea and bannock is extremely common in First Nations and Inuit homes. Though bannock is often homemade, the kneading requirements often make it very difficult for Elders or children to prepare. As a result, ready-made bannock mixes have become a common workaround for many people.[63] Further, when tea and bannock are served, they are often served with margarine and jam. Under the revised NNC eligibility list, bannock mixes, tea, jam, and margarine were all removed from subsidy under the logic that they were insufficiently nutritious foods.

Another elimination of items from the NNC list of eligible foods that contradicted earlier nutrition initiatives in the fifties and sixties under other Indian Affairs schemes was the removal of canned meats from the list of eligibility. NNC made Klik™ —the Canadian version of Spam™—much more expensive in northern communities despite it being a widely eaten product and considered by many to be a comfort food.[64] By removing macaroni and cheese mixes as well as hot dogs (read: "KD and wieners") from eligibility, NNC made an incredibly common low-income meal significantly more expensive. For many families in the north and south, macaroni and cheese, hot dogs, chicken fingers, and other similar foods comprise the core of many children's diets, whether parents want them to or not. Thus, while northern residents could find cheaper avocadoes at the Northern Store following the full implementation of NNC, the most common, cherished, and characteristically northern foods became much more expensive. It is important here to recall Kyla Wazana Tompkins's use of the concept of "racial indigestion to examine the social, symbolic, and material practices through which colonial practices produce and maintain racial (and other systemic) food and social inequalities."[65] Here, foods characterized as "northern foods" were identified as "unhealthy" and, as a result, became prohibitively expensive. Reading the discussions and conversations about those foods receiving higher subsidies and those foods being eliminated under the subsidy due to their so-called perceived nutritional value alongside critical work done on Canada's Food Guide, including the "friendlier" First Nations, Métis, and Inuit version, is essential. Doing so allows us to recognize that these discussions are about more than just "good food/bad food" narratives but as taking place within circumstances informed by settler colonialism, class, race, social, and political contexts.[66] Rather, these discourses work to create false illusions of choice and suggest that there is only one right choice.

Alissa Overend poses the question regarding state efforts to transform the diets of Indigenous people, especially in accordance with the creation of the First Nations, Inuit, and Métis version of Canada's Food Guide, "the question becomes not what is healthy, but who gets to eat well and live well within settler-colonial neoliberal formulations of health?"[67] Overend further argues that "guides and labels are part of the larger epidemic of neoliberal approaches to health, food, and nutrition . . . in shifting the focus onto individual eating habits, systemic and structural accounts of food access, food security, food knowledge, and the time, money, and ability needed to prepare healthy meals are ignored. Such accounts of nutrition not only depoliticize insidious social inequalities that mitigate access to health, but concomitantly feed market purposes where health becomes yet another commodity to be bought and sold."[68] Thus, health is reduced to individual personal choices that are often framed in moralizing ways rather than the outcome of systemic and structural marginalization. Anything identified as lacking in nutritional value was instantly deemed ineligible for the NNC subsidy, which had enormous consequences across the Canadian North. Further, the fascination of southerners with the high cost of Cheez Whiz during the transition to NNC served to obscure rather than reveal the intimate relationship between the federal government and northern retailers.

Unfortunately, the 2014 AG audit did not include in its mandate an investigation of the retailers and their profit margins; however, the lion's share of criticisms in the report centred on this very issue. Indeed, one is left with the impression that the Office of the Auditor General tried quite hard to gain access to NWC data on profit margins and was denied. The 2014 AG's Report heavily criticized the Department of Aboriginal Affairs and Northern Development (AANDC) for failing to stipulate in their agreements with retailers that this kind of information would be subject to any audits and state oversight. For context, the report reviews that roughly $53.9 million of the total $60 million annual budget for NNC had been defined by the department as "contribution agreements."[69] Though the "contribution agreements" specified that the full subsidy must be passed on to the customer, the AG's report lamented that "the department did not specify in the agreements that data on profit margins must be provided" as well.[70] In practice, then, it is rather easy to look up in annual compliance reports the amount of money given to the NWC by the federal government; for example, in the fiscal year ending 31 March 2014 (the year of the federal audit), AANDC reported in a compliance assessment report that the NWC received $31.7 million in transfer payments pursuant to *Funding Agreement no. 1213-01-000019*.[71] However, it is not possible for researchers or even the Auditor General's Office to learn any information whatsoever on the scale of NWC profit margins and mark-ups on subsidized items. In other words, the question of how regularly and to what degree the NWC gouges its customers is not a quantifiable one due to the letter of funding agreements generated by the federal government and agreed to by NWC legal representation and executive leadership. Even so, in its concluding discussion, the AG's report made special mention of this particular issue and underscored that no confirmation could be given to the Canadian government that the full subsidies were indeed being passed on to northern customers at the point of purchase: "The northern retailers have

Figure 15. Nutrition North Canada poster explaining subsidy. Credit: Mandi Chan Peters.

attested to the Department that they do pass on the full subsidy to consumers. If the Department was able to verify that this was the case, some of the public skepticism around the program could be lessened. This would benefit both the program and northern retailers."[72]

To address this oversight in the period leading up to the federal election in the fall of 2015, the Conservative government required northern retailers to indicate NCC subsidy amounts on individual customer receipts. However, this move did not interrogate the profit margins of retailers on unsubsidized products. For example, if the NWC sold a toothbrush at an inflated price well beyond what it costs to acquire, ship, and shelve that product, there was no mandate for the government to intervene or even investigate the matter as toothbrushes were not subsidized by NNC. The receipt policy of the federal government merely checked a box, so to speak, in terms of making the program more transparent and communicative to its recipients. In any case, the Conservative party lost the 2015 federal election, and the NNC schema shifted to the control of a new federal government led by the Liberals.

Since the election of a Liberal federal government under Justin Trudeau, changes have been made to community eligibility for NNC, reverting to the same criteria used under the FMP. Communities are eligible on the basis that they: "lack year-round surface transportation (no permanent road, rail, or marine access), excluding isolation caused by freeze-up and break-up that normally lasts more than four weeks at a time; meet the territorial or provincial definition of a northern community; have an airport, post office, or grocery store; have a year-round population according to the national census."[73] Although the Liberals have once again made all communities eligible for the NNC and included some non-food items, it remains a subsidy paid directly to retailers.

Conclusion

Disproportionately high rates of food insecurity in First Nations and Inuit communities persisted (and in some cases worsened) even after the transition from FMP to NNC. If anything, NNC made it harder for households in the North to purchase necessary household items, which in turn impacted their ability to purchase food. Indeed, Nutrition North Canada has done little to address systemic problems in the current northern retail landscape. Drawing on the neoliberal rationalities outlined in the Dargo report, the federal government's implementation of NNC reinforced a retail system that benefitted the dominant retailer in the region at the expense of Indigenous food sovereignties. Paying subsidies directly to the retailer and creating further barriers to entry only served to solidify an already closed retail system in the North.

Popular discourse in the media further normalized the high cost of food in the North by representing the current situation as "just the cost of doing business in the North," a sentiment frequently echoed by NWC executives.[74] Paying subsidies directly to retailers reinforced the notion that food insecurity in the North could be resolved through market-based solutions offered by benevolent community-minded corporations like the NWC. The federal government's increased funding for harvester support and community food programs in 2020 and 2022, respectively, while extremely important, does not address the systemic inequalities regarding market-based foods. The institution of price caps and controls would be far more effective in controlling the cost of market-based foods and necessary goods; however, such controls would not serve corporate bottom lines. The federal government continues to haphazardly support Indigenous food sovereignties to distract people from the intimate relationship that persists between the state and the NWC.

CONCLUSION

In the summer of 2017, high-ranking board members from the NWC head-quarters in Winnipeg visited Thunder Bay, and because big news travels fast in a small city, it did not take long for rumours to circulate as to why. The scoop quickly became that a local airline and cargo company, North Star Air, had a massive cash deal in the works with the NWC. On 28 April 2017, the NWC issued a media release that confirmed some of these rumours and reported that they had acquired 100 percent of the shares of North Star Air at a cost of $31 million in cash. Further, the company reported that it planned to invest an additional $14 million in airport warehousing throughout northern Manitoba to expand retailing capacity across Nunavut.[1] The next day, *CBC News* ran an article with the headline: "NWC Spends $31 million to buy its own airline."[2]

Though the official acquisition did not take place until 15 June 2017, the outrage across the North was palpable and immediate.[3] Our cell phones, email inboxes, and social media messaging applications were overrun with questions and statements of shock and disbelief. Though many expressed outrage, a particularly acute concern related to the way it appeared that the NWC's expansion was facilitated by federal food subsidy programs. For ex-ample, in the same fiscal year as the airline purchase, the federal government paid $33.1 million in subsidies directly to the NWC.[4] The following year, this number rose to $35.8 million,[5] and according to NNC reporting, the NWC annually receives more than 50 percent of the entire NNC subsidy made available by the federal government.[6] That the company could afford to acquire an airline was, for many people, evidence that the subsidies paid by the federal government operated as corporate welfare, bolstering the operations and profitability of the NWC while leaving northern First Nation and Inuit communities to shoulder the high cost of food. Such perceptions were only fuelled by the NNC's lack of transparency and the NWC's profit margins in the face of rising food costs and food insecurity. Requests from Indigenous politicians, organizations, food sovereigntists/actionists, and the Auditor General of Canada for an accounting of the NNC subsidy and corporate profit margins went unanswered.

Over the last century, the federal government, alongside the Hudson's Bay Company and its offspring, the North West Company, have undermined Indigenous food sovereignties in northern First Nations and Inuit communities to the enormous benefit of both the state and company shareholders. Programs like family allowances, food mail, and NNC, alongside nutrition education initiatives, operated and continue to do so within a broader regulatory framework designed to compel Indigenous families and communities to adopt European-Canadian foodways and domestic practices. Hegemonic nutrition discourses that promoted an "ideal diet" rooted in European-Canadian dietary norms also pathologized Indigenous bodies when they did not conform to the white middle-class settler ideal.[7] Locating the symptoms of settler colonialism within Indigenous bodies justified historical and ongoing state intervention into northern First Nations and Inuit communities. It also provided the HBC and later the NWC with a captive consumer audience to which they could market so-called "healthier lifestyles."[8]

More recent avowals by the federal government to promote access to land- and water-based foods remain largely superficial. Regulations under the Food Mail Program and later Nutrition North Canada's (NNC) Country Foods Initiative made it nearly impossible to ship locally produced foodstuffs or land- and water-based foods between northern communities. Both NNC's Country Foods Initiative and the First Nations, Métis, and Inuit peoples' version of Canada's Food Guide serve largely as performative efforts on the part of the state that provide the appearance of including Indigenous foodways but only so long as they can be enfolded within a capitalist framework and understood and operationalized within the settler state. According to Dawn Morrison, "Indigenous food sovereignty requires a balanced approach to addressing underlying structural issues and inequality in privilege and power, in the policy, planning, and governance of our ancestral homelands, where we hunt, fish, farm, and gather our foods."[9] We argue that this also extends to market-based foods and includes modes and methods of transportation and distribution. If examined in isolation, it can be difficult to see continuities between healthy eating marketing initiatives in grocery stores and schools with historical schemes like the Family Allowance Program or the disruption of Indigenous parenting practices. However, if we examine these policies as part of a system that forms the very architecture of settler colonialism, we can see how food insecurity is both manufactured and maintained in Indigenous communities located in the provincial and far norths. In this context, it is important to highlight the observation of Dene theorist Glen Coulthard who suggests that the newest paradigm of Canadian colonialism functions to "discipline Indigenous life to the cold rationality of market principles," and nowhere is this more evident than in the "market-based solutions" that the Canadian government has conjured up to address food insecurity in the North.[10]

Our book focused on histories of state policy and corporate practices through an examination of governmental and corporate documents. To some degree, this focus risked erasing or at least obscuring the reality of Indigenous resistance and resurgence in response to settler-colonial assaults on Indigenous food sovereignties and community wellness. The focus may also oversell the success of settler colonialism. For these reasons, it is important to emphasize before we conclude that at no point in time did Indigenous nations passively consent to those processes that sought to remove them from their land and access to those resources that had fed their communities for generations. Indigenous peoples did not eagerly welcome the introduction of non-Indigenous foods. For instance, in a 1947 submission to the Special Joint Committee of the Senate and House of Commons, the Chief and Council of the Pas Indian Band stated that Indigenous peoples had been forced "to accept a diet which consists of partly the food of the white man and partly the food of the Indian."[11] They went on to identify several factors as the cause of this: mainly, a shortage of game and the restriction of Indigenous peoples' freedom to pursue land- and water-based harvesting practices. Significantly, the Chief and Council criticized the imposition of regular fees, licences, and royalties on those Indigenous individuals who fish and trap.[12] Nor was this an isolated event. More recently, in regards to the retailing of market-based foods, Chief Donny Morris of Kitchenuhmaykoosib Inninuwug First Nation called out the NWC and its Northern Store chain for "price-gouging" in Indigenous communities.[13] Chief Morris stated that the NWC should pay "reparations for the economic suffering they have inflicted on Indigenous peoples in Canada."[14] Significantly, following a suicide crisis in their community in early 2016, the youth of Attawapiskat First Nation issued a list of demands to the federal government, stating that "there should be a de-privatization of the Northern stores to be able to provide federally assisted food to northern communities."[15] Clearly, the youth council connected preventable losses of life in their community to food sovereignty. In addition to Indigenous political leadership resisting the NWC and calling out the federal government's support of their retailing operations, there are many Indigenous food cooperatives and harvesters doing important work to sustain their communities. First Nations and Inuit communities have engaged in trying to create alternatives to the NWC by establishing their own community-run or member-owned grocery stores, alternative food markets, as well as online grocery stores run by locals.[16] However, the systemic barriers created by the federal government and the NWC remain. Worse still, the NWC building on the foundations of the HBC continues to be the beneficiary of support from the settler state, which it has used to facilitate expansion into postal, financial, pharmaceutical, and transportation services, as well as into other rural regions in Alaska and the Caribbean.

Finally, we return to the story of Sarah. Sarah is a community member who works to enact Indigenous food sovereignty, including bringing market-based foods into her community at cost. Sarah invests much of her time, education, and energy into expanding her community's capacity for food sovereignty; however, the systemic barriers and structural determinants of food access in the North are considerable, and the colonial actors in this context (the NWC and the federal government) have more power, influence, and capital. Even when seeking to bolster community food access and security, Sarah is often forced to use the infrastructure of the NWC. "Every organization buys from the Northern Store," she explains, "from the school, to the band office, to the health centre . . . for simple things like buying food for a workshop to sometimes buying big-time prizes."[17] To put it simply, the way in which the NWC "blankets the north" hinders the development of Indigenous-owned and -run market-based alternatives within northern food systems. At the same time, the discourses employed by the state and corporate actors continue to suggest that better money management skills, nutrition education, and individual responsibility will resolve poverty and address food insecurity in northern First Nations and Inuit communities. As Sarah aptly observes, "there isn't any room for mistakes when the cost of food is so high,"[18] and no amount of money management skills and nutrition education will resolve settler colonialism and neoliberal capitalism. Yet despite significant structural barriers, Indigenous food sovereigntists continue to work on behalf of their communities and nations across the provincial and far norths.

ACKNOWLEDGEMENTS

Kristin Burnett

This book is dedicated to my late uncle Arthur James Burnett. As a child he was affectionately known to me and my cousins as "Big Jim" because he was really tall and everyone called him Jim. He never had kids of his own but Jim parented all of us and was an ever-present person in our lives. Jim died as I was writing the final of chapters of this manuscript, and it was not until that moment that I realized what a constant and supportive presence he had been in my life. Sadly, his passing also signalled what felt like my final move into adulthood. The summer I completed my PhD and quickly moved to Edmonton to take up a post-doctoral fellowship at the University of Alberta, I made frequently trips between Calgary and Edmonton to visit family and complete the research for my first monograph. Jim was my constant travelling companion during that period, keeping me company on the long drives throughout southern Alberta, listening to music, talking, and sharing good food. When I moved to Thunder Bay to take up my first academic job at Lakehead University in January 2007, once again Jim kept me company and helped me wrangle my furry family on the long drive. Jim has always supported me: helping me move, hanging curtains in new apartments, listening to me talk about my work, helping me buy food when I was broke, and visiting and caring for my brother—thank you. "Big Jim" I hope you know how important you were to me and everyone around you, we miss you.

Over the last two decades, my approach to historical research has changed. I have been drawn into community-based work that regularly includes historical components but is no longer solely rooted in an examination of the past in isolation from people and community in the present. In other words, context matters but it serves as an entry point into community-based work and not the sole objective. This project is a reflection of that process of learning how to do historical work properly so that it carries contemporary relevance for people and community. This project was shaped by conversations with community members, knowledge holders, Elders, friends, and colleagues who work every day to assert Indigenous food sovereignties in their territories. These conversations were important because they taught me about the value of relationships and the obligation I carry to ensure my work is done well. I want to express my heartfelt appreciation to those individuals who shared their knowledge and showed me a great deal of patience. Chi-Miigwetch! I also want to thank David Churchill, who recommended I read *Cigarettes Inc.: An Intimate History of Corporate Imperialism* and Lori Chambers, who was a co-applicant on the SSHRC grant for this project and co-authored several preliminary articles.

I owe an enormous debt to several amazing research assistants. The first graduate assistant I ever worked with was Brent Rosborough. Brent liaised with the North West Company and convinced someone to photocopy and mail hard copies of more than twenty years of annual reports to me. Thank you, Brent! I especially want to thank Leah Morton who spent many hours in the Archives of Manitoba perusing HBC records. Without Leah's keen eye and attention to detail this would have been a very different book. The notes and observations Leah wrote were instrumental in writing and theorizing about the role of the HBC.

Thanks to the archivists at Library and Archives Canada and the Archives of Manitoba who offered their assistance and expertise. This project was funded through a grant from the Social Sciences and Humanities Research Council and supported by a Lakehead University Research Chair. In particular, I want to express my gratitude to Susan Wright and Anne Klymenko, from the research office at Lakehead University, for their support.

The people at the University of Manitoba Press have been instrumental in seeing this manuscript to fruition. A special thank you Jill McConkey, who has been very patient. Even though we took twice as long as we promised to deliver the manuscript, she continued to believe in this project. I am deeply appreciative of the careful attention of Glenn Bergen, Sarah Enns, and copyeditor Alicia Hibbert, and the artistic prowess of Sébastien Aubin. I also want to thank the individuals who reviewed this manuscript. Your thoughtful insights and suggestions made this a much better work.

Although I am now a full professor with my own graduate students, I still benefit from the mentors and friends I made as a graduate student. I was fortunate to study with amazing feminist scholars, especially Drs. Kathryn

McPherson and Sarah Carter, who taught me a great deal about the type of scholar and colleague I wanted to become. In this vein, I appreciated the enthusiasm of Travis Hay who started working on this project as a graduate student/research assistant and remained engaged with and committed to this work until the very end. Without Travis's ability to (re)find documents, I doubt we would have finished this manuscript. I particularly want to extend a special thanks to Shannon Stettner—for some reason we hated each other in grad school but since then you have become one of my most valued friends and colleagues. Thank you for reading multiple drafts of everything.

I have also benefitted from the support, expertise, and friendship of many amazing people both at Lakehead University and elsewhere. To name a few: Lana Ray, Barbara Parker, Chris Sanders, Robert Robson, Anna Guttman, Jennifer Chisholm, Denise Baxter, Elizabeth Birmingham, Annette Schroeter, Jackie Fletcher, Rhonda Meekis, Karen Flynn, Joan Metatawabin, Joseph LeBlanc, Renee Southwind, Kathy Loon, Mark Bell, Nadia Verrelli, Perry McLeod-Shabogesic, Kelly Skinner, Tabitha Martens, Cheryl Warsh, Patty Williams, Jane Liu, Debbie Martin, Mary Jane McCallum, Chris Dooley, Adele Perry, Jaime Cidro, Mandi Chan-Peters, and Angie Wong. An awkward hug for Arlene Meekis-Jung and Gigi Veeraraghavan, who are some of my favourite people to hang out with.

Finally, I deeply appreciate the patience of my family: my furry kids who kept my lap warm while I wrote; Robert Thivierge, my cousin, who came to live with me in 2014 and is great company and wonderful to my child; and especially Adrian Thomas Cole Burnett, my beautiful kiddo who fills my world with love and laughter—you are my heart.

Travis Hay

I want to dedicate this book to the memory of my late grandfather and grandmother: James and Rae Hay. I remember them as my Pa and my Grammy. My Pa (himself a local legend) told my favourite story in the world, which involved him buying my Grammy a fur coat store in Thunder Bay, Ontario. Her shop—Rae's Furs—became an iconic installment on Simpson Street and one of the few businesses owned and operated by a woman during those decades. The story sparked my early interest in the fur trade as well as my antipathy to unchecked corporate growth that railroads and bulldozes smaller northern local businesses. Though I lost my Grammy as a very young boy, my Pa passed on more recently in 2021. Though we were lucky to keep him with us for so many years, the loss was and remains very hard on our family. We miss you, Pa, but I bet Grammy did, too, and we are happy you are together again.

This book (and, frankly, anything I do as a historian) would not be possible without the longstanding support and guidance of Kristin Burnett. Kristin had been working on this project for some time when I began as her research assistant in 2013. I had recently completed my master's degree and was devastated to learn that I was not admitted to doctoral programs to continue my graduate studies. Kristin and I were at a community event in Thunder Bay when I received the bad news and, feeling rather sorry for myself I slunk out of the building to have a private self-pity session in my car (which, to make matters worse, was a 2006 PT Cruiser). It was at this point that Kristin came outside in the cold, jacketless. Rather than commiserating with me and offering empty platitudes, Kristin vowed that she would help me, argued against my own protests that I had value as a historian, and that I should not give up on myself. She then found research monies to send me to the HBC archives in Winnipeg and funded my first trip to Congress to present to the Canadian Society for the History of Medicine. As I slowly became something like an academic, she was there to help every step of the way and always reminded me to keep my mind on community, material conditions, and the impacts of my research. When I started to be interviewed for academic positions, Kristin coached me and collected supportive colleagues to form mock job committees where I practised answering those then-terrifying teaching, research, and service questions. Though I am confident she will cringe to see such page-space dedicated to her here, I simply would not be who I am or where I am without this kind of careful tutelage and steadfast support. Sadly, this sort of thing is exceedingly rare in academia, which makes the need to acknowledge Kristin's support even more acute. Neither this book, nor its secondary author, would exist in their current forms without Kristin.

I also want to acknowledge the Nepinak family in Winnipeg. When I first travelled to Winnipeg in 2013 to retrieve records from the HBC archives in the course of researching this book, I met Rebecca Nepinak. I will never forget her laugh and the way it rang off the walls of the archives. We became fast friends and cemented this friendship over our common love of food. I was given a grand tour of The Forks and invited to one of the famous Nepinak Sunday family dinners, where I had the chance to meet Rebecca's mother

Barbara, her father Clarence, and her sisters Melissa, Krystin, and Melanie. From that point forward, I was not allowed to get a hotel in Winnipeg and instead stayed with the Nepinak family. Rebecca's sudden and tragic passing in October of 2022 tore a hole in my heart that has not yet healed. Less than one month later, her father Clarence began his own journey. I hope that this book makes them both proud of me and that they know how much I love and miss them.

Over the course of the last several years, I have also had the honour to work with the Anishinaabe Elder Teri Redsky Fiddler. Teri, who is the busiest person I know, has become like family to me and has been generous with her time. Her teachings, friendship, and example of tireless service to community has been an inspiration to me and I will always try in life to make her proud and to pay her kindness and love forward.

I also want to acknowledge and thank my colleagues in Indigenous Studies at Mount Royal University: Jaime Waucash-Warn, Vicki Bouvier, Ranjan Datta, Gabrielle Weasel Head-Lindstrom, auntie Karen Pheasant-Neganigwane, Jessie Loyer, and Barbara Barnes. I am lucky to be able to work with such brilliant scholars but even luckier that our work together is contoured around our fast-growing friendships and investments in one another's lives and families. When sharing good news or grappling with tragedy, we have been there for one another, which means more than words can communicate.

I would also like to thank the University of Manitoba Press for their continued support. Jill McConkey, Glenn Bergen, Sarah Ens, and David Larsen (among others) have been wonderful to work with. Further, I want to thank and acknowledge Sébastien Aubin, who produced the brilliant cover art for this book. Archivists across the country—but especially at Library and Archives Canada and the HBC archives in Winnipeg—were instrumental in making the research for this book possible. If there were a world run by archivists and librarians, I would happily move there.

These acknowledgements would also be woefully incomplete without a nod to my dear friend and best man Andrew Drainville. Though he moved to France to pursue his own academic career, his constant companionship, intellectual influence, and *joie de vivre* have been a defining feature of my adult life. I also want to thank my friend and colleague Tony McGuire, whose passion for his craft, dedication to telling community stories, and well-timed hugs have been a buoy for my spirits and a beacon for my own life's work. Boyd Cothran, a historian at York University and a dear friend, has also played a similar role as a "north star" in my life. His example (and his correspondence) mean more to me than I am able to articulate. I strive in my life to be the kind of man that Andrew, Tony, and Boyd are.

I will always acknowledge my dad and his rigorous "red pen" for teaching me the importance of clear communication as well as embodying a sense of duty and service to community; similarly, I want to acknowledge and thank my mom for supporting me as a bookworm and for the subversive streak that rests in our bones (for better or worse). My big brother Ryan—who is a skilled hunter and the handiest man I know—has also been a lifeline for me in the past ten years and has kept me in touch with my roots.

I am also blessed to have nieces and nephews that bring me endless joy and laughter. Callia, Zèa, Marek, Evelyn, Ada, Zoe, and Isaac: your uncle loves you! My in-laws—Sunny and Mei Wong—have shown me so much love and support (and fed me so often), that their names must also appear here. My Auntie Myra and Uncle Mike have also helped to make Calgary feel like home and have each kept a keen interest in my work.

To my best friend and wife, Angie Wong: you are everything to me and anything good I do in this world, I do it through your love and support. To my dogs, Kiera and Clyde: thank you for keeping my feet warm and my heart full as I worked on this book.

NOTES

Introduction

1   Interview with community member, 24 August 2017.

2   At the direction of Lakehead University's Research Ethics Board and to prevent any potential repercussions, we avoid naming specific individuals and communities where possible unless identities and affiliations were already part of the public record or historically distant enough that it would be impractical for anyone to pursue. It should also be noted that the NWC has a history of banning people from using the only stores in the community for a variety of reasons including but not limited to critiques of business practices.

3   Nutrition North Canada, "Cost of the Revised Northern Food Basket in 2017–2018"; Leblanc-Laurendeau, *Food Insecurity in Northern Canada: An Overview*, 1–2; and Veeraraghaven, Martin, Burnett, Skinner, Jama, Ramsey, Williams, and Stothart, "Paying for Nutrition: A Report on Food Costing in the North," 4.

4   Interview with community member, 24 August 2017.

5   Gillon (Ngati Awa), "Fat Indigenous Bodies and Body Sovereignty: An Exploration of Re-Presentation"; Mitchinson, *Fighting Fat Canada, 1920–1980*, 45–46.

6   Food sovereignty includes governance over all elements of food systems from production, distribution, cultural knowledge and practices, to the environment. Settee and Shukla, "Introduction," in *Indigenous Food Systems: Concepts, Cases, and Conversations*, 4; and Ray et al., "Examining Indigenous Food Sovereignty," 54–63.

7   Aboriginal Affairs and Northern Development Canada, *The Story of Food Mail*, 2007.

8   We use the term Turtle Island because it is consistent with the nomenclature of the Anishinaabe communities of present-day northwestern Ontario where much of our writing and research took place.

9   Polzer and Power, "Introduction: The Governance of Health in Neoliberal Societies," 4.

10   Coates and Morrison, "Introduction," 1–2.

11   Council of Canadian Academies, *Aboriginal Food Security in Northern Canada: An Assessment of the State of Knowledge: Expert Panel on the State of Knowledge of Food Security in Northern Canada*, 66-67.

12   Nutrition North Canada, "Cost of the Revised Northern Food Basket in 2017–2018"; Leblanc-Laurendeau, *Food Insecurity in Northern Canada: An Overview*, 1–2; and Veeraraghaven et al., "Paying For Nutrition," 4.

13   Garfield, "Food Prices are Insanely High in Rural Canada Where Ketchup Costs $14 and Sunny D Costs $29"; see also Hiebert and Power, "Heroes for the Helpless: A

Critical Discourse Analysis of Canadian National Print Media's Coverage of the Food Insecurity Crises in Nunavut," 120.

14 In 2017–2018, 1/8 households in Canada were food insecure. Proof, "Understanding Household Food Insecurity." This picture looks very different among people living in northern Canada who are Indigenous. For instance, First Nations communities identified as remote (no year-round road access to a service centre and accessible by air for the majority of the year) the rate is 58 percent and in Inuit communities located in the Far North rates of food insecurity are as high as 57 percent. Leblanc-Laurendeau, *Food Insecurity in Northern Canada: An Overview*, 1–2.

15 UN Human Rights Council, "Report of the Special Rapporteur on the Right to Food," 16.

16 Leblanc-Laurendeau, *Food Insecurity in Northern Canada: An Overview*, 1.

17 Jyoti, Frongillo, and Jones, "Food Insecurity Affects School Children's Academic Performance, Weight Gain, and Social Skills," 2831–39; Yangbo et al., "Food Insecurity Is Associated with Cardiovascular and All-Cause Mortality Among Adults in the United States"; Kirkpatrick, McIntyre, and Potestio, "Child Hunger and Long-term Adverse Consequences for Health," 754–62; and Pourmotabbed et al., "Food Insecurity and Mental Health: A Systemic Review and Meta-Analysis."

18 Martin, "The Nutrition Transition and the Public Health Crisis: Aboriginal Peoples on Food and Eating"; Power, "Conceptualizing Food Security for Aboriginal People in Canada," 95–97; and Tobias and Richmond, "That Land Means Everything to Us as Anishinaabe…," 26–33.

19 Settee and Shukla, "Introduction," 4; and Ray et al., "Examining Indigenous Food Sovereignty."

20 Daigle, "Tracing the Terrain of Indigenous Food Sovereignties," 301.

21 Carey and Silverstein, "Thinking with and Beyond Settler Colonial Studies: New Histories after the Postcolonial," 1.

22 Wolfe, "Settler Colonialism and the Elimination of the Native."

23 Wolfe, "Settler Colonialism and the Elimination of the Native."

24 Wolfe, "Settler Colonialism and the Elimination of the Native," 388.

25 Wolfe, "Settler Colonialism and the Elimination of the Native," 388.

26 Moreton-Robinson, *The White Possessive: Property, Power, and Indigenous Sovereignty*, 17.

27 Veracini, *Settler Colonialism: A Theoretical Overview*, 38 and 44.

28 Daigle, "Tracing the Terrain of Indigenous Food Sovereignties," 302.

29 Simpson, "Whither Settler Colonialism," 439. See also Coulthard, *Red Skin, White Masks: Rejecting the Colonial Politics of Recognition*.

30 Morrison, "Indigenous Food Sovereignty: A Model for Social Learning," 100.

31 Veracini, "The Predicaments of Settler Gastrocolonialism," 247–48.

32 Pasternak, "The Fiscal Body of Sovereignty: To 'Make Live' in Indian Country." See also Gettler, *Colonialism's Currency: Money, State and First Nations in Canada, 1820–1950*.

33 Belcourt, "Meditations on Reserve Life," 8.

34 Rose, O'Malley, and Valverde, "Governmentality," 87.

35 See McKay, "The Liberal Order Framework: A Prospectus for a Reconnaissance of Canadian History."

36 Crosby and Monaghan, "Settler Governmentality in Canada and the Algonquins of Barriere Lake," 423.

37 Crosby and Monaghan, "Settler Governmentality in Canada and the Algonquins of Barriere Lake," 423.

38 Biltekoff, *Eating Right in America: The Cultural Politics of Food and Health*, 4.

39 Moreton-Robinson, *The White Possessive: Property, Power, and Indigenous Sovereignty*.

40 Bhabha, *The Location of Culture*, 127–31.

41 Squadrito, "Locke and the Dispossession of the American Indian."

42 Mayes, *Unsettling Food Politics: Agriculture, Dispossession and Sovereignty in Australia*. For a useful example of this kind of work in an Australian context, see Besson, "Confronting Whiteness and Decolonising Global Health Institutions," 2328–29; finally, see Lyons et al., "Nano White Food and the Reproduction of Whiteness."

43 Bonds and Inwood, "Beyond White Privilege: Geographies of White Supremacy and Settler Colonialism," 720. Moreton-Robinson, *The White Possessive: Property, Power, and Indigenous Sovereignty*. Moreton-Robinson uses white possessive logics to describe "a mode of rationalization, rather than a set of positions to reproduce and reaffirm the nation state's ownership control, and domination."

44 Carter, *Capturing Women: The Manipulation of Cultural Imagery in Canada's Prairie West*; Daschuk, *Clearing the Plains: Disease, Politics of Starvation, and the Loss of Aboriginal Life*; and Shewell, *"Enough to Keep Them Alive": Indian Welfare in Canada, 1873–1965*.

45 Mosby, *Food Will Win the War: The Politics, Culture, and Science of Food on Canada's Home Front*, 9.

46 Walters, "A History of Food and Nutrition in Indigenous Communities in Canada, 1962–1985," 52.

47 See, for example, Carter, *Capturing Women: The Manipulation of Cultural Imagery in Canada's Prairie West*; Jacobs, *White Mother to a Dark Race: Settler Colonialism, Maternalism, and the Removal of Indigenous Children in the American West and Australia, 1880–1940*; Raibon, "Living on Display: Colonial Visions of Aboriginal Domestic Spaces"; Rutherdale, *Women and the White Man's God: Gender and Race in the Canadian Mission Field*; Pickles and Rutherdale, eds., *Contact Zones: Aboriginal and Settler Women in Canada's Colonial Past*; Lake, *Progressive New World: How Settler Colonialism and Transpacific Exchange Shaped American Reform*; Haskins, "Domesticating Colonizers: Domesticity, Indigenous Domestic Labor, and the Modern Settler Colonial Nation"; Emmerich, "'Save the Babies!' American Indian Women, Assimilation Policy, and Scientific Motherhood, 1912–1918"; and Simonsen, *Making Home Work: Domesticity and Native American Assimilation in the American West, 1860–1919*.

48 Bohaker and Iacovetta, "Making Aboriginal People Immigrants Too."

49 Iacovetta, Korinek, and Epp, "Introduction," 12.

50 Walters, "'A National Priority': Nutrition Canada's Survey and the Disciplining of Aboriginal Bodies, 1964–1975," 433.

51 Mosby, "Administering Colonial Science," 171.

52 Hackett, Abonyi, and Dyck, "Anthropometric Indices of First Nations Children and Youth on First Entry to Manitoba/Saskatchewan Residential Schools—1919 to 1953."

53 Mosby and Galloway, "'Hunger Was Never Absent': How Residential School Diets Shaped Current Patterns of Diabetes among Indigenous Peoples in Canada," E1043–45.

54 Marcus, *Relocating Eden: The Image and Politics of Inuit Exile in the Canadian Arctic.*

55 Kulchyski and Tester, *Kiumajut (Talking Back): Game Management and Inuit Rights, 1900–70.*

56 Perry, *Aqueducts: Colonialism, Resources, and the Histories We Remember.*

57 Whitney et al., "'Like the Plains People Losing the Buffalo.'"

58 Davies, *Late Victorian Holocausts: El Niño Famines and the Making of the Third World.*

59 Martin, "The Nutrition Transition and the Public Health Crisis: Aboriginal Peoples on Food and Eating."

60 Smith, *Decolonizing Methodologies: Research and Indigenous Peoples*; Wilson, *Research Is Ceremony: Indigenous Research Methods*; Doerfler, Sinclair, and Stark, "Bagijige: Making an Offering," i–vi.

61 Adams et al., *Ceremony at a Boundary Fire: A Story of Indigenist Knowledge*, 17, 24.

62 Wilson and Hughes, "Why Research is Reconciliation," 13.

63 Notable exceptions here include Mary Jane Logan McCallum, Adele Perry, and Brittany Luby.

64 Fraser, "Politics and Personal Experiences: An Editor's Introduction to Indigenous Research in Canada."

65 Gaudry, "Insurgent Research," 132.

66 Simpson, *Mohawk Interruptus: Political Life Across the Borders of Settler States.*

67 The student did not complete their thesis.

68 Mattes, "Wahkootowin, Beading, and Metis Kitchen Table Talks: Indigenous Knowledge and Strategies for Curating Care."

69 Richards, *The Imperial Archive: Knowledge and the Fantasy of Empire*, 6.

70 Stoler, "Colonial Archives and the Arts of Governance," 87.

71 Tuck, "Suspending Damage: A Letter to Communities," 412–13.

72 Proposed in 1993 by Barry Popkin, the nutrition transition refers to rapid shifts that take place in the diets of populations that have experienced growing rates of overweight, obesity, and related chronic disease as a result of increased consumption of "unhealthy" foods. Popkin, Adair, and Ng, "Global Nutrition Transition and the Pandemic of Obesity in Developing Countries," 3–21.

73 Martin, "Nutrition Transition and the Public-Health Crisis: Aboriginal Perspectives on Food and Eating," 209–10.

74 Hiebert and Power, "Heroes for the Helpless: A Critical Discourse Analysis of Canadian National Print Media's Coverage of the Food Insecurity Crises in Nunavut," 120.

75 For example, see Reimer, "Modern-Day Monopoly? North West Company Responds."

76 Reimer, "Modern-Day Monopoly? North West Company Responds."

77 Millington et al., "'Calling out' Corporate Redwashing: The Extractives Industry, Corporate Social Responsibility and Sport for Development in Indigenous Communities in Canada."

Chapter 1: Settler Colonialism and Indigenous Food Sovereignty

1   Morrison, "Indigenous Food Sovereignty: A Model for Social Learning," 97–98.

2   Morrison, "Indigenous Food Sovereignty: A Model for Social Learning," 100.

3   Barker, *Making and Breaking Settler Space: Five Centuries of Colonization in North America*, 12.

4   Veracini, "The Predicaments of Settler Gastrocolonialism," 247–48.

5   Paul, *We Were Not the Savages*.

6   Canada, Treaty Texts – *1752 Peace and Friendship Treaty*, transcribed from R. Simon, 1985; https://www.rcaanc-cirnac.gc.ca/eng/1100100029040/1581293867988.

7   Canada, Treaty Texts – *1752 Peace and Friendship Treaty*, transcribed from R. Simon, 1985; https://www.rcaanc-cirnac.gc.ca/eng/1100100029040/1581293867988.

8   Quoted in Coates, "Reclaiming History Through the Courts: Aboriginal Rights, the *Marshall* Decision, and Maritime History," 318.

9   McMillan, *Truth and Conviction: Donald Marshall Jr. and the Mi'kmaw Quest for Justice*.

10 Parenteau, "'Care, Control, and Supervision': Native People in the Atlantic Salmon Fishery, 1867–1900," 6.

11 Government of Canada, *Treaty Texts – 1850 Robinson Huron-Superior Treaties*, https://www.rcaanc-cirnac.gc.ca/eng/1100100028984/1581293724401?wbdisable=true.

12 Quoted in Parent, "The Indians Would Be Better Off if They Tended to Their Farms Instead of Dabbling in Fisheries," 348.

13 Canada, *Treaty Texts – Treaty No. 3*, https://www.rcaanc-cirnac.gc.ca/eng/1100100028675/1581294028469.

14 Canada, *Treaty Texts – Treaty No. 5*; https://www.rcaanc-cirnac.gc.ca/eng/1100100028699/1581292696320.

15 See Getty and Lussier, eds., *As Long as the Sun Shines and the Rivers Flow: A Reader in Canadian Native Studies*.

16 Quoted in Carter, Hildebrandt, First Rider, and Treaty 7 Elders, *The True Spirit and Original Intent of Treaty 7*, 71.

17 Daschuk, *Clearing the Plains: Disease, Politics of Starvation, and the Loss of Aboriginal Life*.

18 Harring, "'There Seems to Be No Recognized Law,'" 111.

19 Quoted in Harring, "'There Seems to Be No Recognized Law,'" 111.

20 Harring, *White Man's Law: Native People in Nineteenth-Century Canadian Jurisprudence*, 277.

21 Loo, *States of Nature: Conserving Canada's Wildlife in the Twentieth Century*, 15.

22 Tough, "'Powerless to Protect,'" 262–63.

23 Tough, "'Powerless to Protect,'" 262–63.

24 Tough, "'Powerless to Protect,'" 264.

25 Calverley, *Who Controls the Hunt?: First Nations, Treaty Rights, and Wildlife Conservation in Ontario, 1783–1939*, 40.

26 Kerr, *Fish and Fisheries Management in Ontario: A Chronology of Events. Biodiversity Branch*, 21.

27 Kerr, *Fish and Fisheries Management in Ontario: A Chronology of Events. Biodiversity Branch*, 23.

28   Kerr, *Fish and Fisheries Management in Ontario: A Chronology of Events. Biodiversity Branch*, 23.

29   Kerr, *Fish and Fisheries Management in Ontario: A Chronology of Events. Biodiversity Branch*, 23.

30   Kerr, *Fish and Fisheries Management in Ontario: A Chronology of Events. Biodiversity Branch*, 23–24.

31   Kerr, *Fish and Fisheries Management in Ontario: A Chronology of Events. Biodiversity Branch*, 23–24.

32   Kulchyski and Tester, *Kiumajut (Talking Back): Game Management and Inuit Rights, 1900–70*, 27.

33   Piper, "Industrial Fisheries and the Health of Local Communities in the Twentieth-Century Canadian Northwest," 334.

34   Piper, "Industrial Fisheries and the Health of Local Communities in the Twentieth-Century Canadian Northwest," 334.

35   Quoted in Iceton, "'Many Families of Unseen Indians': Trapline Registration and Understandings of Aboriginal Title in the BC-Yukon Borderlands," 165.

36   Ray, "Periodic Shortages, Native Welfare, and the Hudson's Bay Company, 1670–1930."

37   Quoted in Iceton, "'Many Families of Unseen Indians,'" 165.

38   Marchildon, "The Prairie Farm Rehabilitation Administration." Also, see Gray, *Men Against the Desert*.

39   Quoted in Tough, "The Forgotten Constitution."

40   Iceton, "'Many Families of Unseen Indians,'" 165.

41   Iceton, "'Many Families of Unseen Indians,'" 165.

42   Vogt, "'Indians on White Lines,'" 164–65.

43   Loo, *States of Nature: Conserving Canada's Wildlife in the Twentieth Century*, 24.

Chapter 2: Constructing Dependency

1   Simmons, "Custodians of a Great Inheritance," 8–9.

2   Tester and Kulchyski, *Tammarniit (Mistakes): Inuit Relocation in the Eastern Arctic, 1939–63*. The federal government provided the HBC with the funds for annuity payments and reimbursed monies spent on relief and medical services.

3   Tough, "Aboriginal Rights Versus the Deed of Surrender," 229.

4   Tough, "Aboriginal Rights Versus the Deed of Surrender," 229.

5   Hudson's Bay Company History Foundation, "Timeline: From 1673 to 1684, HBC Builds Trading Posts as the Company Expands Along the Hudson and James Bay Routes," 2015; available online, see http://www.hbcheritage.ca/content/timeline.

6   Hudson's Bay Company History Foundation, "Timeline: From 1673 to 1684, HBC Builds Trading Posts as the Company Expands Along the Hudson and James Bay Routes," 2015; available online, see http://www.hbcheritage.ca/content/timeline.

7   *The Other Side of the Ledger: An Indian View of the Hudson's Bay Company*, directed by Martin Defalco and Willie Dunn (NFB, 1972), DVD. See also Ray, *Indians in the Fur Trade*, 61–65.

8   Brown, *Strangers in Blood: Fur Trade Company Families in Indian Country*, 52–57.

9   See Ray, *Indians in the Fur Trade*.

10 See Podruchny and Peers, eds., *Gathering Places: Aboriginal and Fur Trade Histories*; White, *The Middle Ground: Indians, Empires, and Republics in the Great Lakes Region, 1650–1815*; Van Kirk, *Many Tender Ties: Women in Fur-Trade Society, 1670–1870*.

11 Vibert, *Traders' Tales: Narratives of Cultural Encounters in the Columbia Plateau*.

12 Shewell, *"Enough to Keep Them Alive": Indian Welfare in Canada, 1873–1965*, 33–34.

13 The Pemmican Proclamation was a decree issued by the Governor of the Red River Colony, Miles Macdonell, outlawing the export of pemmican and other provisions from Red River. The decree was regarded by Métis traders as an attack on their independence and sovereignty.

14 Quoted in Innis, *The Fur Trade in Canada: An Introduction to Canadian Economic History*, 291.

15 Shewell, *"Enough to Keep Them Alive": Indian Welfare in Canada, 1873–1965*, 35.

16 Arthur Ray quoted in Shewell, *"Enough to Keep Them Alive": Indian Welfare in Canada, 1873–1965*, 35.

17 LeBlanc and Burnett, "What Happened to Indigenous Food Sovereignty in Northern Ontario?," 21.

18 *The Other Side of the Ledger: An Indian View of the Hudson's Bay Company*, directed by Martin Defalco and Willie Dunn (NFB, 1972), DVD.

19 Spraakman, "The First External Auditors of the Hudson's Bay Company, 1866," 60.

20 Oleson, "The Past Hundred Years."

21 Tough, "Aboriginal Rights Versus the Deed of Surrender," 225.

22 Hudson's Bay Company Archives, Provincial Archives of Manitoba, MBGC, 1871, A 2/18, 16, cited in Ray, *The Canadian Fur Trade in the Industrial Age*, 5.

23 Ray, *The Canadian Fur Trade in the Industrial Age*, 39.

24 HBCA, RG3/ 74 A/2 Ungava District Correspondence 1949–50, letter from J.W. Anderson, Indian Affairs, to Post Manager at Fort Chimo, dated 24 November 1949.

25 HBCA, RG3/ 74 A/2 Ungava District Correspondence 1949–50, Letter to R.A. Gibson, Deputy Commissioner, Administration of NWT from R.H. Chesshire, General Manager, Fur Trade Department, dated 16 November 1949. HBCA, RG3/ 74 A/2 Ungava District Correspondence 1949–50, letter from J.W. Anderson to the Manager at Fort Chimo at Frobisher Bay, dated 3 November 1949. HBCA, RG3/ 74 A/2 Ungava District Correspondence 1949–50, letter from J.W. Anderson, Indian Affairs, to Post Manager at Fort Chimo, dated 24 November 1949.

26 Ray, *The Canadian Fur Trade in the Industrial Age*, 210.

27 Ray, *The Canadian Fur Trade in the Industrial Age*, 210.

28 Ray, *The Canadian Fur Trade in the Industrial Age*, 40.

29 For example, see Craig, *Backwoods Consumers and Homespun Capitalists: The Rise of a Market Culture in Eastern Canada*.

30 LAC, RG10, Vol. 4094, File 600552, "Distribution of Sick and Destitute Funds," 1913.

31 Shewell, "Dreaming in Liberal White: Canadian Indian Policy, 1913–2013," 187.

32 High, "Responding to White Encroachment," 26.

33 See Ray, *The Canadian Fur Trade in the Industrial Age*, 199.

34 Hudson's Bay Company History Foundation, "HBC Heritage Timeline: 1907"; available online, see: http://hbcheritage.ca/content/timeline.

35 This will be of extreme relevance later in this chapter when we discuss the NWC's acquisition of food economies in Indigenous communities located outside of Canada.

36 Hudson's Bay Company History Foundation, "HBC Heritage Timeline: 1910"; available online, see: http://hbcheritage.ca/content/timeline.

37 Binnema, *Enlightened Zeal: The Hudson's Bay Company and Scientific Networks, 1670–1870.*

38 HBCA, A.95/58, Development Dept, Native Welfare, "Instructions on Native Welfare," June 1928, 1.

39 HBCA, A.95/58, Development Dept, Native Welfare, "Instructions on Native Welfare," June 1928, 1.

40 HBCA, A.95/58, Development Dept, Native Welfare, "Instructions on Native Welfare," June 1928, 5.

41 Carstairs, Philpott, and Wilmhurst, *Be Wise! Be Healthy!: Morality and Citizenship in Canadian Public Health Campaigns,* 65–66.

42 McLaren, *Our Own Master Race: Eugenics in Canada, 1885–1945,* 30.

43 MacMurchy, *Canadians Need Milk* (Ottawa: Dominion of Canada, 1921) cited in Carstairs, Philpott, and Wilmhurst, *Be Wise! Be Healthy!: Morality and Citizenship in Canadian Public Health Campaigns,* 65.

44 Valverde, *The Age of Light, Soap, and Water: Moral Reform in English Canada, 1885–1925,* 23; Ware, *Beyond the Pale: White Women, Racism, and History*; and Rutherdale, "Cleansers, Cautious Caregivers, and Optimistic Adventurers."

45 Ostry, *Nutrition Policy in Canada, 1870–1939,* 48.

46 Comacchio, *"Nations are Built of Babies": Saving Ontario's Mothers and Children, 1900–1940.*

47 HBCA, A.95/58, Development Dept, Native Welfare, "Instructions on Native Welfare," June 1928, 7–8.

48 HBCA, A.95/58, Development Dept, Native Welfare, "Instructions on Native Welfare," June 1928, 5.

49 HBCA, A.95/53, Northern Stores Department, Development Dossier, Native Welfare, "Report of Medical Service to Indians Located Along the Line of the Canadian National Railways from Cochrane, Ont., to LA Tuque, Que.," June to October 1926, 2–3.

50 HBCA, RG 7/1/1762, Northern Stores Department, Native Welfare, Nutrition Survey, letter from R.H.G. Bonnycastle, Fur Trade Department, to Percy Moore, Acting Superintendent of Medical Services, Dept of Mines and Resources, Indian Affairs Branch, dated 17 August 1943.

51 HBCA, RG 7/1/1762, Northern Stores Department, Native Welfare, Nutrition Survey, Memo from R.H. Chesshire, Fur Trade Department, re "Fortifying Flour for Indians," dated 4 August 1943.

52 HBCA, RG 7/1/1762, Northern Stores Department, Native Welfare, Nutrition Survey, Memo from R.H. Chesshire, Fur Trade Department, re "Fortifying Flour for Indians," dated 4 August 1943.

53 Mosby, *Food Will Win the War: The Politics, Culture, and Science of Food on Canada's Home Front,* 36.

54 HBCA, RG3/ 74 A/2 Ungava District Correspondence 1949–50, Annual Report from Cape Dorset Post (Outfit 269) to District Manager, HBC, dated 31 May 1939.

Chapter 3: "Making Proper Use"

1 Children under the age of five received $5; children between the ages of 6 and 9 received $6; $7 for children between 10 and 12 years of age; and $8 for children between 13 and 15 years. The average payment was $5.94. Guest, "Family Allowance."

2 Milligan, "Finances of the Nation: The Tax Recognition of Children in Canada: Exemptions, Credits, and Cash Transfers," 606.

3 Mosby, *Food Will Win the War: The Politics, Culture and Science of Food on Canada's Home Front*, 162–63.

4 Marshall, *The Social Origins of the Welfare State: Quebec Families, Compulsory Education, and Family Allowances, 1940–1955*, x.

5 See also Blake, *From Rights to Needs: A History of the Family Allowances in Canada, 1929–92*.

6 Adams, *The Trouble with Normal: Postwar Youth and the Making of Heterosexuality*, 20. See also Parr, *The Gender of Breadwinners: Women, Men and Change in Two Industrial Towns, 1880–1950*.

7 McNab, "From the Bush to the Village to the City," 139.

8 Carter, *Ours by Every Law of Right and Justice: Women and the Vote in the Prairie Provinces*, 17.

9 Perry, *On the Edge of Empire: Gender, Race, and the Making of British Columbia, 1849–1871*, 19.

10 Marshall, *The Social Origins of the Welfare State: Quebec Families, Compulsory Education, and Family Allowances, 1940–1955*, 63–66.

11 Marshall, *The Social Origins of the Welfare State: Quebec Families, Compulsory Education, and Family Allowances, 1940–1955*, 63–66.

12 Shewell, *"Enough to Keep Them Alive": Indian Welfare in Canada, 1873–1965*.

13 Quoted in Marshall, *The Social Origins of the Welfare State: Quebec Families, Compulsory Education, and Family Allowances, 1940–1955*, 77.

14 LAC, RG 10, Indian and Northern Affairs, Family Allowances and Mother's Allowances, Indians and Eskimos, file no. 6-38-45 letter to W.C Bethune, Administrative Office, Dept of Citizenship and Immigration from H.M. Jones, dated December 1950.

15 Canada, *Special Joint Committee of the Senate and the House of Commons* (Ottawa: King's Printer, 1947), 1923.

16 LAC, RG10, Indian and Northern Affairs, Family Allowances and Mother's Allowances, Indians and Eskimos, file no. 6-38-4 letter to W.C. Bethune, Administrative Office, Dept of Citizenship and Immigration from H.M. Jones, Superintendent – Welfare Service, dated 5 December 1950.

17 Canada, *Special Joint Committee of the Senate and House of Commons* (Ottawa: King's Printer, 1947), 354–55.

18 LAC, RG 10, Indian and Northern Affairs, Family Allowances, Indians and Eskimos, file no. 6-38-4 letter to W.C. Bethune, Administrative Office, Dept of Citizenship and Immigration, dated 5 December 1950.

19 Ostry, *Nutrition Policy in Canada, 1870–1939*, 67.

20 Mosby, "Administering Colonial Science," 152.

21 LAC RG 10, 13/29-8 volume 1, Family Allowances General, Family Allowance Directive to all Indian Affairs Field Agents, dated 1 January 1950; and Mark Palmer,

Family Allowances in Canada: The Origins and Implementation (Trafford Publishing: 2013), 157–70.

22 LAC RG 10, file 13/29-8 volume 3, Family Allowances Generally, November 1954 to March 1957. Family Allowances Division Circular sent to all Regional Supervisors, Superintendents of Indian Agencies, dated 25 March 1959. Circular #108, pages 1–2.

23 LAC RG 10, file 13/29-8 volume 3, Family Allowances Generally: November 1954 to March 1957. Family Allowances Division, Letter from Fred C. Jackson, Regional Director Family Allowance, to J.T. O'Neil, Indian Superintendent of the Sault Ste Marie Indian Agency, dated 2 June 1958.

24 LAC RG 10, file 13/29-8 volume 3, Family Allowances Generally: November 1954 to March 1957. Family Allowances Division, letter from Fred C. Jackson, Regional Director of Family Allowances, to J.T. O'Neill, Superintendent of Sault Ste Marie Indian Agency, dated 11 June 1958.

25 LAC, RG 10, Indian and Northern Affairs, Family Allowances and Mother's Allowances, Indians and Eskimos, file no. 6-38-4, letter from C.M. Isbister, deputy minister IA, to Dr. J.W. Willard, Deputy Minister of Welfare, dated 17 August 1964.

26 LAC RG 10, file 493/29-8, Family Allowance, January 1961 to June 1977, Memorandum from G.S. Lapp, Regional Director Family Allowances Division, to Superintendents, Northern Ontario region, dated 8 September 1965.

27 LAC, RG 10, Indian and Northern Affairs, Family Allowances and Mother's Allowances, Indians and Eskimos, file no. 6-38-4, Letter from R.F. Battle, Assistant Deputy Minister IA, to David Orlikow, MP house of commons, dated 6 July 1967.

28 LAC, RG 10, Indian and Northern Affairs, Family Allowances and Mother's Allowances, Indians and Eskimos, file no. 6-38-4, Letter from R.F. Battle, Assistant Deputy Minister IA, to David Orlikow, MP house of commons, dated 6 July 1967.

29 LAC, RG10, Indian and Northern Affairs, Family Allowances and Mother's Allowances, Indians and Eskimos, file no. 6-38-4, Memorandum from H.M. Jones, dated 10 March 1960.

30 LAC, RG10, Indian and Northern Affairs, Family Allowances and Mother's Allowances, Indians and Eskimos, file no. 6-38-4, Memorandum from H.M. Jones, dated March 10, 1960,

31 Canada, Department of Mines and Resources, *Annual Report of Indian Affairs Branch for the Fiscal Year Ending March 31, 1947*, 224–26.

32 Canada, *Special Joint Committee of the Senate and the House of Commons* (Ottawa: King's Printer, 1946), 397; Canada, Department of Mines and Resources, *Annual Report of Indian Affairs Branch for the Fiscal Year Ending March 31, 1947*, 224–26.

33 Canada, *Special Joint Committee of the Senate and the House of Commons*, (Ottawa: King's Printer, 1946), 397.

34 LAC RG 10, 13/29-8 volume 1, Family Allowances Generally, Family Allowance Registration Form, Dept of National Health and Welfare, n.d. p. 2. McNab, "From the Bush to the Village to the City," 139.

35 HBCA, RG 7/IA/11, Native Welfare, Correspondence and Reports, 1954–55, RCMP memo re conditions at Pukatawagan, MB, dated July 1954.

36 HBCA, RG 7/IA/11, Native Welfare, Correspondence and Reports, 1954–55, RCMP memo re conditions at Pukatawagan, MB, dated July 1954.

37 HBCA, RG 7/IA/11, Native Welfare, Correspondence and Reports, 1954–55, RCMP memo re conditions at Pukatawagan, MB, dated July 1954.

38 HBCA, RG 7/IA/11, Native Welfare, Correspondence and Reports, 1954–55, RCMP memo re conditions at Pukatawagan, MB, dated July 1954.

39 LAC RG 10, 13/29-8 volume 1, Family Allowances Generally, Letter from H.M. Jones, Supervisor – Family Allowances to all Indian Superintendents, Regional Supervisors of Indian Agents, and the Indian Commissioner Re: Payment of Family Allowances in Kind (Category 'D'), dated 26 January 1949.

40 LAC RG 10, 13/29-8 volume 1, Family Allowances Generally, Letter from H.M. Jones, Supervisor – Family Allowances to all Indian Superintendents, Regional Supervisors of Indian Agents, and the Indian Commissioner Re: Payment of Family Allowances in Kind (Category 'D'), dated 26 January 1949.

41 Carstairs, Philpott, and Wilmhurst, *Be Wise! Be Healthy! Mortality and Citizenship in Canadian Public Health Campaigns*, 123–24.

42 Mosby, "Making and Breaking Canada's Food Rules: Science, the State and the Government of Nutrition, 1942–1949," 410.

43 Wolfe, "Settler Colonialism and the Elimination of the Native."

44 Dawson, "'Food Will Be What Brings the People Together.'"

45 Cornellier, "The 'Indian Thing.'"

46 Wolfe, "Settler Colonialism and the Elimination of the Native," 388.

47 Canada, *Special Joint Committee of the Senate and House of Commons* (Ottawa: King's Printer, 1947), 270. Tisdall also served as a nutrition consultant for the medical branch of the Royal Canadian Air Force.

48 Iacovetta and Korinek, "Jell-O Salads, One-Stop Shopping, and Maria the Homemaker."

49 See Gunn Allen, *The Sacred Hoop;* and Maracle, *I Am Woman: A Native Perspective on Sociology and Feminism.*

50 LAC RG 10, file 493/29-8, Family Allowance, January 1961 to June 1977, letter from A.R. Aquin, Superintendent Sault Ste Marie Agency, to W.F. Hendershot, Regional Director of Family Allowances, dated 29 March 1963; Provincial Archives of Ontario RG 10 file 72/605 vol. 8195. Letter from W.S. Doherty, Regional Welfare Administrator, to unidentified client, dated 13 January 1960.

51 Isaki, "HB 645, Settler Sexuality, and the Politics of Local Asian Domesticity in Hawai'i," 83–84.

52 Isaki, "HB 645, Settler Sexuality, and the Politics of Local Asian Domesticity in Hawai'i," 83–84.

53 LAC, RG 29, Vol. 973, File 388-6-1, "Indian affairs list of special food and clothing, family allowances Act," 27 October 1945. See also: Mosby, "Administering Colonial Science," 156.

54 LAC, DIAND, Deputy Ministers Office, RB 22-1-a volume 845, file 6-38-4 part 2. Family Allowances and Mother's Allowance Indian and Eskimo, Circular Letter, "Combined List of Food and Authorized Goods for Issues under Family Allowances," dated 12 May 1945.

55 LAC, RG 10, Deputy Ministers Office, RB 22-1-a volume 845, file 6-38-4 part 2. Family Allowances and Mother's Allowance Indian and Eskimo, Circular Letter, "Combined List of Food and Authorized for Issues under Family Allowances," dated 12 May 1945.

56 LAC, RG 10, Deputy Ministers Office, RB 22-1-a volume 845, file 6-38-4 part 2. Family Allowances and Mother's Allowance Indian and Eskimo, Circular Letter,

"Combined List of Food and Authorized for Issues under Family Allowances," dated 12 May 1945.

57 LAC, RG10, Deputy Ministers Office, RB 22-1-a volume 845, file 6-38-4 part 2. Family Allowances and Mother's Allowance Indian and Eskimo, Circular Letter, "Combined List of Food and Authorized for Issues under Family Allowances," dated 12 May 1945.

58 LAC, RG29, file 2989, part 1 - Directions for Feeding Indian Babies, Notice entitled "To All Mothers with Small Children," dated 2 April 1947.

59 Mosby, "Administering Colonial Science."

60 HBCA, Northern Stores Department (NSD), Native Welfare, RG 7 box 1, file 1764, letter from General Manager, HBC, to Dr. Percy Moore, dated 1955.

61 HBCA, Northern Stores Department (NSD), Native Welfare, RG 7 box 1, file 1764, letter from General Manager, HBC, to Dr. Percy Moore, dated 1955.

62 Theobald, *Reproduction on the Reservation: Pregnancy, Childbirth, and Colonialism in the Long Twentieth Century*, 49–52. See also Bartlett, "Black Breasts, White Milk? Ways of Constructing Breastfeeding and Race in Australia."

63 Stoler, "State Racism and the Education of Desires: A Colonial Reading of Foucault," 4.

64 Cidro et al., "Breast Feeding Practices as Cultural Interventions for Early Childhood Caries in Cree Communities."

65 LAC, RG29, file 2989, part 1 - Directions for feeding Indian babies, Letter from H.W. Lewis Regional Superintendent for the Eastern Arctic to R.A. Gibson Deputy Commissioner, NWT, dated 28 March 1947.

66 Mosby, "Administering Colonial Science," 156.

67 Tester and Kulchyski, *Taamarniit (Mistakes): Inuit Relocation in the Eastern Arctic*, 69.

68 Harris, "An Archival Administrative History of the Northern Stores Department, Hudson's Bay Company, 1959–1987," 5.

69 Cidro et al., "Breast Feeding Practices as Cultural Interventions for Early Childhood Caries in Cree Communities."

70 Cidro et al., "Breast Feeding Practices as Cultural Interventions for Early Childhood Caries in Cree Communities."

71 LAC, RG29, file 2989, part 1 - Directions for Feeding Indian Babies, letter from L. Black, Director General Program Management, to Dr. C.A. Bently, Regional Director Saskatchewan Region, dated 3 November 1977. See also Cidro et al., "Breast Feeding Practices as Cultural Interventions for Early Childhood Caries in Cree Communities."

72 LAC RG 10, file 493/29-8, Family Allowance, January 1961 to June 1977, Letter from E.R. Bourdon, Assistant Regional Director, Community Affairs, Ontario to District Supervisor Sault Ste Marie, dated 6 May 1974.

73 LAC RG 10, file 493/29-8, Family Allowance, January 1961 to June 1977, Telex from E.R. Bourdon, Assistant Regional Director, Community Affairs Ontario Region, to District Supervisors, dated 27 December 1974.

Chapter 4: "Left at the Trader's Mercy"

1   Belisle, *Retail Nation: Department Stores and the Making of Modern Canada*, 20.

2   Belisle, *Retail Nation: Department Stores and the Making of Modern Canada*, 4.

3   Belisle, *Retail Nation: Department Stores and the Making of Modern Canada*, 236.

4   "H.B.C. Helped Settlers Remain on Land During the Lean Years," *The Beaver* (February 1920): 20. Cited in Belisle, *Retail Nation: Department Stores and the Making of Modern Canada*, 51.

5   Belisle, *Retail Nation: Department Stores and the Making of Modern Canada*, 157; see also Belisle, *Purchasing Power: Women and the Rise of Canadian Consumer Culture*.

6   Belisle, *Purchasing Power: Women and the Rise of Canadian Consumer Culture*, 8.

7   Deutsch, *Building a Housewife's Paradise: Gender, Politics, and American Grocery Stores in the Twentieth Century*, 219.

8   See also: Elvins, *Sales and Celebrations: Retailing and Regional Identity in Western New York State, 1920–1940*.

9   Deutsch, *Building a Housewife's Paradise: Gender, Politics, and American Grocery Stores in the Twentieth Century*, 3.

10 Deutsch, *Building a Housewife's Paradise: Gender, Politics, and American Grocery Stores in the Twentieth Century*, 6.

11 Tester and Kulchyski, *Tammarniit (Mistakes): Inuit Relocations in the Eastern Arctic, 1939–63*; Damas, "Shifting Relations in the Administration of Inuit: The Hudson's Bay Company and the Canadian Government," 5–28.

12 Harris, "An Archival Administrative History of the Northern Stores Department, Hudson's Bay Company," 58.

13 Harris, "An Archival Administrative History of the Northern Stores Department, Hudson's Bay Company," 58.

14 Harris, "An Archival Administrative History of the Northern Stores Department, Hudson's Bay Company," 66.

15 Harris, "An Archival Administrative History of the Northern Stores Department, Hudson's Bay Company," 81.

16 Furs were sold through the Raw Fur Division in the HBC.

17 HBCA, RG7, file 1A/55 Public Relations/Native Credit, 1967, Report, dated 31 January 1967 regarding sales at inland stores.

18 Tester and Kulchyski, *Tammarniit (Mistakes): Inuit Relocations in the Eastern Arctic, 1939–63*; Damas, "Shifting Relations in the Administration of Inuit," 5–28.

19 Deutsch, *Building a Housewife's Paradise: Gender, Politics, and American Grocery Stores in the Twentieth Century*, 154, 183–84.

20 Deutsch, *Building a Housewife's Paradise: Gender, Politics, and American Grocery Stores in the Twentieth Century*, 196.

21 Iacovetta, *Gatekeepers: Reshaping Immigrant Lives in Cold War Canada*, 146–47.

22 Arctic Co-operatives Limited, "Arctic Co-ops Chronological History," https://arctic-coop.com/index.php/about-arctic-co-ops/history/chronological-history/.

23 Burnett et al., "Retail Food Environment Experiences and Purchasing Patterns in Northern Canada."

24   Deutsch, *Building a Housewife's Paradise: Gender, Politics, and American Grocery Stores in the Twentieth Century*, 6.

25   *The Other Side of the Ledger: An Indian View of the Hudson's Bay Company*, directed by Martin Defalco and Willie Dunn (NFB, 1972), DVD.

26   Opp, "Branding 'the Bay/la Baie'," 248.

27   Harris, "An Archival Administrative History of the Northern Stores Department, Hudson's Bay Company," 5. See also: *The Other Side of the Ledger: An Indian View of the Hudson's Bay Company*, directed by Martin Defalco and Willie Dunn (NFB, 1972), DVD.

28   HBCA, RG7/1A/50 Public Relations, 1966–67, Letter from J.R. Murray to Honorable Arthur Laing, Minister of Northern Affairs, dated 20 February 1967.

29   HBCA, RG7/1A/50 public relations, Economic Council of Canada Tour, 1966–67, Letter from Honorable Arthur Laing, Minister of Northern Affairs to J.R. Murray, dated 6 October 1966.

30   LAC RG 10, 13/29-8 volume 1, Family Allowances Generally, Circular issues to Indian Agents, Inspectors of Indian Agents, and the Indian Commissioner of BC from Indian Affairs Bureau, dated 12 May 1945, 1.

31   LAC RG 10, 13/29-8 volume 1, Family Allowances Generally, Circular issues to Indian Agents, Inspectors of Indian Agents, and the Indian Commissioner of BC from Indian Affairs Bureau, dated 12 May 1945, 1.

32   LAC, RG10, Indian and Northern Affairs, Family Allowances and Mother's Allowances, Indians and Eskimos, file no. 6-38-4, Letter from H.M. Jones, Acting Deputy Minister to G.F. Davidson, Deputy Minister, Dept of National Health and Welfare, dated 15 February 1960.

33   Canada, *Special Joint Committee of the Senate and House of Commons* (Ottawa: King's Printer, 1947), 270–71.

34   HBCA, RG 7/1/1764/ Northern Stores Department, Native Welfare, letter from R.H. Chesshire, General Manager, Fur Trade Department to Percy Moore, Indian Health Services, Dept of National Health and Welfare, dated 13 January 1955.

35   Canada, *Special Joint Committee of the Senate and House of Commons* (Ottawa: King's Printer, 1947), 270.

36   HBCA, RG 7/1/1760, Northern Stores Department, Native Welfare, letter from the Office of the Manager of the Western Division, Northern Stores Department to the General Manager, Winnipeg, dated 18 March 1959.

37   HBCA RG 7/1/1760, Northern Stores Department, Native Welfare, letter from H.W. Sutherland to the Manager of the Western Division, dated 23 March 1959.

38   Canada, *Special Joint Committee of the Senate and the House of Commons* (Ottawa: King's Printer, 1947), 200–1.

39   Canada, *Special Joint Committee of the Senate and the House of Commons* (Ottawa: King's Printer, 1947), 206–7.

40   HBCA, RG 7/1/1764, Northern Stores Department, Native Welfare, Letter from H.M. Jones to J. Albert Blais, National Director of Family Allowance, dated 2 November 1959.

41   HBCA, RG 7/1/1764, Northern Stores Department, Native Welfare, letter from R.H. Chesshire, GM of Fur Trade Department, to Office Manager, Western Sections, Fur Trade Department, dated 3 October 1950.

42   HBCA, RG 7/1/1764, Northern Stores Department, Native Welfare, letter from R.H. Chesshire, GM of Fur Trade Department, to D.M. MacKay, Director, Indian Affairs Branch, Dept of Citizenship and Immigration, dated 6 October 1950.

43   HBCA, RG7/1A/11, Native Welfare Correspondence and Reports, 1954–55, letter from J.P.B. Ostrander, Superintendent of Welfare IA, to R.H. Chesshire, General Manager of Fur Trade Department, HBC, dated 18 October 1955; HBCA, RG7/1A/11; HBC, letter from W.J. Cobb, Manager, Central Post Division, to J.P.B. Ostrander, Superintendent of Welfare Dept of Citizenship and Immigration, IA, dated 7 November 1955; HBCA, RG7/1A/11, Native Welfare Correspondence and Reports, 1954–55, letter from R.H. Chesshire to F.J.G. Cunningham, Director, Northern Administration and Lands Branch, Dept of Northern Affairs and National Resources, dated 10 June 1954. HBCA, RG7/1A/11, Native Welfare Correspondence and Reports, 1954–55, archives, letter from J.P.B. Ostrander, Superintendent of Welfare IA, to R.H. Chesshire, General Manager of Fur Trade Department, HBC, dated 18 October 1955.

44   HBCA, RG7/1A/11, Native Welfare Correspondence and Reports, 1954–55, letter from R.H. Chesshire to F.J.G. Cunningham, Director, Northern Administration and Lands Branch, Dept of Northern Affairs and National Resources, dated 10 June 1954.

45   HBCA, RG7/1A/11, memo from R.H. Chesshire to H.M. Jones, Director of Indian Affairs, dated 12 March 1954.

46   HBCA, RG7/1A/11, letter from S. Larson, Superintendent Officer, Commanding G Division, to the Director of Northern Administration and Lands of Dept of Northern Affairs and Natural Resources, dated 14 June 1954; letter from Chesshire to P.A.C. Nichols, dated 6 September 1954.

47   HBCA, R67/76/76, Pikangikum Leases and Documents, Oct. 1948–Sept. 1966.

48   HBCA, R67/76/116116, Attawapiskat Leases and Documents, March 1966–February 1974.

49   Roberts, "41 Below but Getting Warmer," B24.

50   HBCA, H2-273-5-2, Northern Stores Public Affairs Management Correspondence and Subject Files, Nutrition, 1977–81. Nutritionist Annual Report sent to A.R. Huband and M.E. Tiller, dated 17 March 1981.

51   Walters, "A History of Food and Nutrition in Indigenous Communities in Canada, 1962–1985," Chapter 4.

52   McCallum, *Indigenous Women, Work, and History, 1940–1980*.

53   McCallum, *Indigenous Women, Work, and History, 1940–1980*, 120.

54   HBCA, RG7, H2-273-5-2, Northern Stores Public Affairs Manager Correspondence and Subject Files, Nutrition 1977–1981, Marjorie Schurman, "Submission to O.N.E. Newsletter: Job Profile," July 1980, 1.

55   HBCA, RG7, H2-273-5-2, Northern Stores Public Affairs Manager Correspondence and Subject Files, Nutrition 1977–1981, Transcript of CBC interview with Marjorie Schurman, dated 1 December 1980.

56   HBCA, RG7, H2-273-5-2, Northern Stores Public Affairs Manager Correspondence and Subject Files, Nutrition 1977–1981, letter from Marjorie Schurman to the store managers at Tuktoyaktuk, Fort Rae, Fort Simpson, Fort Franklin, dated 12 February 1982.

57   Helen Gage, "Nutritionist Honoured for Work with Native People," *Globe and Mail* (8 April 1981): SB. 10.

58 HBCA, RG7,H2-273-5-2, Northern Stores Public Affairs Manager Correspondence and Subject Files, Nutrition 1977–1981, Marjorie Schurman, "Submission to O.N.E. Newsletter: Job Profile," July 1980, 2.

59 HBCA, RG 7, H2-273-5-2, Northern Stores Public Affairs Manager Correspondence and Subject Files, Nutrition 1977–1981, Marjorie Schurman, "Submission to O.N.E. Newsletter: Job Profile," July 1980, 2.

60 HBCA, RG 7, H2-273-5-2, Northern Stores Public Affairs Manager Correspondence and Subject Files, Nutrition 1977–1981, "News from Nukilik," Number 2, 3.

61 HBCA, RG 7, H2-273-5-2, Northern Stores Public Affairs Manager Correspondence and Subject Files, Nutrition 1977–1981, "News from Nukilik," Number 2, 6.

62 HBCA, RG 7, H2-273-5-2, Northern Stores Public Affairs Manager Correspondence and Subject Files, Nutrition 1977–1981, "News from Nukilik," Number 2, 6.

63 HBCA, RG 7, H2-273-5-2, Northern Stores Public Affairs Management Correspondence and Subject Files, Nutrition, 1977–81. News from Nukilik, Number 1 (1980), 5.

64 HBCA, RG 7, H2-273-5-2, Northern Stores Public Affairs Manager Correspondence and Subject Files, Nutrition 1977–1981, "News from Nukilik," Number 2, 3.

65 Emphasis in original.

66 HBCA, RG 7, H2-273-5-2, Northern Stores Public Affairs Manager Correspondence and Subject Files, Nutrition 1977–1981, Newsletter, "News from Nukilik," Number 1 (1980), 2.

67 Amend, "The Confused Canadian Eater: Quantification, Personal Responsibility, and Canada's Food Guide," 731.

68 HBCA, RG 7, H2-273-5-2, Northern Stores Public Affairs Manager Correspondence and Subject Files, Nutrition 1977–1981, Nutritionist Annual Report, "Statement of the Problem," n.d.

69 HBCA, RG 7, H2-273-5-2, Northern Stores Public Affairs Manager Correspondence and Subject Files, Nutrition 1977–1981, Nutritionist Annual Report, "Statement of the Problem," n.d.

70 HBCA, RG 7, H2-273-5-2, Northern Stores Public Affairs Management Correspondence and Subject Files, Nutrition, 1977–81. Nutritionist Annual Report sent to A.R. Huband and M.E. Tiller, dated 17 March 1981, 2–3.

71 HBCA, RG 7, H2-273-5-2, Northern Stores Public Affairs Management Correspondence and Subject Files, Nutrition, 1977–81. Nutritionist Annual Report sent to A.R. Huband and M.E. Tiller, dated 17 March 1981, 3.

72 HBCA, RG 7, H2-273-5-2, Northern Stores Public Affairs Management Correspondence and Subject Files, Nutrition, 1977–81. Marjorie Schurman, "Manitoba Home Economics Teachers' Association," 5 December 1980, 2.

73 HBCA, RG 7, H2-273-5-2, Northern Stores Public Affairs Manager Correspondence and Subject Files, Nutrition 1977–1981, Marjorie Schurman, "Update on Nutrition Upgrading Program," February 1978, 2.

74 Iacovetta and Korinek, "Jell-O Salads, One-Stop Shopping, and Maria the Homemaker."

75 Magee (Labelle), "'For Home and Country': Education, Activism, and Agency in Alberta Homemaker's Clubs, 1942–1970."

76　HBCA, RG 7, H2-273-5-2, Northern Stores Public Affairs Management Correspondence and Subject Files, Nutrition, 1977–81. Marjorie Schurman, "Nutrition Upgrading Program," 2.

77　HBCA, RG 7, H2-273-5-2, Northern Stores Public Affairs Manager Correspondence and Subject Files, Nutrition 1977–1981, "Abstract Nutrition Upgrading Program," n.d.

78　HBCA, RG 7, H2-273-5-2, Northern Stores Public Affairs Manager Correspondence and Subject Files, Nutrition 1977–1981, "Abstract Nutrition Upgrading Program," n.d.

79　Marcus, *Relocating Eden: The Image and Politics of Inuit Exile in the Canadian Arctic.*

80　Enstad, *Cigarettes, Inc.: An Intimate History of Corporate Imperialism*, ix.

81　Belisle, *Retail Nation: Department Stores and the Making of Modern Canada*, 107.

Chapter 5: "Preferred Perishable Foods"

1　Canada Post, "Services," https://prd11.wsl.canadapost.ca/cpc/en/support/kb/at-the-post-office/services/what-are-air-stage-offices. The Air Stage System refers to remote communities where the mail is delivered by the Post Office via air for at least six months of the year.

2　Indian and Northern Affairs Canada, *Food for the North: Report of the Air Stage Subsidy Review*, 11.

3　Thiessen, *Snacks: A Canadian Food History*, 5.

4　Walters, "A History of Food and Nutrition in Indigenous Communities in Canada, 1962–1985," 52.

5　Amend, "The Confused Canadian Eater: Quantification, Personal Responsibility, and Canada's Food Guide," 721.

6　Gillon (Ngati Awa), "Fat Indigenous Bodies and Body Sovereignty: An Exploration of Re-Presentations."

7　Canada, *Food for the North: Report of the Air Stage Subsidy Review*, 53.

8　Canada, *Food for the North: Report of the Air Stage Subsidy Review*, 11.

9　Canada, *Food for the North: Report of the Air Stage Subsidy Review*, 9.

10　Canada, *Food for the North: Report of the Air Stage Subsidy Review*, 9.

11　Canada, *Food for the North: Report of the Air Stage Subsidy Review*, 10.

12　Canada, *Food for the North: Report of the Air Stage Subsidy Review*, 10.

13　Thobani, "Closing Ranks: Racism and Sexism in Canada's Immigration Policy," 38.

14　INAC, Audit and Evaluation Branch, *Audit of the Food Mail Program*, 1.

15　INAC, Audit and Evaluation Branch, *Audit of the Food Mail Program*, 2.

16　Interview with government employee, 23 August 2013; INAC, Audit and Evaluation Branch, *Audit of the Food Mail Program*, 2.

17　Hiebert and Power, "Heroes for the Helpless."

18　DIAND, *Food Security in Northern Canada: A Discussion Paper on the Future of the Northern Air Stage Program*, 15.

19　Lawn, *Air Stage Subsidy Monitoring Program, Final Report: Food Price Survey*, 3.

20　Majid and Grier, "The Food Mail Program: 'When Pigs Fly'—Dispatching Access and Affordability to Health Food."

21　INAC, *Food for the North: Report of the Air Stage Subsidy Review*, 6.

22　Community conversation, 7 April 2012.

23 Interview with government employee, 23 August 2013; Dargo, *Food Mail Program Review: Findings and Recommendations of the Minister's Special Representative*; Boult, *Hunger in the Arctic: Food (In)Security in Inuit Communities, a Discussion Paper*, 3.

24 Community Conversation, 3 March 2013.

25 Boult, *Hunger in the Arctic: Food (In)Security in Inuit Communities, a Discussion Paper*, 17.

26 Interview with government employee, 23 August 2013.

27 Boult, *Hunger in the Arctic: Food (In)Security in Inuit Communities, a Discussion Paper*, 3.

28 Canada, *Food for the North: Report of the Air Stage Subsidy Review*, 33.

29 Canada, *Food for the North: Report of the Air Stage Subsidy Review*, 33. For more information on nutrition studies please see Walters, "A History of Food and Nutrition in Indigenous Communities in Canada, 1962–1985"; and Mosby, "Administering Colonial Science."

30 Canada, *Food for the North: Report of the Air Stage Subsidy Review*, 33.

31 Canada, *Food for the North: Report of the Air Stage Subsidy Review*, 33–34.

32 Canada, *Food for the North: Report of the Air Stage Subsidy Review*, 34.

33 INAC, *The Revised Northern Food Basket*, 1.

34 INAC, *The Revised Northern Food Basket*, 2.

35 Parker, "Consuming Health, Negotiating Risk, Eating Right," 54.

36 INAC, *The Revised Northern Food Basket*, 4.

37 INAC, *The Revised Northern Food Basket*, 9.

38 Amend, "The Confused Canadian Eater," 720.

39 Canada, *Food for the North: Report of the Air Stage Subsidy Review*, 33.

40 Walters, "A History of Food and Nutrition in Indigenous Communities in Canada, 1962–1985," 180.

41 LaDuke, *Recovering the Sacred: The Power of Naming and Reclaiming*.

42 Dennis and Robin, "Healthy on Our Own Terms," 9.

43 Dennis and Robin, "Healthy on Our Own Terms," 4.

44 Rowse, *White Flour, White Power: From Rations to Citizenship in Central Australia*, 5.

45 Dietary Reference Intakes (DRI) are a "comprehensive set of nutrient reference values for healthy populations that can be used for assessing and planning diets" and reflect the current state of scientific knowledge regarding nutrient requirements. Health Canada, "Dietary Reference Intakes," https://www.canada.ca/en/health-canada/services/food-nutrition/healthy-eating/dietary-reference-intakes.html.

46 Glacken and Hill, *The Food Mail Pilot Projects: Achievements and Challenges*, 20.

47 Glacken and Hill, *The Food Mail Pilot Projects: Achievements and Challenges*, 10.

48 Glacken and Hill, *The Food Mail Pilot Projects: Achievements and Challenges*, 10.

49 Glacken and Hill, *The Food Mail Pilot Projects: Achievements and Challenges*, 10–11.

50 Glacken and Hill, *The Food Mail Pilot Projects: Achievements and Challenges*, 9.

51 Glacken and Hill, *The Food Mail Pilot Projects: Achievements and Challenges*, 9.

52 Glacken and Hill, *The Food Mail Pilot Projects: Achievements and Challenges*, 16.

53 Amend, "The Confused Canadian Eater," 721; and Overend, *Shifting Food Facts: Dietary Discourse in a Post-Truth Culture*.

54   Food and Agriculture Organization of the United Nations, "Hunger and Food Insecurity," http://www.fao.org/hunger/en/. These elements are included in the most widely accepted definition of food security developed by the Food and Agriculture Organization of the United Nations: "Food security exists when all people, at all times, have physical and economic access to sufficient, safe, and nutritious food which meets their dietary needs and food preferences for an active and healthy life."

55   Lawn and Harvey, *The Food Mail Refinements Study*, 19.

56   INAC, *Food for the North: Report of the Air Stage Subsidy Review*, 45.

57   Lawn and Harvey, *The Food Mail Refinements Study*, 19.

58   Lawn and Harvey, *The Food Mail Refinements Study*, 8.

59   Tompkins, *Racial Indigestion: Eating Bodies in the 19th Century*; and Overend, *Shifting Food Facts: Dietary Discourse in a Post-Truth Culture*.

60   The North West Company Inc., *Annual Report for 1990*, 11.

61   Interview with government employee, 3 February 2015.

62   Indian and Northern Affairs Canada, *Food for the North: Report of the Air Stage Subsidy Review*, 32.

Chapter 6: "We Blanket the North"

1   The phrase "we blanket the north" appears in The North West Company Fund, *2001 Annual Report: Vision, Growth, Value*, i.

2   Walmsley, "Retreat from the Frontier."

3   Walmsley, "Retreat from the Frontier."

4   Walmsley, "Retreat from the Frontier."

5   Hudson's Bay Northern Stores Inc., *1987 Annual Report*, 3.

6   Hudson's Bay Northern Stores Inc., *1988 Annual Report*, 2.

7   Hudson's Bay Northern Stores Inc., *1987 Annual Report*, 3.

8   Hudson's Bay Northern Stores Inc., *1989 Annual Report*, 1.

9   The North West Company Inc., *1990 Annual Report*, 4.

10   The North West Company Inc., *1990 Annual Report*, 16.

11   The North West Company Inc., *1991 Annual Report*, 10.

12   The North West Company Inc., *1991 Annual Report*, 1.

13   The North West Company Inc., *1991 Annual Report*, 2.

14   The North West Company Inc., *1990 Annual Report*, 11.

15   The North West Company Fund, *2008 Annual Report*, 5. Emphasis added.

16   The North West Company Inc., *1992 Annual Report*, 6–13.

17   The North West Company Inc., *1992 Annual Report*, 8.

18   The North West Company Fund, *2002 Annual Report*, 6.

19   Northern/NorthMart, WE Financial Services; available online at https://www.northmart.ca/wefinancial.

20   Northern/NorthMart, "Benefits Card," http://www.northmart.ca/financial/financial-benefit-card.php.

21   Northern/NorthMart, "Benefits Card," http://www.northmart.ca/financial/financial-benefit-card.php.

22   Community conversation, 7 April 2012; Community conversation, 2 March 2013; Community conversation, 14 July 2014; Community conversation, 4 October 2015.

23   The North West Company Inc., *1993 Annual Report*, 2.

24   The North West Company Inc., *1994 Annual Report*, 1.

25   George, "Pilot Project Tests Benefits of Lower Food Mail Prices."

26   Freeman, "Fast Food: Oppression through Poor Nutrition."

27   The North West Company Inc., *1993 Annual Report*, 4 and 18.

28   The North West Company Inc., *1993 Annual Report*, 4.

29   The North West Company Inc., *1993 Annual Report*, 4.

30   The North West Company Inc., *1994 Annual Report*, 7.

31   The North West Company Inc., *1994 Annual Report*, 6.

32   The North West Company Inc., *1994 Annual Report*, 8.

33   The North West Company Inc., *1995 Annual Report*, 22.

34   The North West Company Inc., *1995 Annual Report*, 22.

35   The North West Company Inc., *1993 Annual Report*, 7.

36   The North West Company Inc., *1996 Annual Report*, 2 and 18.

37   The North West Company Fund, *2000 Annual Report*, 20.

38   The North West Company Inc., *1996 Annual Report*, 10.

39   The North West Company Inc., *1997 Annual Report*, 20.

40   The North West Company Inc., *1997 Annual Report*, 9.

41   The North West Company Fund, *1999 Annual Report*, 3.

42   The North West Company Fund, *1999 Annual Report*, 3.

43   The North West Company Fund, *1999 Annual Report*, 4.

44   The North West Company Fund, *2001 Annual Report*, i.

45   The North West Company Fund, *2002 Annual Report*, 11.

46   The North West Company Fund, *2005 Annual Summary Report*, 1.

47   In March of 2020, the *Winnipeg Free Press* reported that the NWC was planning to sell 34 of its 46 Giant Tiger locations in a $45 million deal. Martin Cash reported that "130 positions…will be cut, about 86 people will be laid off and 40 positions will be eliminated through attrition." See Martin Cash, "NWC Sells all but 12 Giant Tiger Stores," *Winnipeg Free Press*, 12 March 2020, https://www.winnipegfreepress.com/business/2020/03/12/nwc-sells-all-but-12-giant-tiger-stores. The sale was completed in July of 2020 when Giant Tiger Stores Limited acquired these 34 stores. The NWC annual report for the fiscal year of 2021 noted that the Company retained five key stores in the northern market, closed four locations, and converted one store to a Valu Lots Clearance Centre. Northwest Company Inc., *Annual Report 2021*, 10, https://www.northwest.ca/uploads/documents/2021%20Q4%20-%20Annual%20Report%20-%20APR13-22.pdf (accessed 27 January 2023).

48   The North West Company Fund, *2003 Annual Summary Report*, 14.

49   The North West Company Fund, *2003 Annual Summary Report*, 3. Emphasis added.

50   The North West Company Fund, *2004 Annual Report*, 12.

51   The North West Company Fund, *2004 Annual Report*, 12.

52   The North West Company Fund, *2005 Annual Summary Report*, 1 and 4.

53   Auditor General of Canada, "Report 4 – Access to Health Services in Remote First Nations Communities" (Spring 2015).

54 The North West Company Fund, *2005 Annual Summary Report,* 1 and 4.

55 The North West Company Fund, *2006 Annual Summary Report*, 4.

56 The North West Company Fund, *2006 Annual Summary Report*, 9.

57 The North West Company Fund, *2007 Annual Report*, 5.

58 The North West Company Fund, *2007 Annual Report*, 5.

59 McCallum, "The Last Frontier: Isolation and Aboriginal Health."

60 McCallum, "This Last Frontier: Isolation and Aboriginal Health," 115.

61 The North West Company Inc., *1993 Annual Report*, 7.

62 The North West Company Inc., *1993 Annual Report*, 7.

63 McCallum, "This Last Frontier: Isolation and Aboriginal Health," 115.

64 The North West Company Inc., *1993 Annual Report*, 4.

65 The North West Company Inc., *1993 Annual Report*, 4.

66 The North West Company Fund, *2007 Annual Report*, 7.

67 The North West Company Fund, *2007 Annual Report*, 10.

68 The North West Company Inc., *1991 Annual Report*, 7.

69 The North West Company Inc., *1992 Annual Report*, 3–4.

70 The North West Company Inc., *1991 Annual Report*, 13.

71 The North West Company Inc., *1990 Annual Report*, 8.

72 The North West Company Inc., *1990 Annual Report*, 11.

73 The North West Company Inc., *2001 Annual Report*, 7.

74 Anderson, *The Cultivation of Whiteness: Science, Health, and Racial Destiny in Australia*, 31.

75 The North West Company Inc., *1993 Annual Report*, 4.

76 The North West Company Fund, *2006 Annual Report*, 9.

77 The North West Company Inc., *1991 Annual Report*, 7.

78 The North West Company Inc., *1993 Annual Report*, 7.

79 Amend, "The Confused Canadian Eater," 721.

80 The North West Company Inc., *1993 Annual Report*, 7.

81 Canada, *Working with Grocers to Support Healthy Eating*, 36.

82 NWC, "Health Happy Program Launches in Northern and NorthMart Stores."

83 Northern/NorthMart, "Health Happy" https://www.northmart.ca/health-happy.

84 Canada, *Working with Grocers to Support Healthy Eating*, 36.

85 North West Company, "Kids in Kugluktuk Learn About Being Healthy and Happy."

86 North West Company, "Health Happy Taste Test Raises Awareness of Healthy Lifestyle Options in Kuujjuaq."

87 Interview with community member, 24 August 2017; Community conversation, 3 March 2013.

88 Timiskaming Health Unit, *Northern Fruit and Vegetable Program.*

Chapter 7: "Direct, Effective, and Efficient"

1 Galloway, "Is the Nutrition North Canada Retail Subsidy Meeting the Goal," e395–97.

2 Overend et al., "Introduction to 'Against Healthisms,'" 1.

3 Scrinis, "On the Ideology of Nutritionism," 40–41.

4   Glacken and Hill, *The Food Mail Pilot Projects: Achievements and Challenges.*

5   de Souza, *Feeding the Other: Whiteness and Privilege and Neoliberal Stigma in Food Pantries*, 224; see also Zoller, "Health Activism: Communication Theory and Action for Social Change," 341–64.

6   Socha et al., "Food Security in a Northern First Nation Community; see also Socha et al., "Food Availability, Food Store Management, and Food Pricing in a Northern First Nation Community."

7   Dargo, *Food Mail Program Review: Findings and Recommendations of the Minister's Special Representative.*

8   Burnett et al., "Retail Food Environments, Shopping Experiences, First Nations, and the Provincial Norths," 336.

9   Burnett et al., "Retail Food Environments, Shopping Experiences, First Nations, and the Provincial Norths," 336.

10 NNC, "Northern Food Retail Data Collection & Analysis by Enrg Research Group," https://www.nutritionnorthcanada.gc.ca/eng/1424364469057/1424364505951#h6.

11 Alex Roslin, "Northern Gets Boot in Big Trout Lake," *The Nation Archives*, http://www.nationnewsarchives.ca/article/northern-gets-boot-in-big-trout-lake/.

12 Dargo, *Food Mail Program Review: Findings and Recommendations of the Minister's Special Representative*, 24.

13 Enstad, *Cigarettes, Inc.: An Intimate History of Corporate Imperialism*, 264.

14 Parlee and Wray, "Gender and the Social Dimensions of Changing Caribou Populations in the Western Arctic."

15 Dargo, *Food Mail Program Review: Findings and Recommendations of the Minister's Special Representative*, 16–17.

16 Dargo, *Food Mail Program Review: Findings and Recommendations of the Minister's Special Representative*, 16–17.

17 Duignan, Moffat, and Martin-Hill, "Be Like the Running Water," 114864. Also see Boyd "No Taps, No Toilets: First Nations and the Constitutional Right to Water in Canada." Finally, see Boulet et al., *Beyond the Fields: The Value of Forest and Freshwater Foods in Northern Ontario.*

18 Dargo, *Food Mail Program Review: Findings and Recommendations of the Minister's Special Representative*, 38.

19 Dargo, *Food Mail Program Review: Findings and Recommendations of the Minister's Special Representative*, 9.

20 Dargo, *Food Mail Program Review: Findings and Recommendations of the Minister's Special Representative*, 3.

21 Evidence of Dargo's employment was uncovered by Galloway in "Canada's Northern Food Subsidy Nutrition North Canada: A Comprehensive Program Evaluation," 15.

22 Canada, *From Food Mail to Nutrition North Canada: Report of the Standing Committee on Aboriginal Affairs and Northern Development*, 1.

23 Interview with government employee, 23 August 2013; Burnett et al., "From Food Mail to Nutrition North Canada: Reconsidering Federal Food Subsidy Programs for Northern Ontario," 141–56.

24 Auditor General, *Report of the Auditor General of Canada: Nutrition North Canada – Aboriginal Affairs and Northern Canada. Chapter Six.* (Ottawa: Queen's Printer, 2014): https://www.oag-bvg.gc.ca/internet/English/parl_oag_201411_06_e_39964.html.

25 Interview with government employee, 23 August 2013.

26 Interview with government employee, 3 February 2015.

27 Interview with government employee, 3 February 2015.

28 Dargo, *Food Mail Program Review: Findings and Recommendations of the Minister's Special Representative,* 4.

29 Burnett, Skinner, and LeBlanc, "From Food Mail to Nutrition North Canada," 148; and Achtemichuk, "Addressing a Northern Food Crisis: Process Evaluation of Nutrition North Canada," 1–8.

30 NNC, "2018-2019: Full Fiscal Year," https://www.nutritionnorthcanada.gc.ca/eng/1583247671449/1583247805997#chp6.

31 Canada, "Statement by Minister Valcourt on the NNC Advisory Board's Recommendations for the Wider Application of a Point-Sale System" (4 June 2015): https://www.canada.ca/en/news/archive/2015/06/statement-minister-valcourt-nnc-advisory-board-recommendations-wider-application-point-sale-system.html.

32 Burnett, Skinner, and LeBlanc, "From Food Mail to Nutrition North Canada," 146.

33 Burnett, Skinner, and LeBlanc, "From Food Mail to Nutrition North Canada"; see also Galloway, "Canada's Northern Food Subsidy Nutrition North Canada."

34 Auditor General of Canada, *2014 Fall Report: Chapter 6 – Nutrition North Canada; Aboriginal Affairs and Northern Development Canada,* August 2014.

35 Auditor General of Canada, *2014 Fall Report: Chapter 6 – Nutrition North Canada; Aboriginal Affairs and Northern Development Canada,* August 2014.

36 Auditor General of Canada, *2014 Fall Report: Chapter 6 – Nutrition North Canada; Aboriginal Affairs and Northern Development Canada,* August 2014.

37 NNC, "For Retailers and Suppliers," https://www.nutritionnorthcanada.gc.ca/eng/1415626422397/1415626591979.

38 NNC, "For Retailers and Suppliers," https://www.nutritionnorthcanada.gc.ca/eng/1415626422397/1415626591979.

39 Jim Bell, "Igloolik-Based Online Upstart Offers Lower-Cost Food in Baffin," *Nunatsiaq News,* 12 September 2017, https://nunatsiaq.com/stories/article/65674igloolik-based_online_upstart_offers_lower-cost_food_in_baffin/#:~:text=Igloolik%2C%20known%20for%20decades%20as,to%20get%20store%2Dbought%20food.

40 Interview with community member, 24 August 2017.

41 Aboriginal Affairs and Northern Development Canada, "Changes to the List of Items Eligible for Shipment."

42 Interview with community member, 24 August 2017.

43 Chambers, "Boil Water Advisories and Federal (in)Action."

44 North West Company Fund, *2004 Annual Report* and North West Company Fund, *2005 Annual Report.*

45 Aboriginal Affairs and Northern Development Canada, "Changes to the List of Items Eligible for Shipment."

46 Canada, "Country Foods a Priority Under Nutrition North Canada," 17 March 2011. Ref. #2-3477. https://www.canada.ca/en/news/archive/2011/03/country-foods-priority-under-nutrition-north-canada.html.

47 Burnett, Skinner, and LeBlanc, "From Food Mail to Nutrition North Canada."

48 Gombay, "Sharing or Commoditising?"

49   NNC, "For Retailers and Suppliers," https://www.nutritionnorthcanada.gc.ca/eng/14 15626422397/1415626591979.

50   Canada, "Country Foods a Priority Under Nutrition North Canada," 17 March 2011. Ref. #2-3477. https://www.canada.ca/en/news/archive/2011/03/country-foods-priority-under-nutrition-north-canada.html.

51   Canada, "A Northern moment: Minister Vandal chats with Natan Obed and Aluki Kotierk about the Harvesters Support Grant (video)," https://www. nutritionnorthcanada.gc.ca/eng/1596227913010/1596278942676.

52   Nutrition North Canada, "Support for hunting, harvesting, and community-led food programs," https://nutritionnorthcanada.gc.ca/eng/1586274027728/ 1586274048849#sec1.

53   Nutrition North Canada, "Support for hunting, harvesting, and community-led food programs," https://nutritionnorthcanada.gc.ca/eng/1586274027728/ 1586274048849#sec1.

54   Nutrition North Canada, "Support for hunting, harvesting, and community-led food programs," https://nutritionnorthcanada.gc.ca/eng/1586274027728/1 586274048849#sec1.

55   Tsuji et al., "Harvest Programs in First Nations of Subarctic Canada"; Kamal et al., "A Recipe for Change"; Natcher, Castro, and Felt, "Hunter Support programs and the Northern Social Economy"; and Gombay, "Making a Living: Place and the Commoditisation of Country Foods in a Nunavik Community."

56   INAC, *Food for the North: Report of the Air Stage Subsidy Review*, 31. For a more detailed analysis of the cost of hunting and barriers faced by community members participating in hunting activities, see Pal, Haman, and Robidoux, "The Costs of Food Procurement in Two Northern Indigenous Communities in Canada"; and Randazzo and Robidoux, "The Costs of Local Food Procurement in a Northern Canadian First Nation Community."

57   Duncan quoted in Murphy, "$1M a month Arctic Food Subsidy Extended."

58   Jose Kusugak quoted in House of Commons Canada, *From Foodmail to Nutrition North Canada: Report of the Standing Committee on Aboriginal Affairs and Northern Development*, March 2011, 16; available online at http://publications.gc.ca/collections/ collection_2011/parl/XC35-403-1-1-02-eng.pdf.

59   Interview with NWC employee, 26 June 2014. See also Ford, Clark, and Naylor, "Food Insecurity in Nunavut: Are We Going from Bad to Worse?"

60   St-Germain, Galloway, and Tarasuk, "Food Insecurity in Nunavut Following the Introduction of Nutrition North Canada."

61   "PHOTOS: $29 Cheez Whiz? High Arctic Food Costs."

62   "PHOTOS: $29 Cheez Whiz? High Arctic Food Costs."

63   Luppens and Power, "'Aboriginal Isn't Just About What Was Before, It's What's Happening Now.'"

64   Community conversation, 4 October 2015; Interview with community member, 24 August 2017b.

65   Tompkins, *Racial Indigestion: Eating Bodies in the Nineteenth Century*; Overend, *Shifting Food Facts: Dietary Discourse in a Post-Truth Culture*, 44.

66   Overend, *Shifting Food Facts: Dietary Discourse in a Post-Truth Culture*, 32.

67   Overend, *Shifting Food Facts: Dietary Discourse in a Post-Truth Culture*, 46–47.

68 Overend, *Shifting Food Facts: Dietary Discourse in a Post-Truth Culture*, 46–47 and 50. Robert Crawford coined the term *healthism* in 1980 to mean a "preoccupation with personal health as a primary—often the primary—focus for the definition and achievement of well-being" that could only be achieved through the right personal lifestyle choices." Crawford, "Healthism and the Medicalization of Everyday Life," 368.

69 Auditor General of Canada, *2014 Fall Report: Chapter 6 – Nutrition North Canada; Aboriginal Affairs and Northern Development Canada.*

70 Auditor General of Canada, *2014 Fall Report: Chapter 6 – Nutrition North Canada; Aboriginal Affairs and Northern Development Canada.*

71 Aboriginal Affairs and Northern Development Canada, *Compliance Assessment Report: Northwest Company for Funding Agreement n°. 1213-01-000019.*

72 Auditor General of Canada, *2014 Fall Report: Chapter 6 – Nutrition North Canada; Aboriginal Affairs and Northern Development Canada.*

73 NNC, "Eligible Communities," https://www.nutritionnorthcanada.gc.ca/eng/1415540731169/1415540791407#tpc1.

74 Derek Reimer, "Modern-Day Monopoly? North West Company Responds, CBC News, 17 December 2014, https://www.cbc.ca/news/canada/manitoba/modern-day-monopoly-north-west-company-responds-1.2877058.

Conclusion

1 "NWC Spends $31 Million to Buy Its Own Airline," *CBC News*, https://www.cbc.ca/news/canada/north/north-west-company-purchases-airline-1.4091988.

2 "NWC Spends $31 Million to Buy Its Own Airline."

3 The North West Company, *Report to Shareholders: Quarterly Period Ending April 30, 2017*, https://www.northwest.ca/uploads/documents/2017-06-14-q1-report-2017.pdf.

4 Nutrition North Canada, *2015–2016 Fiscal Year*, https://www.nutritionnorthcanada.gc.ca/eng/1491402892387/1491402911878#h6.

5 See Nutrition North Canada, *2016–2017 Fiscal Year*, https://www.nutritionnorthcanada.gc.ca/eng/1524237277832/1524237310943.

6 NNC, *Reports*, https://www.nutritionnorthcanada.gc.ca/eng/1415647255632/1415647437113#tpc2.

7 See Walters, "'A National Priority': Nutrition Canada's Survey," 433–34; and Mosby, "Making and Breaking Canada's Food Rules," 421–22.

8 Biltekoff, *Eating Right in America: The Cultural Politics of Food and Health*; see also Hay, *Inventing the Thrifty Gene: The Science of Settler Colonialism.*

9 Morrison, "Reflections and Realities: Expressions of Food Sovereignty in the Fourth World," 27.

10 Coulthard, *Red Skin, White Masks: Rejecting the Colonial Politics of Recognition in Canada.*

11 Canada, *Special Joint Committee of the Senate and the House of Commons*, 655.

12 Canada, *Special Joint Committee of the Senate and the House of Commons*, 668.

13 Narine, "'Business Monopoly has Inflicted Economic Suffering in Northern Communities,' says Chief."

14 Narine, "'Business Monopoly has Inflicted Economic Suffering in Northern Communities,' says Chief."

15   Attawapiskat Youth Council, "Official Demands to the Federal Government from Attawapiskat Youth," 21 April 2016, https://www.indiantime.net/story/2016/04/21/news/attawapiskat-youth-council-makes-demands/21030.html.

16   Bell, "Igloolik-Based Online Upstart Offers Lower-Cost Food in Baffin."

17   Interview with community member, 24 August 2017.

18   Interview with community member, 24 August 2017.

BIBLIOGRAPHY

Archival Collections

Hudson's Bay Company Archives, Provincial Archives of Manitoba, Winnipeg

RG 7, Records of the Northern Stores Department
RG 9, Records of the Hudson's Bay Company Head Office
Hudson's Bay Company Annual Reports and Proceedings, 1870–1989

Library Archives Canada, Ottawa

Department of Indian Affairs, Record Group 10
Department of National Health and Welfare, Record Group 29

Oral Interviews and Community Conversations

Community conversation, 7 April 2012
Community conversation, 3 March 2013
Community conversation, 14 July 2014
Community conversation, 4 October 2015
Interview with community member, 24 August 2017
Interview with community member, 24 August 2017b
Interview with government employee, 23 August 2013
Interview with government employee, 3 February 2015
Interview with North West Company employee, 26 June 2014

Newspapers

CBC News
Globe and Mail
Indigenous Business and Finance Today
Insider
Maclean's

Nunatsiaq News
The Nation Archives
The Peterborough Examiner
WindSpeaker News

Published Primary Sources

Aboriginal Affairs and Northern Development Canada. *The Story of Food Mail*. Report of Aboriginal Affairs and Northern Development Canada, 2007. http://www.aad-nc-aandc.gc.ca/eng/1100100035774 (accessed 2012).

Boult, David. *Hunger in the Arctic: Food (In)Security in Inuit Communities, A Discussion Paper*. National Aboriginal Health Organization, October 2004.

Canada. *1752 Peace and Friendship Treaty*, Transcribed from R. Simon [1985]. https://www.rcaanc-cirnac.gc.ca/eng/1100100029040/1581293867988.

———. *1850 Robinson Huron-Superior Treaties*. https://www.rcaanc-cirnac.gc.ca/eng/1100100028984/1581293724401?wbdisable=true.

———. Aboriginal Affairs and Northern Development Canada, *Compliance Assessment Report: Northwest Company For Funding Agreement n°. 1213-01-000019*. Ottawa: Deloite LPP, 7 November 2015.

———. Audit and Evaluation Branch. *Audit of the Food Mail Program*. June 2008.

———. Auditor General. *Report 4—Access to Health Services in Remote First Nations Communities*. Spring 2015.

———. Auditor General. *Chapter 6 – Nutrition North Canada; Aboriginal Affairs and Northern Development Canada*. August 2014.

———. "Country Foods a Priority Under Nutrition North Canada." 17 March 2011. Ref. #2- 3477. https://www.canada.ca/en/news/archive/2011/03/country-foods-priority-under-nutrition-north-canada.html

———. *Food for the North: Report of the Air Stage Subsidy Review*. Ottawa: INAC, 1991.

———. *Food Security in Northern Canada: A Discussion Paper on the Future of the Northern Air Stage Program*. Ottawa: DIAND, 1994.

———. *From Food Mail to Nutrition North Canada: Report of the Standing Committee on Aboriginal Affairs and Northern Development*. Ottawa: House of Commons, March 2011.

———. House of Commons. *Sessional Papers*.

———. House of Commons. *Special Joint Committee of the Senate and the House of Commons Appointed to Examine and Consider the Indian Act. Minutes of Proceedings and Evidence*. Ottawa: King's Printer, 1947.

———. Indian Affairs *Annual Reports*, 1864–1990.

———. "A Northern moment: Minister Vandal chats with Natan Obed and Aluki Kotierk about the Harvesters Support Grant (video)." https://www.nutritionnorthcanada.gc.ca/eng/1596227913010/1596278942676 (accessed 23 August 2022).

———. *The Revised Northern Food Basket*. Ottawa: INAC, 2007.

———. *Treaty No. 3*. https://www.rcaanc-cirnac.gc.ca/eng/1100100028675/1581294028469.

———. *Treaty No. 5.* https://www.rcaanc-cirnac.gc.ca/eng/1100100028699/158129269 6320.

———. *Working with Grocers to Support Healthy Eating.* Ottawa: Health Canada, 2013.

Dargo, Graeme. *Food Mail Program Review: Findings and Recommendations of the Minister's Special Representative.* Ottawa: Dargo and Associates, 2008.

Glacken, Jody B., and Frederick Hill. *The Food Mail Pilot Projects: Achievements and Challenges.* Ottawa: INAC, 2009.

Lawn, Judith. *Air Stage Subsidy Monitoring Program, Final Report: Food Price Survey.* Volume 1. Prepared for the Department of Indian Affairs and Northern Development, December 1993.

Lawn, Judith, and Dan Harvey. *The Food Mail Refinements Study.* Ottawa: INAC, January 1996.

North West Company. *Annual Reports, 1987–2020.*

Online Sources

Aboriginal Affairs and Northern Development Canada. "Changes to the List of Items Eligible for Shipment." 2013. http://www.aadnc-andc.gc.ca/eng/1100100015868 /1100100015870.

Arctic Co-operatives Limited. "Arctic Co-ops Chronological History." https://arctic-coop.com/index.php/about-arctic-co-ops/history/chronological-history/ (accessed 29 October 2021).

Canada. "Statement by Minister Valcourt on the NNC Advisory Board's Recommendations for the Wider Application of a Point-Sale System." 4 June 2015. https://www.canada.ca/en/news/archive/2015/06/statement-minister-valcourt-nnc-advisory-board-recommendations-wider-application-point-sale-system.html.

Canada Post Corporation. "Services." https://prd11.wsl.canadapost.ca/cpc/en/support/kb/at-the-post-office/services/what-are-air-stage-offices (accessed 6 August 2021).

Food and Agriculture Organization of the United Nations. "Hunger and Food Insecurity." http://www.fao.org/hunger/en/ (accessed 28 August 2021).

Guest, Dennis. "Family Allowance." *The Canadian Encyclopedia.* 18 December 2013. https://www.thecanadianencyclopedia.ca/en/article/family-allowance.

Health Canada. "Dietary Reference Intakes." https://www.canada.ca/en/health-canada/services/food-nutrition/healthy-eating/dietary-reference-intakes.html (accessed 5 August 2021).

Hudson's Bay Company History Foundation. "Timeline: From the Fur Trade to Fifth Avenue." http://www.hbcheritage.ca/content/timeline (accessed 17 November 2015).

North West Company. "Health Happy Taste Test Raises Awareness of Healthy Lifestyle Options in Kuujjuaq." https://www.northwest.ca/community/community-engagement/303/health-happy-taste-test-raises-awareness-of-healthy-lifestyle-options-in-kuujjuaq (accessed 25 November 2021).

———. "Kids in Kugluktuk Learn About Being Healthy and Happy." https://www.northwest.ca/community/community-engagement/82/article-82 (accessed 25 November 2021).

Northern/NorthMart, "Benefits Card." http://www.northmart.ca/financial/financial-benefit-card.php (accessed 8 November 2016).

———. "Health Happy." https://www.northmart.ca/health-happy (accessed 25 November 2021).

———. "WE Financial Services." https://www.northmart.ca/wefinancial (accessed 8 January 2022).

Nutrition North Canada. "2015–2016 Fiscal Year." https://www.nutritionnorthcanada.gc.ca/eng/1491402892387/1491402911878#h6 (accessed 26 June 2019).

———. "2016–2017 Fiscal Year." https://www.nutritionnorthcanada.gc.ca/eng/1524237277832/1524237310943 (accessed 26 June 2019).

———. "2018–2019: Full Fiscal Year." https://www.nutritionnorthcanada.gc.ca/eng/1583247671449/1583247805997#chp6 (accessed 30 November 2021).

———. "Eligible Communities." https://www.nutritionnorthcanada.gc.ca/eng/1415540731169/1415540791407#tpc1 (accessed 29 November 2021).

———. "For Retailers and Suppliers." https://www.nutritionnorthcanada.gc.ca/eng/1415626422397/1415626591979 (accessed 29 November 2021).

———. "Northern Food Retail Data Collection & Analysis by Enrg Research Group." https://www.nutritionnorthcanada.gc.ca/eng/1424364469057/1424364505951#h6 (accessed 30 November 2021).

———. *Reports.* https://www.nutritionnorthcanada.gc.ca/eng/1415647255632/1415647437113#tpc2 (accessed 31 January 2022).

———. "Support for hunting, harvesting, and community-led food programs." https://nutritionnorthcanada.gc.ca/eng/1586274027728/1586274048849#sec1 (accessed 23 August 2022).

Proof. "Understanding Household Food Insecurity." https://proof.utoronto.ca/food-insecurity/ (accessed 25 August 2022).

Timiskaming Health Unit. "Northern Fruit and Vegetable Program." https://www.timiskaminghu.com/454/northern-fruit-vegetable-program (accessed 2 December 2021).

UN Human Rights Council. "Report of the Special Rapporteur on the Right to Food, Olivier De Schutter: Addendum, Mission to Canada." 24 December 2012, A/HRC/22/50/Add.1, p.16. http://www.reforld.org/docid/511cb0422.html (accessed 3 January 2015).

Films

The Other Side of the Ledger: An Indian View of the Hudson's Bay Company. Directed by Martin Defalco and Willie Dunn. NFB, 1972.

Blog

Fraser, Crystal. "Politics and Personal Experiences: An Editor's Introduction to Indigenous Research in Canada." *Active History.* 11 January 2016. http://activehistory.ca/2016/01/politics-and-personal-experiences-an-editors-introduction-to-indigenous-research-in-canada/.

Secondary Sources

Achtemichuk, Lauren. "Addressing a Northern Food Crisis: Process Evaluation of Nutrition North Canada." *University of Saskatchewan Undergraduate Research Journal* 2, no. 2 (2016): 1–8.

Adams, Dawn, Shawn Wilson, Ryan Heavy Head, and Edmund Gordon. *Ceremony at a Boundary Fire: A Story of Indigenist Knowledge.* Sydney, Australia: eScholarship Repository, 2015.

Adams, Mary Louise. *The Trouble with Normal: Postwar Youth and the Making of Heterosexuality.* Toronto: University of Toronto Press, 1997.

Amend, Elyse. "The Confused Canadian Eater: Quantification, Personal Responsibility, and Canada's Food Guide." *Journal of Canadian Studies* 52, no. 3 (2018): 718–41.

Anderson, Warwick. *The Cultivation of Whiteness: Science, Health, and Racial Destiny in Australia.* New York: Basic Books Publishing, 2003.

Barker, Adam. *Making and Breaking Settler Space: Five Centuries of Colonization in North America.* Vancouver: UBC Press, 2021.

Bartlett, Alison. "Black Breasts, White Milk? Ways of Constructing Breastfeeding and Race in Australia." *Australian Feminist Studies* 19, no. 45 (November 2004): 341–55.

Belcourt, Billy-Ray. "Meditations on Reserve Life, Biosociality, and the Taste of Non-Sovereignty." *Settler Colonial Studies* 8, no. 1 (2018): 1–15.

Belisle, Donica. *Retail Nation: Department Stores and the Making of Modern Canada.* Vancouver: UBC, 2011.

———. *Purchasing Power: Women and the Rise of Canadian Consumer Culture.* Toronto: University of Toronto Press, 2020.

Besson, Emilie Koum. "Confronting Whiteness and Decolonising Global Health Institutions." *The Lancet* (British Edition) 397, no. 10292 (2021): 2328–29.

Bhabha, Homi K. *The Location of Culture.* New York: Routledge Publishing, 1994.

Biltekoff, Charlotte. *Eating Right in America: The Cultural Politics of Food and Health.* Durham: Duke University Press, 2013.

Binnema, Theodore. *Enlightened Zeal: The Hudson's Bay Company and Scientific Networks, 1670–1870.* Toronto: University of Toronto Press, 2014.

Blake, Raymond. *From Rights to Needs: A History of the Family Allowances in Canada, 1929–92.* Vancouver: UBC Press, 2009.

Bohaker, Heidi, and Franca Iacovetta. "Making Aboriginal People Immigrants Too: A Comparison of Citizenship Programs for Newcomers and Indigenous Peoples in Postwar Canada, 1940s–1960s." *The Canadian Historical Review* 90, no. 3 (2009): 450–1.

Bonds, Anne, and Joshua Inwood. "Beyond White Privilege: Geographies of White Supremacy and Settler Colonialism." *Progress in Human Geography* 40, no. 6 (2016), 715–33.

Boulet, Alex, Julee Boan, Rike Burkhardt, and Lynn Palmer. *Beyond the Fields: The Value of Forest and Freshwater Foods in Northern Ontario.* Toronto: Ontario Nature, 2014.

Boyd, David R. "No Taps, No Toilets: First Nations and the Constitutional Right to Water in Canada." *McGill Journal of Law* 57, no. 1 (2011): 81–134.

Brown, Jennifer. *Strangers in Blood: Fur Trade Company Families in Indian Country.* Vancouver: UBC Press, 1980.

Burnett, Kristin, Kelly Skinner, and Joseph LeBlanc. "From Food Mail to Nutrition North Canada: Reconsidering Federal Food Subsidy Programs for Northern Ontario." *Canadian Food Studies* 2, no. 1 (2015): 141–56.

Burnett, Kristin, Kelly Skinner, Travis Hay, Joseph LeBlanc, and Lori Chambers. "Retail Food Environment Experiences and Purchasing Patterns in Northern Canada." *Health Promotion and Chronic Disease Prevention in Canada (HPCDP)* 37, no. 10 (2017): 333–41.

Calverley, David. *Who Controls the Hunt?: First Nations, Treaty Rights, and Wildlife Conservation in Ontario, 1783–1939.* Vancouver: UBC Press, 2018.

Carey, Jane, and Ben Silverstein. "Thinking with and Beyond Settler Colonial Studies: New Histories after the Postcolonial." *Postcolonial Studies* 23, no. 1 (2020): 1–20.

Carstairs, Catherine, Bethany Philpott, and Sara Wilmhurst. *Be Wise! Be Healthy!: Morality and Citizenship in Canadian Public Health Campaigns.* Vancouver: UBC Press, 2018.

Carter, Sarah. *Capturing Women: The Manipulation of Cultural Imagery in Canada's Prairie West.* Montreal: McGill-Queen's University Press, 1997.

———. *Ours by Every Law of Right and Justice: Women and the Vote in the Prairie Provinces.* Vancouver: UBC Press, 2020.

Carter Sarah, Walter Hildebrandt, Dorothy First Rider, and Treaty 7 Elders. *The True Spirit and Original Intent of Treaty 7.* Montreal: McGill-Queen's University Press, 1996.

Chambers, Lori. "Boil Water Advisories and Federal (in)Action: The Politics of Potable Water in Pikangikum First Nation." *Journal of Canadian Studies* 51, no. 2 (2017): 289–310.

Cidro, Jaime, Lynelle Zahayko, Herenia P. Lawrence, Samantha Folster, Margaret McGregor, and Kristen McKay. "Breast Feeding Practices as Cultural Interventions for Early Childhood Caries in Cree Communities." *BMC Oral Health* 15, no. 49 (2015): 0.1186/s12903-015-0027-5.

Coates, Kenneth S. "Reclaiming History Through the Courts: Aboriginal Rights, the Marshall Decision, and Maritime History." In *Roots of Entanglement: Essays in the History of Native-Newcomer Relations*, edited by Myra Rutherdale, Kerry Abel, and P. Whitney Lackenbauer, 313–36. Toronto: University of Toronto Press, 2018.

Coates, Kenneth, and William Morrison. "Introduction." In *The Forgotten North: A History of Canada's Provincial Norths*, 1–10. Toronto: James Lorimer and Company, 1992.

Comacchio, Cynthia. *"Nations Are Built of Babies": Saving Ontario's Mothers and Children, 1900–1940.* Montreal: McGill-Queen's University Press, 1993.

Cornellier, Bruno. "The 'Indian Thing': On Representation and Reality in the Liberal Settler Colony." *Settler Colonial Studies* 3, no. 1 (2013): 49–64.

Coulthard, Glen. *Red Skin, White Masks: Rejecting the Colonial Politics of Recognition in Canada.* Vancouver: UBC Press, 2014.

Craig, Béatrice. *Backwoods Consumers and Homespun Capitalists: The Rise of a Market Culture in Eastern Canada.* Toronto: University of Toronto Press, 2009.

Crawford, Robert. "Healthism and the Medicalization of Everyday Life." *International Journal of Health Services* 10, no. 3 (1980): 365–88.

Crosby, Andrew, and Jeffrey Monaghan. "Settler Governmentality in Canada and the Algonquins of Barriere Lake." *Security Dialogue* 43, no. 5 (2012): 421–38.

Daigle, Michelle. "Tracing the Terrain of Indigenous Food Sovereignties." *The Journal of Peasant Studies* 46, no. 2 (2019): 297–315.

Damas, David. "Shifting Relations in the Administration of Inuit: The Hudson's Bay Company and the Canadian Government." *Études Inuit Studies* 17, no. 2 (1993): 5–28.

Daschuk, James. *Clearing the Plains: Disease, Politics of Starvation, and the Loss of Aboriginal Life.* Regina: University of Regina Press, 2013.

Davies, Mike. *Late Victorian Holocausts: El Niño Famines and the Making of the Third World.* London: Verso, 2001.

Dawson, Leslie. "'Food Will Be What Brings the People Together': Constructing Counternarratives from the Perspective of Indigenous Foodways." In *Indigenous Food Systems: Concepts, Cases, and Conversations*, edited by Priscilla Settee and Shailesh Shukla, 83–95. Toronto: Canadian Scholars, 2020.

Dennis, Mary Kate, and Tabitha Robin. "Healthy on Our Own Terms: Indigenous Wellbeing and the Colonized Food System." *Journal of Critical Dietetics* 5, no. 1 (2020): 4–11.

de Souza, Rebecca. *Feeding the Other: Whiteness and Privilege and Neoliberal Stigma in Food Pantries.* Cambridge: MIT Press, 2019.

Deutsch, Tracey. *Building a Housewife's Paradise: Gender, Politics, and American Grocery Stores in the Twentieth Century.* Chapel Hill: North Carolina Press, 2010.

Doerfler, Jill, Niigaanwewidam James Sinclair, and Heidi Kiiwetinepineskiik Stark. "Bagijige: Making an Offering." In *Centering Anishinaabeg Studies: Understanding the World Through Stories*, edited by Jill Doerfler, Niigaanwewidam James Sinclair, and Heidi Kiiwetinepineskiik Stark, i–vi. Winnipeg: University of Manitoba Press, 2013.

Duignan, Sara, Tina Moffat, and Dawn Martin-Hill. "Be Like the Running Water: Assessing Gendered and Age-Based Water Insecurity Experiences with Six Nations First Nation." *Social Science and Medicine* 298 (2022): 114864.

Elvins, Sarah. *Sales and Celebrations: Retailing and Regional Identity in Western New York State, 1920–1940.* Athens: Ohio University Press, 2004.

Emmerich, Lisa. "'Save the Babies!' American Indian Women, Assimilation Policy, and Scientific Motherhood, 1912–1918." In *Writing the Range: Race, Class, and Culture in the Women's West*, edited by Elizabeth Jameson and Susan Armitage, 393–409. Norman: University of Oklahoma Press, 1997.

Enstad, Nan. *Cigarettes, Inc.: An Intimate History of Corporate Imperialism.* Chicago: University of Chicago Press, 2018.

Ford, James D., Dylan Clark, and Angus Naylor. "Food Insecurity in Nunavut: Are We Going from Bad to Worse?" *Canadian Medical Association Journal* 191, no. 20 (2019): E550–51.

Freeman, Andrea. "Fast Food: Oppression through Poor Nutrition." *California Law Review* 95, no. 6 (December 2007): 2221–60.

Galloway, Tracey. "Canada's Northern Food Subsidy Nutrition North Canada: A Comprehensive Program Evaluation." *Journal of Circumpolar Health* 76, no. 1 (2017): 1279451–19.

———. "Is the Nutrition North Canada Retail Subsidy Meeting the Goal of Making Nutritious and Perishable Food More Accessible and Affordable in the North?" *Canadian Journal of Public Health* 105, no. 5 (2014): e395–57.

Gaudry, Adam. "Insurgent Research." *Wicazo Sa Review* 26, no. 1 (Spring 2011): 113–36.

George, Jane. "Pilot Project Tests Benefits of Lower Food Mail Prices." *Nunatsiaq News* 4 January 2002, https://nunatsiaq.com/stories/article/pilot_project_tests_bene-fits_of_lower_food_mail_prices/.

Gettler, Brian. *Colonialism's Currency: Money, State and First Nations in Canada, 1820–1950.* Montreal: McGill-Queen's University Press, 2020.

Getty, Ian, and Antoine Lussier, eds. *As Long as the Sun Shines and the Rivers Flow: A Reader in Canadian Native Studies.* Vancouver: UBC Press, 1995.

Gillon, Ashlea (Ngati Awa). "Fat Indigenous Bodies and Body Sovereignty: An Exploration of the Representations." *Indigenous Sociology: Contemporary Theoretical Perspectives* 56, no. 2 (2020): 213–28.

Gombay, Nicole. "Making a Living: Place and the Commoditisation of Country Foods in a Nunavik Community." PhD diss., Queen's University, 2003.

———. "Sharing or Commoditising? A Discussion of Some of the Socio-Economic Implications of Nunavik's Hunter Support Program." *Polar Record* 45, no. 233 (2009): 119–32.

Gray, James H. *Men Against the Desert.* Saskatoon: Western Producer Prairie Book, 1967.

Gunn Allen, Paula. *The Sacred Hoop.* Boston: Beacon Press, 1986.

Hackett, Paul, Sylvia Abonyi, and Roland F. Dyck. "Anthropometric Indices of First Nations Children and Youth on First Entry to Manitoba/Saskatchewan Residential Schools—1919 to 1953." *International Journal of Circumpolar Health* 75, no. 1 (2016): 30734–39.

Harring, Sidney. *White Man's Law: Native People in Nineteenth-Century Canadian Jurisprudence.* Toronto: University of Toronto Press, 1998.

———. "'There Seemed to be No Recognized Law': Canadian Law and the Prairie First Nations." In *Laws and Societies in the Canadian Prairie West, 1670–1940,* edited by Louis A. Knafla and Jonathan Swainger, 92–126. Vancouver: UBC Press, 2005.

Harris, Geraldine Alton. "An Archival Administrative History of the Northern Stores Department, Hudson's Bay Company, 1959–1987." MA thesis, University of Manitoba, 1995.

Haskins, Victoria. "Domesticating Colonizers: Domesticity, Indigenous Domestic Labor, and the Modern Settler Colonial Nation." *American Historical Association* 124, no. 4 (2019): 1290–1301.

Hay, Travis. *Inventing the Thrifty Gene: The Science of Settler Colonialism.* Winnipeg: University of Manitoba Press, 2021.

Hiebert, Bradley, and Elaine Power. "Heroes for the Helpless: A Critical Discourse Analysis of Canadian National Print Media's Coverage of the Food Insecurity Crises in Nunavut." *Canadian Food Studies* 3, no. 2 (December 2016): 142–61.

High, Steven. "Responding to White Encroachment: The Robinson-Superior Treaty and the Capitalist Labour Economy: 1880–1914." *Thunder Bay Historical Museum Society Papers and Records* 22 (1994): 23–39.

Iacovetta, Franca. *Gatekeepers: Reshaping Immigrant Lives in Cold War Canada.* Toronto: Between the Lines, 2006.

Iacovetta, Franca, and Valerie J. Korinek. "Jell-O Salads, One-Stop Shopping, and Maria the Homemaker: The Gender Politics of Food." In *Sisters or Strangers? Immigrant, Ethnic, and Racialized Women in Canadian History.* 2nd edition, edited by Marlene Epp and Franca Iacovetta, 432–54. Toronto: University of Toronto Press, 2016.

Iacovetta, Franca, Valerie Korinek, and Marlene Epp. "Introduction." In *Edible Histories, Cultural Politics: Towards a Canadian Food History*, edited by Franca Iacovetta, Valerie Korinek, and Marlene Epp, 3–29. Toronto: University of Toronto Press, 2012.

Iceton, Glenn. "'Many Families of Unseen Indians': Trapline Registration and Understandings of Aboriginal Title in the BC-Yukon Borderlands." *BC Studies* 201 (2019): 67–91.

Innis, Harold. *The Fur Trade in Canada: An Introduction to Canadian Economic History.* Second Edition. Toronto: University of Toronto Press, 1999.

Isaki, Bianca. "HB 645, Settler Sexuality, and the Politics of Local Asian Domesticity in Hawai'i." *Settler Colonial Studies* 2, no. 1 (2011): 82–102.

Jacobs, Margaret. *White Mother to a Dark Race: Settler Colonialism, Maternalism, and the Removal of Indigenous Children in the American West and Australia, 1880–1940.* Lincoln: University of Nebraska Press, 2009.

Jyoti, Diana, Edward Frongillo, and Sonya Jones. "Food Insecurity Affects School Children's Academic Performance, Weight Gain, and Social Skills." *Journal of Nutrition* 135, no. 12 (2005): 2831–39.

Kamal, Asfia Gulrukh, Rene Linklater, Shirley Thompson, Joseph Dipple, and Ithinto Mechisowin Committee. "A Recipe for Change: Reclamation of Indigenous Food Sovereignty in O-Pipon-Na-Piwin Cree Nation for Decolonization, Resource Sharing, and Cultural Restoration." *Globalizations* 12, no. 4 (2015): https://doi.org/10.1080/14747731.2015.1039761.

Kerr, S.J. *Fish and Fisheries Management in Ontario: A Chronology of Events. Biodiversity Branch.* Peterborough, ON: Ontario Ministry of Natural Resources, 2010.

Kirkpatrick, Sharon, Lynn McIntyre, and Melissa Potestio. "Child Hunger and Long-term Adverse Consequences for Health." *Archives of Pediatric and Adolescent Medicine* 164, no. 8 (2010): 754–62.

Kulchyski, Peter, and Frank J. Tester. *Kiumajut (Talking Back): Game Management and Inuit Rights, 1900–70.* Vancouver: UBC Press, 2007.

LaDuke, Winona. *Recovering the Sacred: The Power of Naming and Reclaiming.* Toronto: Between the Lines, 2016.

Lake, Marilyn. *Progressive New World: How Settler Colonialism and Transpacific Exchange Shaped American Reform.* Cambridge: Harvard University, 2019.

LeBlanc, Joseph, and Kristin Burnett. "What Happened to Indigenous Food Sovereignty in Northern Ontario?: Imposed Political, Economic, Socio-Ecological, and Cultural Systems Changes." In *A Land Not Forgotten: Indigenous Food Security and Land-Based*

Practices in Northern Ontario, edited by Michael Robidoux and Courtney Mason, 16–33. Winnipeg: University of Manitoba Press, 2017.

Leblanc-Laurendeau, Olivier. *Food Insecurity in Northern Canada: An Overview.* Publication no. 2020-47-E. Canada, Library of Parliament, 1 April 2020.

Loo, Tina. *States of Nature: Conserving Canada's Wildlife in the Twentieth Century.* Vancouver: UBC Press, 2006.

Luppens, Lise, and Elaine Power. "'Aboriginal Isn't Just About What Was Before, It's What's Happening Now': Perspective of Indigenous Peoples on the Foods in Their Contemporary Diets." *Canadian Food Studies* 5, no. 2 (2018): 142–61.

Lyons, Kristen, Bronwyn Fredericks, Abraham Bradfield, Christopher Mayes, and Catherine Koerner. "Nano White Food and the Reproduction of Whiteness: Impacts for Indigenous Health and Relationships with Food." *Borderlands* 20, no. 1 (2021): 207–35.

Magee (Labelle), Kathryn. "'For Home and Country': Education, Activism, and Agency in Alberta Homemaker's Clubs, 1942–1970." *Native Studies Review* 18, no. 2 (2009): 27–49.

Majid, Kashef, and Sonja Grier. "The Food Mail Program: 'When Pigs Fly'—Dispatching Access and Affordability to Health Food." *Social Marketing Quarterly* 16, no. 3 (2010): 78–95.

Maracle, Lee. *I Am Woman: A Native Perspective on Sociology and Feminism.* New York: Global Professional Publishing, 1996.

Marchildon, Gregory. "The Prairie Farm Rehabilitation Administration: Climate Crisis and Federal–Provincial Relations During the Great Depression." *The Canadian Historical Review* 90, no. 2 (2009): 275–301.

Marcus, Alan R. *Relocating Eden: The Image and Politics of Inuit Exile in the Canadian Arctic.* Hanover: University Press of New England, 1995.

Marshall, Dominique. *The Social Origins of the Welfare State: Quebec Families, Compulsory Education, and Family Allowances, 1940–1955.* Waterloo: Wilfrid Laurier University Press, 2006.

Martin, Debbie. "The Nutrition Transition and the Public Health Crisis: Aboriginal Peoples on Food and Eating." In *Critical Perspectives in Food Studies*, edited by Mustafa Koc, Jennifer Sumner, and Anthony Winson, 208–22. Don Mills: Oxford University Press, 2012.

Mattes, Cathy. "Wahkootowin, Beading, and Metis Kitchen Table Talks: Indigenous Knowledge and Strategeies for Curating Care." In *Radicalizing Care: Feminist and Queer Activism in Curating*, edited by Elke Krasny, Sophie Lingg, Lena Fritsch, Birgit Bosold, and Vera Hofmann, 132–43. London: Sternberg Press, 2021.

Mayes, Christopher. *Unsettling Food Politics: Agriculture, Dispossession and Sovereignty in Australia.* London: Rowman and Littlefeld International, 2018.

McCallum, Mary Jane. *Indigenous Women, Work, and History, 1940–1980.* Winnipeg: University of Manitoba Press, 2014.

———. "This Last Frontier: Isolation and Aboriginal Health." *Canadian Bulletin of Medical History* 22, no. 1 (2005): 103–20.

McKay, Ian. "The Liberal Order Framework: A Prospectus for a Reconnaissance of Canadian History." *The Canadian Historical Review* 102, no. 8 (2022): s1133–58.

McLaren, Angus. *Our Own Master Race: Eugenics in Canada, 1885–1945*. Toronto: McClelland and Stewart, 1990.

McMillan, L. Jane. *Truth and Conviction: Donald Marshall Jr. and the Mi'kmaw Quest for Justice*. Vancouver: UBC Press, 2018.

McNab, Miriam. "From the Bush to the Village to the City: Pinehouse Lake Aboriginal Women Adapt to Change." In *"Other" Voices: Historical Essays on Saskatchewan Women*, edited by David De Brou and Aileen Moffat, 131–43. Regina: Canadian Plains Research Center, 1995.

Milligan, Kevin. "Finances of the Nation: The Tax Recognition of Children in Canada: Exemptions, Credits, and Cash Transfers." *Canadian Tax Journal* 64, no. 3 (2016): 606–18.

Millington, Rob, Audrey Giles, Lyndsay Hayhurst, Nicolien van Luijk, and Mitchel McSweeney. "'Calling out' Corporate Redwashing: The Extractives Industry, Corporate Social Responsibility and Sport for Development in Indigenous Communities in Canada." *Sport in Society* 22, no. 2 (1999): 2122–40.

Mitchinson, Wendy. *Fighting Fat Canada, 1920–1980*. Toronto: University of Toronto Press, 2018.

Moreton-Robinson, Aileen. *The White Possessive: Property, Power, and Indigenous Sovereignty*. Minneapolis: University of Minnesota Press, 2015.

Morrison, Dawn. "Indigenous Food Sovereignty: A Model for Social Learning." In *Food Sovereignty in Canada: Creating Just and Sustainable Food Systems*, edited by H. Wittman, A. Desmarais, and N. Wiebe, 97–112. Black Point, NS: Fernwood Publishing, 2011.

———. "Reflections and Realities: Expressions of Food Sovereignty in the Fourth World." In *Indigenous Food Systems: Concepts, Cases, and Conversations*, edited by Priscilla Settee and Shailesh Shukla, 17–38. Toronto: Canadian Scholars, 2020.

Mosby, Ian. "Administering Colonial Science: Nutrition Research and Human Biomedical Experimentation in Aboriginal Communities and Residential Schools, 1942–1952." *Histoire sociale/Social History* 46, no. 1 (May 2013): 145–72.

———. *Food Will Win the War: The Politics, Culture, and Science of Food on Canada's Home Front*. Vancouver: UBC Press, 2014.

———. "Making and Breaking Canada's Food Rules: Science, the State and the Government of Nutrition, 1942–1949." In *Edible Histories, Cultural Politics: Towards a Canadian Food History*, edited by Franca Iacovetta, Marlene Epp, and Valerie Korinek, 409–32. Toronto: University of Toronto Press, 2012.

Mosby, Ian, and Tracy Galloway. "'Hunger Was Never Absent': How Residential School Diets Shaped Current Patterns of Diabetes among Indigenous Peoples in Canada." *Canadian Medical Association Journal* 189, no. 32 (August 2017): E1043–45.

Murphy, Jessica. "$1M a month Arctic Food Subsidy Extended." *The Peterborough Examiner*, 10 March 2011, B1.

Narine, Shari. "'Business Monopoly has Inflicted Economic Suffering in Northern Communities', says Chief." *Windspeaker News*, 27 August 2018, https://windspeaker.com/news/windspeaker-news/business-monopoly-has-inflicted- economic-suffer-ing-in-northern-communities-says-chief.

Natcher, David, Damian Castro, and Lawrence Felt. "Hunter Support Programs and the Northern Social Economy." In *Northern Communities Working Together: The Social Economy of Canada's North*, edited by Chris Southcott, 183–97. Toronto: University of Toronto Press, 2014.

NWC. "Health Happy Program Launches in Northern and NorthMart Stores." Press Release, 5 September 2017. *Indigenous Business and Finance Today*, https://ibftoday. ca/health-happy-program-launches-in-northern-and-northmart-stores/.

———. *Report to Shareholders: Quarterly Period Ending April 30, 2017*. https://www.north-west.ca/uploads/documents/2017-06-14-q1-report-2017.pdf.

Oleson, Robert. "The Past Hundred Years." *The Beaver* (Spring 1970): 14–22.

Opp, James. "Branding 'the Bay/la Baie': Corporate Identity, The Hudson's Bay Company, and the Burden of History in the 1960s." *The Canadian Historical Review* 96, no. 2 (2015): 223–56.

Ostry, Aleck. *Nutrition Policy in Canada, 1870–1939*. Vancouver: UBC Press, 2006.

Overend, Alissa. *Shifting Food Facts: Dietary Discourse in a Post-Truth Culture*. London: Routledge, 2021.

Overend, Alissa, Meredith Bessey, Adele Hite, and Andrea Noriega. "Introduction to 'Against Healthisms': Challenging the Paradigm of 'Eating Right.'" *Journal of Critical Dietetics* 5, no. 1 (2020): 1–3.

Pal, Shinjini, François Haman, and Michael Robidoux. "The Costs of Food Procurement in Two Northern Indigenous Communities in Canada." *Food and Foodways* 21 (2013): 132–52.

Parent, Gabrielle. "The Indians Would Be Better Off if They Tended to Their Farms Instead of Dabbling in Fisheries." In *Aboriginal History: A Reader*, edited by Kristin Burnett and Geoff Read, 334–50. Don Mills: Oxford University Press, 2012.

Parenteau, Bill. "'Care, Control, and Supervision': Native People in the Atlantic Salmon Fishery, 1867-1900." *The Canadian Historical Review* 79, no. 1 (1998): 1–34.

Parker, Barbara. "Consuming Health, Negotiating Risk, Eating Right: Exploring the Limits of Choice Through a Feminist Intersectional Lens." *Journal of Critical Dietetics* 5, no. 1 (2020): 46–57.

Parlee, Brenda, and Kristine Wray. "Gender and the Social Dimensions of Changing Caribou Populations in the Western Arctic." In *Living on the Land: Indigenous Women's Understanding of Place*, edited by Nathalie Kermoal and Isabel Altamirano-Jiménez, 69–190. Edmonton: Athabasca University Press, 2016.

Parr, Joy. *The Gender of Breadwinners: Women, Men and Change in Two Industrial Towns, 1880–1950*. Toronto: University of Toronto Press, 1990.

Pasternak, Shiri. "The Fiscal Body of Sovereignty: To 'Make Live' in Indian Country." *Settler Colonial Studies* 6, no. 4 (2016): 317–38.

Paul, Daniel N. *We Were Not the Savages*. Halifax, N.S: Fernwood, 2000.

Perry, Adele. *Aqueducts: Colonialism, Resources, and the Histories We Remember*. Winnipeg: ARP Books, 2016.

———. *On the Edge of Empire: Gender, Race, and the Making of British Columbia, 1849–1871*. Toronto: University of Toronto Press, 2001.

"PHOTOS: $29 Cheez Whiz? High Arctic Food Costs." *CBC News*. 10 February 2011. https://www.cbc.ca/news/canada/north/photos-29-cheez-whiz-high-arctic-food-costs-1.1027737 (accessed 13 June 2019).

Pickles, Katie, and Myra Rutherdale. eds. *Contact Zones: Aboriginal and Settler Women in Canada's Colonial Past*. Vancouver: UBC Press, 2005.

Piper, Liza. "Industrial Fisheries and the Health of Local Communities in the Twentieth-Century Canadian Northwest." In *Aboriginal History: A Reader*, edited by Kristin Burnett and Geoff Read, 332–40. Don Mills: Oxford University Press, 2012.

Podruchny, Carolyn, and Laura Peers, eds. *Gathering Places: Aboriginal and Fur Trade Histories*. Vancouver: UBC Press, 2010.

Polzer, Jessica, and Elaine Power. "Introduction: The Governance of Health in Neoliberal Societies." In *Neoliberal Governance and Health: Duties, Risks, and Vulnerabilities*, edited by Jessica Polzer and Elaine Power, 3–42. Montreal: McGill-Queen's Press, 2016.

Popkin, Barry, Linda Adair, and Shu Wen Ng. "Global Nutrition Transition and the Pandemic of Obesity in Developing Countries." *Nutrition Review* 70, no. 1 (2012): 3–21.

Pourmotabbed, Ali, Sajjad Moradi, Atefeh Babaei, Abed Ghavami, Hamed Mohammadi, Cyrus Jalili, Michael Symonds, and Maryam Miraghajani. "Food Insecurity and Mental Health: A Systemic Review and Meta-Analysis." *Public Health Nutrition* 10 (2020): 1778–90.

Power, Elaine. "Conceptualizing Food Security for Aboriginal People in Canada." *Canadian Journal of Public Health* 99, no. 2 (2008): 95–97.

Raibon, Paige. "Living on Display: Colonial Visions of Aboriginal Domestic Spaces." *BC Studies* 140 (2003/2004): 69–89.

Randazzo, Michael Leibovitch, and Michael Robidoux. "The Costs of Local Food Procurement in a Northern Canadian First Nation Community: An Affordable Strategy to Food Security?" *Journal of Hunger and Environmental Nutrition* 14, no. 5 (2019): 662–82.

Ray, Arthur. *The Canadian Fur Trade in the Industrial Age*. Toronto: University of Toronto Press, 1990.

———. *Indians in the Fur Trade*. Toronto: University of Toronto Press, 1974; reprint 1998.

———. "Periodic Shortages, Native Welfare, and the Hudson's Bay Company, 1670–1930." In *The Subarctic Fur Trade: Native Social and Economic Adaptation*, edited by Shepard Krech III, 1–20. Vancouver: UBC Press, 1984.

Ray, Lana, Kristin Burnett, Anita Cameron, Serena Joseph, Joseph LeBlanc, Barbara Parker, Angela Recollet, and Catherine Sergerie. "Examining Indigenous Food Sovereignty as a Conceptual Framework for Health in Two Urban Communities in Northern Ontario, Canada." *IUHPE - Global Health Promotion* 26, supp. 3 (2019): 54–63.

Richards, Thomas. *The Imperial Archive: Knowledge and the Fantasy of Empire*. London: Verso, 1993.

Roberts, David. "41 Below but Getting Warmer: The Store in Sandy Lake Signals a New Relationship Between the North's Dominant Retailer and the Native Indians and Inuit Who Are Its Main Customers." *Globe and Mail*, 1 February 1994, B24.

Rose, Nikola, Pat O'Malley, and Mariana Valverde. "Governmentality." *Annual Review of Law and Social Sciences* 2, no. 1 (2006): 83–104.

Rowse, Tim. *White Flour, White Power: From Rations to Citizenship in Central Australia.* New York: Cambridge University Press, 1998.

Rutherdale, Myra. "Cleansers, Cautious Caregivers, and Optimistic Adventurers: A Proposed Typology of Arctic Canadian Nurses, 1945–1970." In *Place and Practice in Canadian Nursing History*, edited by Jayne Elliott, Meryn Stuart, and Cynthia Toman, 53–70. Vancouver: UBC Press, 2008.

———. *Women and the White Man's God: Gender and Race in the Canadian Mission Field.* Vancouver: UBC Press, 2002.

Scrinis, Gyorgy. "On the Ideology of Nutritionism." *Gastronomica* 8, no. 1 (Winter 2008): 39–48.

Settee, Priscilla, and Shailesh Shukla. "Introduction." In *Indigenous Food Systems: Concepts, Cases, and Conversations*, edited by Priscilla Settee and Shailesh Shukla, 1–16. Toronto: Canadian Scholars, 2020.

Shewell, Hugh. "Dreaming in Liberal White: Canadian Indian Policy, 1913–2013." In *Aboriginal History: A Reader*, edited by Kristin Burnett and Geoff Read, 170–78. Second edition. Toronto: Oxford University Press, 2016.

———. *"Enough to Keep Them Alive": Indian Welfare in Canada, 1873–1965.* Toronto: University of Toronto Press, 2004.

Simmons, Deidre. "Custodians of a Great Inheritance: An Account of the Making of the Hudson's Bay Company Archives." MA thesis, University of Manitoba, 1994.

Simonsen, Jane. *Making Home Work: Domesticity and Native American Assimilation in the American West, 1860–1919.* Chapel Hill: University of North Carolina Press, 2006.

Simpson, Audra. *Mohawk Interruptus: Political Life Across the Borders of Settler States.* Durham: Duke University Press, 2014.

———. "Whither Settler Colonialism?" *Settler Colonial Studies* 6, no. 4 (2016): 1–8.

Socha, T., L. Chambers, M. Zahaf, R. Abraham, and T. Fiddler, "Food Availability, Food Store Management, and Food Pricing in a Northern First Nation Community." *International Journal of Humanities and Social Science* 1, no. 11 (2011): 49–61.

Socha, T., M. Zahaf, L. Chambers, R. Abraham, and T. Fiddler. "Food Security in a Northern First Nation Community: An Exploratory Study on Food Availability and Accessibility." *Journal of Aboriginal Health* 8, no. 2 (2012): 5–14.

Spraakman, Gary. "The First External Auditors of the Hudson's Bay Company, 1866." *Accounting Historians Journal* 38, no. 1 (June 2011): 57–80.

Squadrito, Kathy. "Locke and the Dispossession of the American Indian." *American Indian Culture and Research Journal* 20, no. 4 (1996): 145–81.

St-Germain, Andrée-Anne Fafard, Tracey Galloway, and Valerie Tarasuk. "Food Insecurity in Nunavut Following the Introduction of Nutrition North Canada." *Canadian Medical Association Journal* 191, no. 20 (21 May 2019): E553–58. doi: 10.1503/cmaj.181617.

Stoler, Ann Laura. "Colonial Archives and the Arts of Governance." *Archival Science* 2 (2002): 87–109.

———. "State Racism and the Education of Desires: A Colonial Reading of Foucault." In *Deep Histories: Gender and Colonialism in Southern Africa*, edited by Wendy Woodward, Patricia Hayes, and Gary Minkley, 3–31. New York: Editions Rodopi B.V., 2002.

Tester, Frank, and Peter Kulchyski. *Tammarniit (Mistakes): Inuit Relocation in the Eastern Arctic, 1939–63*. Vancouver: UBC Press, 1994.

Theobald, Brianna. *Reproduction on the Reservation: Pregnancy, Childbirth, and Colonialism in the Long Twentieth Century*. Chapel Hill, NC: University of North Carolina Press, 2019.

Thiessen, Janis. *Snacks: A Canadian Food History*. Winnipeg: University of Manitoba Press, 2017.

Thobani, Sunera. "Closing Ranks: Racism and Sexism in Canada's Immigration Policy." *Race and Class* 42, no. 1 (2000): 35–55.

Tobias, Joshua, and Chantelle Richmond. "'That Land Means Everything to Us as Anishinaabe': Environmental Dispossession and Resilience on the North Shore of Lake Superior." *Health and Place* 29 (September 2014): 26–33.

Tompkins, Kyla Wazana. *Racial Indigestion: Eating Bodies in the 19th Century*. New York: Nork University Press, 2012.

Tough, Frank. "Aboriginal Rights Versus the Deed of Surrender: The Legal Rights of Native People's and Canada's Acquisition of the Hudson's Bay Company Territory." *Prairie Forum* 17, no. 2 (Fall 1992): 225–50.

———. "The Forgotten Constitution: The Natural Resources Transfer Agreements and Indian Livelihood Rights, ca. 1925–1933." *The Alberta Law Review* 41, no. 4 (2004): 999–1048.

———. "'Powerless to Protect': Ontario Game Protection Legislation, Unreported and Indetermined Case Law, and the Criminalization of Indian Hunting in the Robinson-Treaty Territories, 1892–1931." In *Roots of Entanglement: Essays in the History of Native-Newcomer Relations*, edited by Myra Rutherdale, Kerry Abel, and P. Whitney Lackenbauer, 259–88. Toronto: University of Toronto Press, 2018.

Tsuji, Leonard, Stephen Tsuji, Aleksandra Zuk, Roger Davey, and Eric Liberda. "Harvest Programs in First Nations of Subarctic Canada: The Benefits Go Beyond Addressing Food Security and Environmental Sustainability Issues." *Environmental Research and Public Health* 17, no. 21 (2020): 8113. doi:10.3390/ijerph17218113.

Tuck, Eve. "Suspending Damage: A Letter to Communities." *Harvard Educational Review* 79, no. 3 (Fall 2009): 412–13.

Tuhiwai Smith, Linda. *Decolonizing Methodologies: Research and Indigenous Peoples*. London: Zed Books, 1999.

Valverde, Mariana. *The Age of Light, Soap, and Water: Moral Reform in English Canada, 1885–1925*. Toronto: McClelland and Stewart, 1991.

Van Kirk, Sylvia. *Many Tender Ties: Women in Fur-Trade Society, 1670–1870*. Oklahoma: University of Oklahoma Press, 1983.

Veeraraghaven, Gigi, Debbie Martin, Kristin Burnett, Kelly Skinner, Aliya Jama, Megan Ramsey, Patty Williams, and Christopher Stothart. "Paying For Nutrition: A Report on Food Costing in the North." Food Secure Canada, 2016. https://foodsecure-canada.org/sites/foodsecurecanada.org/files/201609_paying_for_nutrition_fsc_report_final.pdf (accessed 27 January 2023).

Veracini, Lorenzo. "The Predicaments of Settler Gastrocolonialism." In *"Going Native?" Settler Colonialism and Food*, edited by Alejandro Colás, Daniel Monterescu, and Ronald Ranta, 247–60. Cham, Switzerland: Springer Nature, 2022.

———. *Settler Colonialism: A Theoretical Overview.* London: Palgrave McMillan, 2010.

Vibert, Elizabeth. *Traders' Tales: Narratives of Cultural Encounters in the Columbia Plateau.* Norman: University of Oklahoma Press, 1997.

Vogt, David. "'Indians on White Lines': Bureaucracy, Race, and Power on Northern British Columbian Traplines, 1925–1950." *Journal of the Canadian Historical Association* 26, no. 1 (2015): 163–90.

Walmsley, Ann. "Retreat from the Frontier." *Maclean's,* 16 February 1987. https://archive.macleans.ca/article/1987/2/16/retreat-from-the-frontier.

Walters, Krista. "A History of Food Nutrition in Indigenous Communities in Canada, 1962–1985." PhD diss., University of Manitoba, 2020.

———. "'A National Priority': Nutrition Canada's Survey and the Disciplining of Aboriginal Bodies, 1964–1975." In *Edible Histories, Cultural Politics: Towards a Canadian Food History*, edited by Franca Iacovetta, Valerie Korinek, and Marlene Epp, 433–52. Toronto: University of Toronto: 2012.

Ware, Vron. *Beyond the Pale: White Women, Racism, and History.* London: Verso, 1992.

White, Richard. *The Middle Ground: Indians, Empires, and Republics in the Great Lakes Region, 1650–1815.* Cambridge: Cambridge University Press, 1991.

Whitney, Charlotte, Alejandro Frid, Barry K. Edgar, Jennifer Walkus, Peter Siwallace, Iris L. Siwallace, and Natalie C. Ban. "'Like the Plains People Losing the Buffalo': Perceptions of Climate Change Impacts, Fisheries Management, and Adaptation Actions by Indigenous Peoples in Coastal British Columbia, Canada." *Ecology and Society* 25, no. 4 (2020): 3–21.

Wilson, Shawn. *Research Is Ceremony: Indigenous Research Methods.* Halifax, NS: Fernwood, 2008.

Wilson, Shawn, and Margaret Hughes. "Why Research Is Reconciliation." In *Research and Reconciliation: Unsettling Ways of Knowing Through Indigenous Relationships*, edited by Shawn Wilson, Andrea Breen, and Lindsay Dupre, 5–20. Toronto: Canadian Scholars, 2019.

Wolfe, Patrick. "Settler Colonialism and the Elimination of the Native." *The Journal of Genocide Research* 8, no. 4 (2006): 387–409.

Yangbo, Sun, Buyun Liu, Shuang Rong, Yang Du, Guifeng Xu, Linda Snetselaar, Robert Wallace, and Wei Bao. "Food Insecurity Is Associated with Cardiovascular and All-Cause Mortality Among Adults in the United States." *Journal of the American Heart Association*, 25 September 2020. https://doi.org/10.1161/JAHA.119.014629.

Zoller, Heather. "Health Activism: Communication Theory and Action for Social Change." *Communication Theory* 15, no. 4 (2005): 341–64.

INDEX

than FMP, 148; view of high costs, 158; view of itself, 115–17, 130–34; and Vision +2000, 127
North West Fund, 125–26
Northcote, Stafford, 39
Northern Air Stage Program (Food Mail Program), 73, 97–98
Northern Food Basket (NFB), 104–9
Northern Fruit and Vegetable Program, 137
Northern Stores Department (NSD): and cashing cheques, 87; creation of, 80; innovations of, 80–81; lack of competition for, 81–82; new name of Fur Trade Department, 73; and Nutrition Upgrading Program, 93; setting of food shipment routes, 37; sold by HBC, 115, 117–18. *See also* North West Company (NWC) (formerly Northern Stores Department)
NorthMart, 123
Northwest Rebellion (1885), 24
Nukilik (cartoon character), 90–91
Numbered Treaty System, 21–23
Nutrition North Canada (NNC): AGs report on in 2014, 145, 147–48, 156–57; assessment of its failure, 158; changes to under Liberal government, 157–58; and Community Food Program, 151–53; and country food, 150–51; criticism of, 145, 153–54; Dargo Report audit which led to, 142–44; eligibility requirements of, 146–48; excessive bureaucracy of, 146–47, 148–49; and food insecurity, 141, 147, 154, 158; and how much of subsidy goes to NWC, 159–60; and ineligible foods important to Indigenous under, 154–55; necessary items ineligible for subsidy under, 149–50; start of program, 139–40, 145
Nutrition Upgrading Program, 89–95
nutrition/nutritional science: beneficial to HBC's profits, 95; changing guidelines of, 108; and cultural vision of Canadian citizenship, 63; data collected from Indigenous peoples on, 108–9, development of, 45; experiments in, 56–57; and Food Mail Pilot Project, 109–10; and Food Mail Program, 98–99, 102–3; and HBC's role in, 43–44; as inconsequential to real problems, 114, 163; Indian Affairs recommendations on, 81; and logic of Indigenous elimination,

9; neoliberal view of, 155–56; and Nutrition Upgrading Program, 89–95; in NWC's healthy living campaign, 134–35; as part of Northern Food Basket, 105–8; as part of Nutrition North Canada, 140; as part of settler colonialism, 160; and purchase lists, 66, 69–71; racism of its guidelines, 155; view of in Dargo Report, 144. *See also* Nutrition North Canada (NNC)

O
obesity, 99, 107
O'Neill, J.T., 59
Ontario, Government of, 25–27
Ostrander, J.P.B., 87
Ottawaska, Wilson, 26

P
Pablum, 56, 68, 69–71
Pass System, 24
Peace and Friendship Treaty of 1752, 19
Peace and Friendship Treaty of 1760, 20
Pemmican Proclamation, 36, 177n13
People of the Deer (Mowat), 95
pharmacies, 129
pollution, 26, 27
Prairie Farm Rehabilitation Administration, 29
price gouging, 114, 156, 162
purchasing lists: conception of idea for, 56, 58, 64; as danger to Indigenous lives, 71–72; Indigenous complaints about, 86–87; and Indigenous food choices, 66–68, 82, 83–86; and Pablum, 69–71; as part of family allowance, 49, 64, 66–67, 71–72; and prohibitive cost of food, 72

R
racism: and beliefs about Indigenous peoples as consumers, 79; and Cheez Whiz affair, 153; of family allowance policies, 69, 71; of FMP, 104; of nutritional guidelines, 155
rationing, 11, 108
RCMP (Royal Canadian Mounted Police), 87, 88
recuperating Indigeneity, 64
Reed, Hayter, 41
residential schools, 8, 12, 57, 62, 94
retail capitalism, 75–76. *See also* market economies
Revised Northern Food Basket (RNFB), 105–7
Rickford, Greg, 150–51
Robinson-Superior Treaty of 1850, 20, 26

9 781772 840490